SPEAKING OF THE U.S.A.

A Reader for Discussion

BERTHA C. NEUSTADT
Boston University

Harper & Row, Publishers
New York   Evanston   San Francisco   London

To Guy and Vittoria and Stefan and Kunio
and the hundreds of other students
for whom this book was written.

Sponsoring Editor: George J. Telecki
Project Editor: Cynthia Hausdorff
Designer: Andrea Clark
Production Supervisor: Will C. Jomarrón
Picture Editor: Myra Schachne

Speaking of the U.S.A.: A Reader for Discussion

Library of Congress Cataloging in Publication Data

Neustadt, Bertha C
   Speaking of the U. S. A.; a reader for discussion.
   Bibliography: p.
   1. English language—Text-books for foreigners.
2. Readers—United States.   I. Title.
PE1128.N38   428'.6'4   74-13009
ISBN 0-06-044798-2

Cover photo: Bob Combs, Rapho Guillumette

Speaking of the U.S.A.

Contents

Preface

This book is the product of teaching. It has grown out of fifteen years of experience in teaching English as a foreign language at Columbia and Boston Universities. At both universities the teaching was done in programs designed for students from many different countries, who were often highly educated in their own languages. Most of these students were preparing themselves for further study at American institutions of higher learning.

Speaking of the U.S.A. is meant to fill a gap in the textbooks available to students like mine. I have written an introduction, nineteen chapters, each discussing a specific aspect of American society, and two concluding chapters. Each chapter is written to be read and then discussed in English by students of disparate language backgrounds. The subjects have been chosen to engage and hold the interest of adults. Presentation is intended to facilitate discussion as an outgrowth of reading.

The book has three specific aims: first, to improve the student's understanding and use of written and spoken English; second, to develop skills for university study; and, third, to introduce the contemporary United States with some relevant historical background.

The subjects of the various chapters reflect the interests of my students over the years. Topics range from American voting patterns to women's liberation to trends in American architecture. The information presented is based on extensive research and provides opportunities for informative, cross-cultural comparisons in class.

The book is divided into six sections. Each has been tested in the classroom by instructors of students at different levels of English proficiency. The reading materials have proved suitable for both intermediate and advanced students. Each reading assignment is followed by a number of exercises that offer practice in reading and listening comprehension and vocabulary building, with emphasis on word formation. Special exercises stress training in note-taking (for lectures) and in group discussion (for seminars). Library assignments require the use of research facilities as well as the writing of research reports. The exercises for each section are of varying difficulty and offer the instructor the opportunity to choose those most appropriate to the needs of a particular class.

SUGGESTED USES FOR THIS TEXT

Each section is a self-contained unit of two or more chapters, and therefore the instructor may present the sections in any order. However, since library assignments appear throughout the text, the library section (Section I) should be introduced first. Instructors may find that the material on the American government (Section II) satisfies the students' interest in politics, *except* in important election years. During those years they may decide to add Section VI, Political Parties and the Election Process. When Section VI is used, it should *follow* Section II, which introduces a number of basic political terms and concepts.

Each reading assignment is followed by a number of different exercises of varying difficulty. During the first part of the semester instructors of students at intermediate levels should emphasize vocabulary, reading comprehension, and dictation drills. After two or three sections have been completed, intermediate students should be able to handle additional exercises of greater complexity.

Advanced students will benefit from emphasis on listening comprehension exercises and discussion and writing topics. Most of the glossed vocabulary will present no problem to these students, but they should review the pronunciation of each glossed word and additional uses of words marked with asterisks. (See the suggested uses of vocabulary.)

The vocabulary exercises at the end of each section should be done orally in class, although some exercises may be prepared initially as written assignments.

The length of time spent on a section will vary with different classes. Most groups who have worked with this material have spent between ten and fifteen class hours on each section.

I. Reading and Glossed Vocabulary

Students should read the text of each chapter before class, without referring to the glossary. Each glossed word is printed in boldface type once in the reading selection. Advanced students will have little difficulty with the vocabulary. Intermediate students should be encouraged to guess the meaning of unfamiliar words and to try to get a general idea of the content of the chapter before referring to the glossary.

In class the instructor should review the pronunciation of each glossed word and indicate when the word is uncountable.

Since words are usually defined as they are used in the text, words with at least one other common meaning are marked with asterisks. The instructor and students should discuss and illustrate the other uses of such words. For example, the verb *to run* is defined in Section VI as a political term: to seek office. The meaning of this verb may be expanded to include: to manage, to move one's legs rapidly, to be in working order, to drip, and so on. Intermediate and advanced students should add their own definitions and illustrative sentences.

Some instructors have varied the introduction of glossed vocabulary by reading the illustrative sentences aloud and then asking students to frame an appropriate definition. Instructors may choose to spend class time on a few words in the glossary and expect students to study the complete list outside of class. Since most of the vocabulary will be familiar to advanced students, they will spend minimum time on the glossary, but all students should do the vocabulary review exercises and quizzes that follow the glossary before they begin the comprehension and thought questions. Intermediate students should reread the text after they have studied the glossary.

II. Reading Comprehension and Thought Questions;
Discussion and Writing Topics

Some students prefer to write answers to the comprehension and thought questions and to prepare written outlines for the discussion topics before the class meetings. This approach gives them a relaxed opportunity to think about their responses and to organize complex ideas. These exercises should be done orally in class as well, and students should be encouraged to use new vocabulary as often as possible. Whenever time permits, students should also discuss orally the topics they have prepared as compositions.

Many of the discussion topics call for comparisons of the different countries represented by students in the class. Native-born Americans whose first language is not English may discuss the countries from which their ancestors came. They should be encouraged to do library research to fill in any gaps in their information.

III. Listening Exercises

Dictation and listening comprehension exercises for each chapter appear at the end of the book, beginning on p. 243. They should be introduced at any time after the glossed vocabulary for the chapter has been reviewed. Students should not look at this material until after the dictation has been given or the listening comprehension questions have been answered and discussed.

At the start of each listening comprehension exercise some words that are not found in the text of the chapter are defined. The instructor should pronounce and explain them. They have been chosen on the assumption that the sections will be introduced in the sequence presented in the text. If the instructor changes this sequence, he should be sure to explain any additional unfamiliar words or concepts.

The listening exercises serve the dual purpose of vocabulary review and practice in note-taking. They should be read at a normal speaking pace, and the instructor should discourage interruptions during the reading.

IV. Other Suggestions

A number of books and recordings are recommended to the users of this book at relevant points in the text. It is advisable that these materials be made available in a convenient library. (Detailed information on the recordings can be found in the *Schwann Record and Tape Guide,* Boston, Schwann, current semiannual supplement.)

Section III
RECORDS (spoken)

Speeches by Presidents Roosevelt, Truman, Eisenhower, Johnson, and Nixon	Kennedy-Nixon debates "War of the Worlds"

Section IV
BOOKS

Reading list on architecture (see pp. 150-151)
Printed texts of recommended plays (see pp. 128-129)
RECORDS (music)

My Fair Lady	*Showboat*
Oklahoma	*West Side Story*

RECORDS (spoken)
Recorded plays (see pp. 128-129)

Section V
BOOKS
Reading list on the American family (see pp. 189-190)

In teaching the materials included in this book, I have found it very useful to supplement classroom instruction with field trips. I can recommend trips of the following sorts to be taken in conjunction with the indicated sections of the book.

Section I
A guided tour through a library; often libraries offer film strips on how to use library facilities.

Section III
A visit to a local newspaper or broadcasting station.

Section IV
A tour of an art museum, especially the section on American art if there is one.

Section V
A visit to a day-care center and/or a nursery school.

Acknowledgments

Many friends and colleagues contributed to this book.

I am especially grateful to four of my associates at Boston University: George Draper, Francine Stieglitz, Abbey Mason, and Robert Saitz, who reviewed draft chapters and gave me a great deal of good advice. Dr. Stieglitz also read and constructively criticized the penultimate draft. Mr. Draper and Ms. Mason tested materials in their classes, for which I am particularly appreciative. Instructors in two other programs reviewed drafts: Mary Dobbie of Columbia University and Isabel Halsted of the City College of New York. I am grateful for their helpful comments. Three graduate teaching assistants tested materials under my supervision: Linda Ferrari, Michaela Ford, and Anita Reiner. Their interest, enthusiasm, and suggestions were of real importance.

Special thanks are owed to my friend Babette Spiegel for her painstaking editorial assistance. I could not have completed this work without her help.

Others gave me indispensable advice on subject matter in their fields of expertise. I owe thanks especially to Doris Kearns of the Government Department of Harvard University and to Joan Cohen of the Museum School of the Boston Museum of Fine Arts.

Federal agencies responded to my inquiries with promptness and much useful information. Let me thank my correspondents at the Federal Communications Commission, the Civil Service Commission, the Office of Education, the Bureau of the Census, and the office of Congressman Thomas P. O'Neill, House majority leader.

My research was done mainly at four libraries: the Mugar Library of Boston University, the Gutman Library of the Harvard School of Education, and the Boston and Cambridge Public Libraries. At all four the librarians were uniformly helpful, often far beyond the call of duty. Thanks are owed and gratefully given.

Thanks are also due to others who made special contributions—Bill and Betsy Olsen of the Villa Serbelloni, Victor Brudney, Susan Davidson, Pat Follett, Penny Gouzoule, Inge Hoffman, Margaret Johnson, Margaret Rector, Barbara Schwartz, Corinne Shelling, Desmond Simon, Janet Sondheim, and Pam Thomure.

For permission to use copyrighted materials I thank Geno Ballotti of *Daedalus* and Nicholas Johnson, formerly of the Federal Communications Commission.

Finally, I want to thank my husband and my son, Richard E. and Richard M. Neustadt respectively, and my daughter, Elizabeth Neustadt, for their comments on subjects in their special fields of interest. They helpfully read the manuscript and bore with its production.

Bertha C. Neustadt

Introducing You to the United States

This book was written to introduce you to some aspects of the United States and the people who live here. It begins with an introduction to the United States. This is followed by a section on libraries, because many of you will study at American schools where you will have to write papers that involve using libraries. Therefore, throughout the book there are library assignments to give you practice in doing library work.

Because it would be impossible to include chapters on everything you might want to know about this country and its people, I have chosen subjects in which many foreign students have been particularly interested. I hope these selections will interest you, too.

The United States extends 3000 miles from the Atlantic to the Pacific Oceans and over 1000 miles from Canada to Mexico. When you cross the country, you pass through four separate time zones. This means that when it is nine o'clock in New York, it is three hours earlier, or six o'clock in San Francisco. From north to south the climate changes greatly. On the same day in January ten or twelve inches of snow may fall in parts of Minnesota and Maine, while people in southern California and Florida are swimming and enjoying warm sunshine.

More than 200 million people live in the United States. Except for the American Indians, these Americans originally came from countries all over the world. The names in any telephone directory provide examples of their various national backgrounds—from Abbott (England) to Hsu (China) to Zyskowski (Poland). The names of American cities also show that people from many different nations have shared

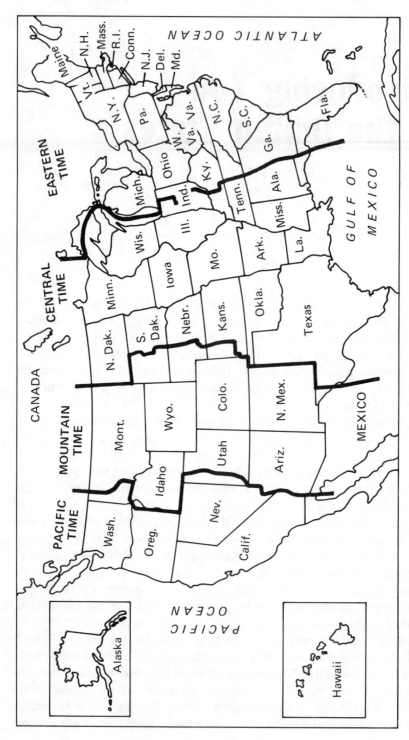

Map of the United States showing time zones.

in the development of this country: Boston (England), St. Louis (France), Brooklyn (the Netherlands), San Francisco (Spain).

The history of the United States begins with the exploration of the New World by Europeans. In 1492 Christopher Columbus, an Italian who sailed under the Spanish flag, landed in the Bahamas, which are islands southeast of Florida. Nine years later Amerigo Vespucci, an Italian for whom the Americas were named, sailed along the northern coast of South America. During the next two centuries the Spanish, French, Swedish, Dutch, and the English explored large portions of North America, and many settled there.

The first permanent English colony was founded in Jamestown, Virginia, in 1607, and soon the British controlled what is now the eastern United States. In 1776 these colonists declared their independence from Great Britain. Following a revolutionary war, which lasted from 1776 to 1781, they established a new nation, the United States. The people of the United States have always called themselves Americans, and they often call their country America. Although these terms really belong to all the people of both American continents, we shall use them in this book as they are used in the United States.

In 1800 there were 5.5 million Americans, living mostly in the eastern part of the young country. Nearly 1 million of them were Blacks who had been brought from Africa to work as slaves on southern cotton, sugar, and tobacco plantations (very large farms). During the next half-century the country expanded westward to the Pacific. By 1850 the population had reached 23 million, and ten years later it had grown to over 31 million. More than 6 million people came from Europe between 1800 and 1860, and an unknown number of slaves also arrived during that period. Slavery continued throughout the South until 1865, when the slaves were freed after a long and bloody civil war between the northern and southern states. Although that war was fought more than 100 years ago, its effects are still being felt and will be mentioned in several sections of this book.

During the first half of the nineteenth century the United States had been primarily an agricultural country, but following the Civil War the economy became industrialized rapidly. From the 1860s to the early 1900s more than 28 million immigrants came to the United States. Although some were farmers who moved west to the Mississippi valley, most went to work in the new and expanding factories. In addition, many Americans left the farms, and by the early 1900s more than half the population lived in cities and worked in nonagricultural occupations.

Every ten years the national government conducts a census. That is, the government gathers statistical information about the American people. The 1970 census reports that there are about 205 million Americans. Almost 38 percent are less than twenty-one years old. Approximately 10 percent are sixty-five or over. Eleven percent of all Americans are black.[1] Approximately 35 percent live in or near cities with populations of at least 50,000.

Americans are movers. Each year one of every five moves from one home to another, either within the same city or to a different one.

Almost 79 million people are employed, and 4 million more are unemployed and looking for work.[2] Table 1 presents some figures that show how Americans earn their living.

Table 1.   1970 Employment in Nonagricultural Industries

Industry	Percentage of Total
Manufacturing	27.4
Wholesale and retail trade	21.1
Government (federal, state, local)	17.8
Services*	16.5
Transportation and public utilities	6.4
Finance, insurance, and real estate	5.2
Construction	4.7
Mining	0.9

*Includes many different kinds of businesses, such as hotels and restaurants, laundries, advertising agencies, automobile and television repair shops.

Source: *Statistical Abstract of the United States, 1972,* Washington, D.C., U.S. Bureau of the Census, 1972, p. 225.

More than 50 percent of all employed persons are called "white-collar workers." They include professional people such as doctors, lawyers, nurses, and engineers, as well as managers, salespersons, and people who work in offices. More than 34 percent are "blue-collar workers." They usually perform manual jobs that require special work clothes. More than 10 percent are service workers who hold jobs such as maids in private homes, waiters, cooks, and bartenders. Fewer than 4 percent work on farms. Ten percent of all working Americans are self-employed. The rest work for someone else. Table 2 gives information about the money income of American families.

1. For additional information on race and religion see Section V, Chapter 16.

2. These are the census figures for 1970. Five years later, during a period of economic recession, more than 8 million people were unemployed.

Table 2. Money Incomes of Families in 1970

Annual Income Level	Percentage of All Families
Under $1,000	1.5
$1,000–2,999	7.3
$3,000–3,999	5.1
$4,000–4,999	5.3
$5,000–0,999	11.8
$7,000–9,999	19.9
$10,000–14,999	26.8
$15,000 and over	22.3

Source: *Statistical Abstract of the United States, 1972,* Washington, D.C., U.S. Bureau of the Census, 1972, p. 322.

LIBRARIES

Public and Private Libraries

The earliest libraries existed thousands of years ago in China, Egypt, and Assyria, where collections of records on tablets of baked clay were kept in temples and royal palaces. In the Western world, libraries were first established in ancient Greece. Aristotle had a **research** library in the third century B.C., and this collection probably inspired the great libraries of Alexandria in Egypt and Pergamum in Asia Minor.

Roman generals brought home Greek libraries as prizes of war. In the late years of the Roman republic, Greek and Latin private libraries became an important part of Roman home life and a fashionable way to display wealth. In later years the Roman emperors established public libraries. By the fourth century A.D., there were twenty-eight public libraries in Rome and many more in provincial cities. When Constantinople became the capital of the Roman Empire in 330 A.D., the Emperor Constantine established a library there, and Christian literature was admitted to an imperial collection for the first time.

As Christianity expanded, religious-library collections became an important part of church organization. Throughout Europe during the Middle Ages (from approximately the fifth century to the tenth or eleventh century), monks carefully copied and decorated religious manuscripts. During the same time Arabs and Moors established great Arabic libraries in Baghdad, Cairo, Tripoli, and Spain. These Muslims introduced paper to the Western world by way of Constantinople and Spain.

By the fourteenth and fifteenth centuries there were so many volumes in the European monasteries that they had to be **stored** in special rooms or libraries. Scholars and students were allowed to use these books, and, following the procedures of the monastic libraries,

Seventeenth-century woodcut—La bibliothèque de l'université de Leyde. *The New York Public Library Picture Collection*

newly established colleges also provided books for their students. Students could borrow certain books. Others were available in a kind of **reference** section. These books were fastened by chains to desks for use within the library. Today chains are still used on a few books in the Bodleian Library at Oxford University. In the famous library of the Escorial, built by Philip II of Spain in 1584, there were no chains, and for the first time books were placed in bookcases along the walls.

The Renaissance saw a great revival of interest in literature and a significant increase in book collecting, but modern library history truly begins with the invention of printing. The first Gutenberg Bible was printed with a mechanical hand press in the mid-fifteenth century. Important improvements in printing techniques soon followed. By the seventeenth and eighteenth centuries most of the cultural and intellectual centers of Europe featured royal, national, and academic libraries. By the 1800s many town libraries had been established on the Continent and in Britain.

The first library in this country was a private library, which could be used only by **authorized** readers. In 1638 Reverend John Harvard gave money and more than 300 books to a newly established college in Massachusetts. In gratitude the legislature voted that the school be named Harvard College. The librarian, who was **in charge**

of the books, set the rules for the new library. Only college students and faculty members could use the books. No book could be lent for more than one month. Anyone who mistreated a book had to pay a **fine** and was forbidden to borrow books in the future. The librarian was responsible for the care of the books, having the library swept,

Main reading room of the Library of Congress.   *Courtesy The Library of Congress*

and "keeping the books clean and orderly and in their proper places."[1]

The earliest public library was established in Philadelphia in 1731. Although this library was open to everyone, all readers had to pay a membership or subscription fee in order to borrow books. Very few subscription libraries exist today. Some book and stationery stores maintain small rental libraries where anyone may borrow books for a daily charge.

The first truly free public library that **circulated** books to everyone at no cost was started in a small New England town in 1833. Today there are more than 7000 free public libraries in **communities** throughout the United States. They contain approximately 160 million books, which are circulated to over 52 million readers. Most of these libraries are supported by local taxes, **supplemented** by aid from the federal government. Some public libraries also receive money from private organizations.

Historically, the major purpose of free public libraries was educational. They were expected to provide adults with the opportunity to continue their education after they left school. Melville Dewey, a mid-nineteenth-century librarian who played an important role in library development, described the function of a public library as "less a reservoir [a place where water is stored] than a fountain." In other words, emphasis was to be placed on wide circulation, rather than on collecting and storing books.

Over the years library services have greatly expanded. In addition to their continuing and important educational role, public libraries provide culture and recreation, and they are trying to fill many changing community needs. In order to make books easily available, most city libraries maintain neighborhood branches, divisions of the main library that serve the residents of small, limited geographic areas. Traveling, or mobile, libraries carry books on trucks to rural areas and to inner-city[2] residents, to encourage book borrowing.

Most libraries offer **browsing** rooms where readers can relax on comfortable chairs and read current newspapers and magazines. Many also circulate music records. Library programs of films, lectures, reading clubs, and concerts also attract library users. Gaily decorated children's rooms offer special books and story hours for children, in which stories are read aloud to them.

In addition to books, records, **periodicals,** and reference material, libraries provide technical information, such as books and **pamphlets** on gardening, carpentry, and other specialized fields of interest.

1. Louis Shores, *Origins of the American College Library,* Nashville, Tenn., Peabody College Press, 1934, p. 182.
2. An old central part of a large city, occupied by very poor people.

President Dwight D. Eisenhower (r) at the Dwight D. Eisenhower Library.
Courtesy Dwight D. Eisenhower Library

Books in Braille[3] and specially recorded "talking books" are available for the blind. Neighborhood branches are reaching out to the inner-city poor and ethnic minorities. They are offering literacy-test materials and easy-to-read books for adults on subjects such as driving a car or preparing balanced meals. Some libraries even offer discussion programs on such subjects as nutrition and how parents can help children with their homework.

The largest public library in the United States is the Library of Congress. It was originally planned as a reference library for the federal legislature. Today, in addition to that important function, it serves as a reference library for the public and sends out many books to other libraries on an interlibrary loan system. On 270 miles (435 kilometers) of shelves, the library stores books, manuscripts, maps, photographs, prints, records, and some publications of other countries. Two copies of every copyrighted item must be sent to the library within ten days after publication. A copyright is a legal right held by the author of a work for a certain number of years, which prevents others from copying from it without his permission. A special library **cataloging** system records every book currently published in the United States.

Another major federal public library system is run abroad by the

3. A system of printing that enables blind people to read by touch.

United States Information Service (USIS). Many foreign readers are familiar with such libraries as the American Cultural Center, Amerika Haus, Biblioteca Lincoln, and Casa Americana. These libraries in foreign countries make available American books, magazines, pamphlets, and government publications.

A third federal library system is operated by the National Archives, the official storehouse of unpublished government materials. The National Archives is also in charge of all presidential libraries, which contain the papers of former presidents. There are now four presidential libraries, and a fifth is being built.[4]

Unlike free public libraries, which are open to everyone, private libraries can be used only by authorized readers. Many industrial and scientific organizations and business firms have collections of books, journals, and research **data** for their staffs. Several private historical associations have research collections of special interest to their members. In addition, many elementary and secondary schools operate libraries for use by students and teachers. Prisons and hospitals maintain libraries, also.

The largest and most important private libraries are operated by colleges and universities and are used by students, faculty members, and occasionally by visiting scholars. Many universities have special libraries for research in particular fields such as law, medicine, and education. Recent surveys report that more than 300 million books are available in these academic libraries and that they are regularly used by over eight million students.

VOCABULARY

to authorize	to approve and permit
authorization	You may not use the National Archives without special permission. An official must **authorize** you to use the Archive materials. You must have **authorization.**
to browse (through)	to read casually for interest and enjoyment (usually parts of a book or books)
	He **browsed** through several magazines, reading only the articles that interested him.

4. These libraries are worth sight-seeing visits. If you plan such a trip, you should write directly to the director of the library and request an appointment for a tour. The Franklin D. Roosevelt Library is in Hyde Park, New York; the Harry S. Truman Library in Independence, Missouri; the Dwight D. Eisenhower Library in Abilene, Kansas; and the Lyndon B. Johnson Library in Austin, Texas. The John F. Kennedy Library will be located in a city in Massachusetts.

a catalog
  to catalog

a list of names, books, etc. arranged in a particular order

The main **catalog** in the library contains alphabetically arranged cards for all books, periodicals, and other printed items in the library.

The librarian **cataloged** the new magazines. She added the names to the magazine card file.

in charge of

responsible for

That librarian is responsible for all new library books. She must catalog them and supervise their use. She is **in charge of** the new books.

*to circulate
  circulation*

to move about (as books move in and out of a library); to lend library books

Library books often **circulate** for two-week periods. Readers may borrow books for two weeks but must return them by the fourteenth day.

Public librarians want more people to read library books. They want to increase the **circulation** of library books.

*a community

a group of people who live in the same area and who often have the same religious, racial, or national background

Libraries provide books written in Spanish for members of Spanish-speaking **communities** in many large cities.

data *información*

facts ("data" is plural)

A scientist draws conclusions from the facts he learns from his research. He draws conclusions from his research **data.**

a fine *multar*
  to fine

a money penalty

The punishment for returning a library book late is a small **fine.**

The librarian **fined** the student ten cents.

a pamphlet

a small paper-covered book, often on a subject of current interest

The U.S. Government Printing Office publishes hundreds of government **pamphlets** on various subjects, including health care for children, labor statistics, improved farming methods, and services offered by different government agencies.

a periodical	a magazine or journal published at regular time intervals (not daily newspapers)

Time and *Newsweek* are two popular weekly news **periodicals.** *Harper's* is a monthly **periodical.**

*a reference
   to refer — something consulted for information

Books used for **reference,** such as dictionaries and encyclopedias, are found in the **reference** room of the library.

We **refer** to dictionaries for the correct spelling and definitions of words.

research — investigation and study
   to research

He is studying the causes of cancer. He is doing **research** on cancer. He is **researching** the causes of cancer.

to store — to collect and hold for safekeeping
   storage

Dewey thought that libraries should not hold books but should encourage their circulation. He believed that libraries should not simply **store** books. He thought libraries should not be just space for the **storage** of books.

to supplement — to add to something
   a supplement

Teachers often **supplement** their incomes by writing textbooks. They earn additional money by writing textbooks.

A new volume is usually added to the *Encyclopedia Britannica* each year to bring it up to date. An annual *supplement* is added to the *Encyclopedia Britannica.*

Vocabulary Review

A. Change the following sentences by substituting words from the vocabulary list for the words in heavy type. You may make words plural, and you may change the tense of any verb.

Vocabulary List

a. periodical g. research
b. supplement h. browse
c. fine i. in charge of
d. community j. circulate
e. store k. data
f. authorize

EXAMPLE   1. The librarian **gave** him **permission** to use the new books.
            The librarian (f) **authorized** him to use the new books.

2. He reads several **magazines and journals** every week.
3. Most of the library books **are lent** for two-week periods.
4. Vitamin pills are sometimes a necessary **addition** to one's regular diet.
5. She **collected and kept** all the heavy woolen clothes in a large clean box during the summer.
6. The book is based on a great deal of **careful study and investigation.**
7 The head librarian was **responsible for** the entire library,
8. He spent hours in the library getting **facts and figures** on the oil situation.
9. Take the book back this week, or you'll have to pay a large **penalty.**
10. There is a good branch library, which serves **the people who live in this area.**

B. Match each noun in Column I with a word in Column II that has a similar meaning.

EXAMPLE   1. authorization   h. permission

I	II
1. authorization _____	a. magazine
2. supplement _____	b. study and investigation
3. circulation _____	c. list or record
4. catalog _____	d. facts
5. research _____	e. money penalty
6. data _____	f. easy movement
7. fine _____	g. addition
8. periodical _____	h. permission
	i. responsibility

Comprehension and Thought Questions

1. Who owned a famous ancient research library? Where? When?
2. Who introduced paper to the Western world?
3. Why is it said that the history of the modern library begins with the invention of the printing press?

4. How did Harvard College get its name?
5. Historically, the purpose of free public libraries was education. Do you think this is still true? How have library services been expanded?
6. What is the Library of Congress? List some of its functions. Can you think of any functions that community libraries have that the Library of Congress does not have?
7. How are presidential papers stored? How are official papers stored in your country?
8. Who is authorized to use libraries operated by colleges and universities?
9. Name a few different kinds of organizations or institutions that maintain private libraries. Why do these organizations maintain private libraries when books and periodicals can be obtained from free public libraries?

Discussion and Composition Topics

1. Free public libraries have been called "the people's universities." Do you think this description is accurate? Explain your answer.
2. If you have used a USIS library in your country, describe how it was organized. What kinds of publications were available? What information were you looking for? Did you find it?
3. Visit your nearest public library. Apply for a library card. Often you must give the name and telephone number of someone who lives in the community and who knows you, so be sure to take that information with you.

    Prepare a report on your impressions of the library. Describe the browsing room, the children's section, and the section with musical and spoken recordings (if the library has these sections). Tell whether this library is the main library or a branch. Who was using the library when you were there? Find out about special activities that take place in the library: concerts, lectures, discussion groups, films. Most libraries have free, printed materials about special events. If you cannot find such materials, ask the librarian for them.

Listening Exercises for Chapter 1 begin on p. 243.

How to Use
a Library

Academic libraries are designed primarily for research and study. To illustrate the use of a college library, let us choose a research topic and follow the step-by-step procedure of preparing a **bibliography.** Your assignment is to write a paper on the American author Ernest Hemingway. You may want to include a brief **biography,** a list of his books and his magazine articles, and comments by literary **critics** on his influence on the development of American fiction.

The initial step is to go to the main catalog, which consists of large wooden or metal cabinets containing drawers or trays of hundreds of cards arranged in alphabetical order. These cards are printed references to all materials available in the library. Each publication is **indexed** in three ways: by subject, by author (family name first), and by title. Title cards are cataloged by the first word of the book title, omitting the words *a, an,* and *the.*

First, **look up** Hemingway, Ernest. A separate card lists each of his books by title, with date and place of publication, publisher, and number of pages. Another **classification** of Hemingway material contains cards that list books about him. This **category** is subdivided into sections, one including biographies of Hemingway and another for literary criticism of his works. The cards in each section are arranged in alphabetical order by author and contain publication details. Frequently books have been printed more than once, occasionally with revisions or changes in later printings or editions. It is important to note which edition you want to read.

In an upper corner of each card is the **call number,** the numerical code that indicates where the book is located in the library. On tables near the catalog there are usually small sheets of paper called "call slips." In order to obtain the books you need, you must fill out a call slip for each book, indicating the call number, author, title, edition, and your name.

Most libraries have open and closed **stacks.** Open-stack books, arranged by call number, are shelved in readily accessible areas and are available for immediate use by the reader. Many large libraries keep most of their books in closed stacks, which are accessible only to authorized library staff. To borrow a book from the closed stacks, you must present your call slip to a librarian at the circulation desk. Often he will give you a number, which will be announced when the book has been located and is ready for you. Many libraries have an electric board on which your number appears when the book is at the desk. Graduate students may often obtain stack passes that permit them to enter the stacks and look for the books themselves.

If the book is **out,** you may request that you be notified when it is available and that it be **reserved,** or kept, for you. If the book is **in** and you wish **to take it out,** you must fill out a "charge slip" and present it with your university identification card to the librarian. The book will be charged to you, and the **due date,** the day on which it must be returned, will be stamped on a slip in the back of the book. It is important to take books back by the due date; otherwise you will have to pay a fine.

Some books are kept on reserve. These are books assigned to particular classes for reading during limited periods. These books circulate in the library for short periods of time during the day and usually may be taken out only overnight.

If you have not finished your book by the due date, you may often request a **renewal,** permission to take it out again. If no one else has requested the book, the librarian at the circulation desk will stamp it for another loan period.

In addition to books by Hemingway and about him, you will want **to look at** periodical and newspaper articles. First, you must go to the reference section, where dictionaries, directories, encyclopedias, atlases, and periodical reference volumes such as the *Readers' Guide to Periodical Literature* are located. A citation, or reference, to an article on Hemingway or by him will include the title of the article, the author (if the article is signed), the name of the magazine, the date, the volume, and the page number. The *New York Times* also publishes a detailed subject index of all the articles that have appeared in that newspaper. These reference collections are published at regular intervals during the year and then collected in single volumes annually. In order to have an adequate list of magazine and newspaper references to Hemingway, you may have to consult indexes covering the period from 1923, the date of his first publication, to the present time.

Current periodicals and newspapers are kept in the periodical room.[1] After a certain length of time, magazines and journals are bound between hard covers to protect them and to make them easier to shelve. Some newspapers and journals are microfilmed to save storage space and to preserve them. They are put on small rolls of film, or on cards called "microfiche," and they are read on machines that enlarge the films to their original size.

For more detailed research, additional reference **sources** are available. For example, abstracts and annotated bibliographies give descriptive information about the contents of articles and books. An abstract is a brief summary of the main points of a book or article, without critical evaluation. An annotated bibliography is a list of publications on a specific subject, with a short descriptive criticism of each item. *The Guide to Reference Books* lists approximately 7500 reference books in English and other languages on many different subjects. Several organizations, known as clearinghouses, provide abstracts of specific research projects and help scholars to contact people who may have information that the scholars need.

It is important to remember that the librarians will help you locate books, use reference materials, and arrange interlibrary loans if you need books that are not in your library collection. For your Hemingway project, however, you will undoubtedly be able to prepare an adequate bibliography by using the main catalog, a periodical reference guide, and the *New York Times Index*. Next, you must **look over** these materials and decide what you want to use. Then you will **take notes,** on which your paper will be based.

A short bibliography for a report on Hemingway might include the following:

Novels by Ernest Hemingway

Across the River and into the Trees, New York, Scribner's, 1950.
Death in the Afternoon, New York, Scribner's, 1932.
A Farewell to Arms, New York, Scribner's, 1929.
For Whom the Bell Tolls, New York, Scribner's, 1940.
The Green Hills of Africa, New York, Scribner's, 1935.
The Old Man and the Sea, New York, Scribner's, 1952.
The Sun Also Rises, New York, Scribner's, 1926.
To Have and Have Not, New York, Scribner's, 1937.

Short Stories by Ernest Hemingway

In Our Times, New York, Scribner's, 1953.
A Moveable Feast, New York, Scribner's, 1964.
Short Stories, New York, Scribner's, 1966.

---

1. Foreign students may often find newspapers from their own countries in the periodical room.

Other Books by Ernest Hemingway

By-Line: Selected Articles by Ernest Hemingway, William White (ed.) New York, Scribner's, 1967.

Books About Ernest Hemingway

Hemingway, Leicester, *My Brother, Ernest Hemingway,* Cleveland, World Publishing, 1962.

Hotchner, A. E., *Papa Hemingway,* New York, Random House, 1966.

Hovey, Richard B., *The Inward Terrain,* Seattle, University of Washington Press, 1968.

Lewis, Robert W., *Hemingway on Love,* Austin, University of Texas Press, 1965.

Stephens, Robert O., *Hemingway's Non-fiction,* Chapel Hill, University of North Carolina Press, 1968.

Periodical Articles by Ernest Hemingway

"Hemingway Reports Spain," *New Republic,* May 5, 1937, **90,** 376–379; January 12, 1938, **93,** 273–276; April 27, 1938, **94,** 350–351; June 8, 1938, **95,** 124–126.

Periodical Articles About Ernest Hemingway

Campbell, K., "Appreciation of Hemingway," *American Mercury,* July, 1938, **44,** 288–291.

Cowley, M., "Mister Papa," *Life,* January 10, 1949, **26,** 86–90.

"Life of Hemingway," *Time,* October 18, 1937, **30,** 80–81, 83–85.

"Portrait," *Saturday Review of Literature,* October 15, 1938, **18,** 6.

VOCABULARY

a bibliography	a list of publications, usually on one subject or by one author
	The assignment is to prepare a **bibliography** on Ernest Hemingway, including a list of his works and books and articles about him.
a biography	the history of someone's life, written by someone else
	Many people enjoy reading **biographies** of famous historical personalities.
a call number	a special library code that indicates where the book is shelved
	When you request a library book, you must fill out a slip indicating the **call number,** author, and title.
a category *to categorize*	a division in a system that groups things by certain common qualities or characteristics
	The broad subject of literature may be divided into several separate topics. These include such

categories as novels, short stories, poetry, plays, and essays. Novels, short stories, poetry, plays, and essays may be **categorized** as different kinds of literature.

to classify *a classification*	to arrange by special group Library books are **classified** by subject. Other **classifications** include authors and titles.

to criticize
    a critic
    (a) criticism
    critical
	to give a judgment or opinion
	Theater reviewers **criticize** new plays. These **critics** express their opinions on the quality of the productions. Sometimes their **criticisms** are favorable, but often they find fault with the writing or acting.
	"It is easier to be **critical** than to be correct."
	        Benjamin Disraeli, British
	        Prime Minister, speech, 1860.

a due date	the day on which a book must be returned to the library If you do not return your book by the **due date,** you must pay a fine.
*in/out	The book is on the library shelf and may be borrowed. The book is **in.** The book is not on the library shelf. Someone has probably borrowed it. The book is **out.**
an index *to index*	a classification or list of names, subjects, or references in special order, usually alphabetical A subject **index** appears at the end of a book and indicates the specific subjects mentioned in the text and the pages on which these subjects are discussed. The author **indexed** his book carefully. He listed every major subject included in the text and the appropriate page numbers. (The plural of **index** is either **indexes** or **indices.**)
to look at	to direct one's eyes to something; to read casually I **looked at** several library books, but none of them interested me, so I didn't borrow any.
*to look over	to examine Please **look over** this lesson carefully and study the new vocabulary.
*to look up	to search for; to consult a reference book You should **look up** unfamiliar words in a dictionary.

*to renew *a renewal*	to obtain again; to continue to have He wanted to continue to receive the magazine. He had only paid for one year, so at the end of the year he had to **renew** his subscription. He sent a check to pay for the **renewal.**
to reserve *on reserve*	to set aside for special use Some books have been **reserved** for special class use. The librarian has put them aside for use by the students. They are **on reserve.**
a source	a place from which something comes or is obtained A newspaper is a good **source** of information about what is happening in the world.
*a stack	a wood or metal frame with shelves for books **Closed stacks** refer to bookshelf sections in a library that cannot be used without special permission. **Open stacks** refer to library bookshelf sections from which books may be taken without special permission.
to take notes	to write down facts and information It is difficult **to take notes** during a lecture when the speaker talks very quickly.
to take out (a book)	to borrow a book from a library I wanted **to take out** *The Old Man and The Sea* by Ernest Hemingway, but it wasn't in.

Vocabulary Review

Substitute words or phrases from the vocabulary lists of Chapters 1 and 2 for the words in heavy type in the following sentences. Make other changes in the sentences when necessary.

EXAMPLE The assignment was to prepare **a list of books and articles** on Melville Dewey.
          The assignment was to prepare a **bibliography** on Melville Dewey.

1. The National Archives is the federal agency that **collects and holds** unpublished government materials. It also is **responsible for managing** all presidential libraries.
2. In 1764 the Harvard library had approximately five thousand books.

Today it has more than five million volumes, as well as hundreds of **magazines and journals.**

3. The **sections of bookshelves** are open to graduate students **who have special permission.**
4. Some books are **set aside** for special classroom assignments.
5. When a student **borrows** a book, **the date on which it must be returned** is stamped on a slip in the back. If he returns the book after that date, he must pay a **financial penalty.**
6. He had not finished the book, so he asked the librarian **to lend it to him again.**
7. The Sunday *New York Times Book Review* contains **opinions and judgments** of new books.
8. The yellow pages of a telephone book contain the names, addresses, and telephone numbers of businesses in a particular area. The names are **arranged in special groups,** according to the type of business, and then are printed alphabetically.

Comprehension and Thought Questions

1. How are library card calalogs organized?
2. What information must be written on a call slip?
3. What can you do if you have not finished your book by the due date?
4. What happens if you take back a book after the due date?
5. Where are current periodicals kept? bound periodicals?
6. What kinds of library reference sources are available for use in research? Compare the library reference materials described in the text with reference materials available in libraries in your country. How are newspaper and magazine articles indexed in libraries in your country?
7. In what ways is the procedure for taking out library books in your country similar to or different from the procedure described in the text?

Discussion and Composition Topics

1. Spend a half-hour browsing in the periodical room of your school library. List a few of the magazines and newspapers that are available. Look for any that are printed in your native language. Prepare a report on what you find.
2. Do you prefer to read fiction or non fiction? Discuss your favorite author who writes in English and your favorite author who writes in your native language.
3. There is a school in New York City that is attended by children of people who work for the United Nations. Pretend that you are going to give a book and a subscription to a newspaper or magazine, both published in your native language, to the library of the high school at this UN school. What book and paper or periodical will you give? Describe and explain your choices.

Library Assignment 1

From the following list choose one or more questions that interest you. Each student should report to the class every step involved in doing the assignment. Suggested sources are in parentheses. The librarian will assist you if you need help.

Research in the Card Catalog and Stacks

1. What books by Yukio Mishima, the Japanese writer, are in the library collection? Write the title, the call number, and the date of publication of each book.
2. How many books on archery are in the library?
3. Who wrote **The Magic Mountain?** List two other books by the same author and give their call numbers.
4. Who wrote **Man's Fate?** What is the call number? How long is the book? If it is in the open stacks, find out the title of the book directly to the right.
5. How many books entitled **Memoirs** are included in the library collection? List three authors who have written their memoirs (short autobiographies) and the call numbers of the three books.

Research in the Periodical and Reference Rooms

6. In 1973 a short story by the Colombian writer Gabriel García-Marquez appeared in **The Atlantic,** a monthly magazine. Find out the title of the story, the month in which it appeared, and the page on which the story begins. (Use the *Readers' Guide.*)
7. How many recent foreign-language (not English) newspapers or magazines are in the library? List the names of three, the date on which each current copy was published, and the language in which each is printed.
8. Poems by Jorge Luis Borges, the Argentine writer, were published in the magazine *Poetry* in August 1970. Find the name of one poem.
(Use the *Readers' Guide.*)
9. In 1971 Iran celebrated an important event. What was the event? A large state banquet was given at the time. How many guests attended?
(Use the *New York Times Index.*)
10. What is the population of California? (Use U.S. Census, *Statistical Abstract;* be sure to look at the most recent edition.)
11. When was Gerald Ford born? (Use *Who's Who.*)
12. Pablo Neruda, a Chilean poet, won the Nobel Prize for literature in 1971. When was this award announced in the *New York Times?* On what page? (Use the *New York Times Index.*)

Record Library

13. Aaron Copland is a modern American composer. How many recordings of his compositions are in the music library? What is the name of one composition?

14. Find out if the library has a recording of *Othello* by William Shakespeare. If so, tell when the recording was made and the names of the leading actor and actress.

Library Assignment 2

Prepare a short bibliography on a subject that interests you. Discuss the subject with your instructor before you begin your library work. Be sure to include at least five books and five articles from periodicals or newspapers.

Listening Exercises for Chapter 2 begin on p. 244.

Vocabulary Exercises for Section I

Exercise I   Compounds

A. Compound words are single words in which two or more words are combined.

EXAMPLES   blackboard
            overwork

A compound noun usually has the stronger stress on the first part of the word. A compound verb usually has the stronger stress on the second part. There are no absolute rules about the use of the hyphen in most compound words. If you are not sure, you should look up the word in the dictionary.

Here are some compound words that were used in Section I. Read them aloud with your instructor to review stress patterns.

bookstore	storehouse
homework	newspaper
bookshelf	clearinghouse
copyright	Spanish-speaking

B. A special compound structure is used to indicate weight, amount, and measure.

EXAMPLES   I can keep the library book for two weeks. It is a **two-week** library book.
            The book was late, and I had to pay a fine of ten cents. I had to pay a **ten-cent** fine.

Observe that in this structure the modifying compound is always singular and a hypen is used. There is equal stress on both parts of the compound.

C. From the words below make appropriate compounds. Read them aloud to review stress patterns.

1. an assignment five pages long
2. a brick building that has five stories
3. a college program that lasts four years
4. a store where drugs are sold
5. a case that holds books
6. an encyclopedia consisting of ten volumes
7. a traffic fine amounting to twenty dollars
8. a package that weighs five pounds
9. a book bound in paper
10. a book in which to write notes

Exercise II   Suffixes

The suffix **-al** changes some verbs to nouns; it is added to some nouns to form adjectives. The stress is usually not affected. Notice that the final **-e** is dropped when this suffix is added.

EXAMPLES   to renew   renewal
           culture   cultural

A. Change the following verbs to nouns by adding the suffix **al.** Pronounce each new word.

    propose arrive
    revive refuse
    approve dismiss

B. Change the following nouns to adjectives by adding the suffix **-al.** Pronounce each new word.

    recreation
    education
    origin (note the stress change)
    function
    nation (note the pronunciation change)
    supplement (note the stress change)
    rent
    addition
    tradition
    critic

C. The suffix **-ial** or **-ual** is added to some nouns to form adjectives. The stress then changes to the syllable before the suffix.

EXAMPLE   president   presidential
          intellect   intellectual
          industry   industrial
          office   official

Read these words aloud with your instructor. Notice the pronunciation changes.

Exercise III   Prefixes

Prefixes are added to the beginnings of some words.

A. inter- among or between
Through **interlibrary** loans, one library borrows books from another library.

B. re-   again
When you write a paper again, you **rewrite** it.

C. sub-   under; indicating lower position or importance
The subject index in the catalog is **subdivided** into many related categories.

Note: Letter combinations that are used for prefixes and suffixes do not always carry the prefix or suffix meaning but may be part of the root word.

EXAMPLES   reason
subtle

Pronounce the following words, which are related to vocabulary in the text. Addition of the prefixes does not change the pronunciation of the words or the stress.

recharge	interstate
subclassification	subtitle
international	interracial
reclassify	research

Exercise IV   *Pronunciation of Identical Nouns and Verbs*

A. Some two-syllable words stress the first syllable when used as nouns and the second syllable when used as verbs.

EXAMPLES   The text referred to music *récords* in the library. It also stated that the Library of Congress cataloging system *recórds* every book published in the United States.

Some other examples:

Noun	Verb
ábstract	abstráct
cónduct	condúct
óbject	objéct
cónflict	conflíct
cóntest	contést
cóntrast	contrást
ímport	impórt
próduce	prodúce
íncrease	incréase

B. Some words keep the same stress when used as nouns or verbs. Examples from the text:

	Noun	**Verb**
	fúnction	fúnction
	reviéw	reviéw
	cátalog	cátalog
	résearch	résearch
or	reseárch	reseárch
	índex	índex

Read the words in A and B above aloud with your instructor.

Exercise V Nouns are often used to modify other nouns

EXAMPLES reference book
library desk

In Chapter 1 find at least ten nouns that modify other nouns.

II
THE AMERICAN GOVERNMENT

The Constitution and the Presidency

Two hundred years ago the American colonies declared their independence from Great Britain. From 1776 to 1781 they fought a revolutionary war, and when the war ended they established a new nation, the United States of America. Their experience under colonial rule had left the people pulled in opposite directions. On the one hand, they wanted a strong government that would unite the new country. On the other hand, they feared a strong government that might lead to another king. After much debate **representatives** of the states (as the colonies now called themselves) wrote a **constitution,** which generally satisfied these opposite points of view.

The Constitution set up a federal system of government. Under this system some important powers were given to the federal or national government. All the rest of the powers were kept by the states. The national government was made up of three branches: the **executive,** the **legislative,** and the **judicial.** Certain powers were given to each of the branches, but these powers **overlapped** in such a way that the powers of one branch were limited by the powers of the others. This arrangement is known as the system of **checks** and **balances.** It is a basic part of the structure of the American governmental system. No one person or institution can have unlimited **authority.** Each branch of the national government shares and limits some of the powers of the other branches. (In several parts of this section you will find examples of the ways in which the system of checks and balances affects the three branches of the federal government.)

The national government's powers were limited by the powers that were kept by the states. The powers of the national and state governments were further limited by certain constitutional **guarantees** of **civil liberties** for individual citizens. These guarantees are known as the Bill of Rights. They forbid the government from restricting or limiting such civil liberties as freedom of speech, of religion, and of the press, and they guarantee to all citizens certain legal procedures and other rights.

The Constitution begins with this statement of purpose:

> We the People of the United States, in Order to form a more perfect Union, establish Justice, insure domestic Tranquility, provide for the common defence, promote the general welfare, and secure the Blessings of Liberty to ourselves and our Posterity, do ordain and establish this Constitution for the United States of America.

The powers that were given to the national or federal government under the Constitution include the right to make war; the right to tax; the right to borrow and coin money, and to **regulate** its value; the right to regulate commerce between the states (interstate commerce); and the right to maintain a postal system.

The states, too, may tax and borrow money, but they may not coin money or regulate its value. Each state government may control education, regulate corporations and businesses within the state (intrastate commerce), determine most election procedures, and regulate local governments. The states may also make and **administer** civil and criminal laws. (Civil laws are concerned with citizens' private rights, such as contract and property. Criminal laws deal with crimes like theft and murder.)

The powers of the federal government have expanded enormously since the early days of the new nation, largely because of the way in which the federal courts have interpreted the Constitution. The courts have ruled that the responsibilities of the national government extend far beyond those that were **specifically** mentioned in the original document. In addition, federal powers have been increased by constitutional changes called amendments.

The Constitution has been amended twenty-six times. Specific steps must be followed in order to amend the Constitution. Any amendment must be approved by the federal legislature and three-fourths of all the state legislatures. The first ten amendments are the Bill of Rights; later ones deal with great issues like **civil rights** for Blacks. Changes through interpretation by the courts and through amendment have made the Constitution a "living" document, one that has met the tests of governing for almost two hundred years.

The Constitution combines the federal system with a presidential system. Originally, the executive, legislative, and judicial branches were supposed to have equal powers. However, emergencies, crises, and the demands of modern society have made the President, as chief executive, the most important government figure.

The President performs many of the functions of both the British prime minister and king. He is head of the government and chief of state. Subject to approval by the Senate (the upper house of the federal legislature), he negotiates foreign treaties and appoints government officials, including ambassadors, judges, and department heads. He commands the armed forces and sends and receives diplomatic officials. In effect, he makes foreign policy. He performs the ceremonial duties of chief of state, including giving state dinners and receiving foreign visitors. As head of the executive branch he sees to it that laws enacted by the legislature are **carried out**. He is also the leader of his political party, and at the same time he serves as "the voice of the people." The President and the Vice-President are the only officials chosen in a nationwide election.

The Constitution requires the President to be a citizen born in U.S. territory and at least thirty-five years old. It specifies that he may not serve more than two terms of four years each. It also describes how the President can be removed from office and the circumstances under which his duties will be carried out by the Vice-President. The President's annual taxable salary is $200,000; he also receives $50,000 for work-related expenses and $40,000 for tax-free travel.

The official presidential residence, the White House, is located in Washington, D.C. It is the oldest public building in the city and was originally painted gray. During the War of 1812 between the United States and Great Britain, it was badly damaged by British troops, and in 1814 it was repainted white. In his original plans James Hoban, the architect of the White House, had called the building "the Palace." This name offended the opponents of royalty, and the name was changed to "the President's House." Since 1814, however, the executive mansion has been known as "the White House." The President lives and works in this building, and the offices of most of his staff are located there also.

The members of the President's staff handle his appointments schedule, help write his speeches, summarize information and documents for him, assist at press conferences and television appearances, prepare studies and reports on government programs, and keep in touch with Congress and the many parts of the executive branch.

The executive branch consists of eleven departments and many independent agencies, including the postal service. The department heads, called secretaries, form the President's Cabinet. The Cabinet is one source of advice and assistance to the President. He has many

The White House as it looks today.   *Courtesy The White House*

other sources, both private and public, including other representatives of the departments and agencies. Recent presidents have relied increasingly on members of their own White House staffs. For such reliance President Nixon, in particular, was severely criticized.

The section at the end of this chapter summarizes the functions of the various departments and of some of the major agencies of the executive branch.

Almost three million civilians work in the departments and agencies of the executive branch. This number exceeds the total employed by America's seven largest corporations. These government employees make up the federal bureaucracy. Most of them are civil servants, hired under a system in which merit and training are supposed to be the bases of employment and promotion. There are approximately ten thousand civil-service job classifications, which range from bridge engineer to librarian to clerk. Ten percent of these federal employees, or bureaucrats, work in Washington, D.C., 6 percent work outside the United States, and the rest are located throughout the fifty states.

In spite of what seems to be an enormously powerful position involving many responsibilities, the President's powers are not unlimited; most of them are shared with and restricted by the other branches of government. The system of checks and balan‿ clearly illustrated by the President's working relations with the le‿ lature. The President proposes legislation, but the legislature does n‿ have to enact it. He cannot put a treaty into effect without approval by two-thirds of the Senate. In 1973 the legislature limited his powers as commander in chief by forbidding him to keep any armed forces abroad for combat without specific Congressional approval. The Senate must approve most of his appointments to the executive and judicial branches. Because the President cannot command the legislators to do what he wishes, he must try to **persuade** them.

The President's strength and power really depend on his ability to persuade others in the government to carry out the policies and actions he proposes. His ability to persuade increases when he has support of citizens throughout the country. To keep the support of the people he must present an image of honesty, authority, and leadership.

VOCABULARY

to administer *administration* *administrative*	to manage; to govern The secretary of each department of the executive branch of the government **administers** his department. He is the chief **administrative** official of the department and is responsible for its **administration.**
the Administration	In the United States the **Administration** consists of the President, his staff, and his department heads during his time in office.
*authority	the power or right to give orders and to make others obey them The Constitution gives the President the **authority** to choose the Supreme Court judges, but this **authority** is limited by the requirement that the Senate approve his choices.
*a balance *to balance*	a condition in which opposing forces are kept equal In international relations a **balance** of power exists when no one country or group of countries is stronger than another. Their powers are **balanced.**
*to carry out	to perform; to put into practice It is often easier to make plans than to **carry** them **out.**

*a check

   to check

a control; a restraint

The legislature must approve all money that is used to pay for programs which are administered by the executive branch. In this way the legislature exercises an important **check** on the executive branch and on the power of the President. The money power of the legislature **checks** the spending power of the President.

civil liberties

the legal promises or assurances to the individual of certain freedoms such as the freedom of religion, speech, and press

civil rights

equality of treatment under the law without discrimination based on race, nationality, religion, or sex

Since the end of slavery in the United States there has never been a question about a Black's freedom of religion—**a civil liberty.** At the same time, Blacks have been restricted in such matters as schools they could attend or public facilities they could use—restrictions of their **civil rights.**

*a constitution

the laws and principles that establish a system of government

The United States **Constitution** is a written document that declares how the government is to function.

an executive

   *to execute

   executive

a person who is responsible for making decisions and shaping policy

The President is the chief **executive** of the United States government. He has **executive** responsibilities. He must carry out government policy. He must **execute** government policy.

to guarantee

   a guarantee

to promise; to assure without question or condition

The Constitution **guarantees** certain basic liberties such as freedom of speech and freedom of religion. Constitutional **guarantees** include those of freedom of speech and freedom of religion.

judicial

relating to a judge or a court of law

The federal **judicial** system is composed of three separate levels of courts.

legislative

   legislation

   a legislature

lawmaking

The Senate and the House of Representatives constitute the **legislative** branch of the federal

a legislator
to legislate

government. They are the federal **legislature.** Their role is to **legislate,** to pass laws or to enact **legislation.** The members of Congress are federal **legislators.**

to overlap

an overlap

to cover or extend partly over something

Here are two circles. The dark area indicates where these circles **overlap.** The dark area is the **overlap.**

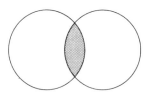

to persuade

persuasion

to convince or to reason successfully with someone to do something or to believe something

President Harry S. Truman, who was President from 1945 to 1953, said, "I sit here all day trying to **persuade** people to do the things they ought to have sense enough to do without my **persuading** them. . . . That's all the powers of the President amount to."

Richard E. Neustadt, *Presidential Power,* New York, Wiley, 1960, p. 10

President Truman said that presidential power is limited to the power of **persuasion.**

*to regulate

a regulation
regulatory
regular
regularly

to control in an orderly way

Traffic laws are designed to **regulate** the use of automobiles and trucks. **Regulatory** traffic laws set speed limits. Traffic laws establish driving **regulations.**

Many students come to class every day. They never miss a session. Their attendance is **regular.** They attend classes **regularly.**

*to represent

a representative
representative
representation

to act or speak for

The President **represents** all the people. He is the people's **representative.**

Elections by the people are supposed to guarantee **representative** government. Elections are held throughout the country to assure **representation** of all the people.

A **representative,** also called a congressman, is a member of the House of **Representatives,** one of the two houses of the legislature.

specific   detailed and precise
   to specify   The teacher gave the students **specific** instruc-
   specifically   tions about their homework. She explained
                             exactly how they were to do it.
                       The doctor advised his patient not to eat meat.
                             He **specified** that the patient was never to eat
                             steak. He **specifically** warned him not to eat
                             steak.

Vocabulary Review

A. Put a plus sign (+) in front of the word in list II if it has a meaning that
is the same as or similar to the corresponding word in list I. Put a minus
sign (−) in front of the word in list II if it has a different meaning.

	I	II
EXAMPLE	1. legislate	+____ pass laws
	2. specify	____ generalize
	3. amend	____ change
	4. carry out	____ execute
	5. check	____ allow
	6. administer	____ manage
	7. guarantee	____ refuse
	8. persuade	____ command
	9. balance	____ equalize
	10. overlap	____ partly extend over

B. Choose words from the list below to complete the following sentences.
You may make the word plural or change the tense of any verb if necessary.
Use a word only once.

a. authority	g. judicial
b. balance	h. overlap
c. check	i. persuade
d. carry out	j. regulation
e. execute	k. representative
f. guarantee	l. specific

EXAMPLE   Because the boat was not properly (b) **balanced,** it turned over.

1. You can depend on him. He always _____ instructions carefully.

2. The watch broke the first time I wore it. Fortunately, it was _____ to run properly for a year, so I did not have to pay for the repair work.

3. She continued to cry. She could not _____ her tears.

4. The directions were so _____ that we found the house with no trouble.

5. They had planned to stay home, but he _____ them to go to the movies.

6. Policemen have the _____ to give parking tickets.

7. He spoke for all the people in that community. He was their

   _____.

8. The library has strict _____ concerning areas where smoking is permitted.

9. They see each other at school when their class schedules

   _____.

10. The President is expected to have all federal laws properly

    _____.

Comprehension and Thought Questions

1. What are checks and balances? Why are they important in the United States system of government?
2. List some powers granted to the national government by the Constitution. What powers were kept by the states?
3. How does the procedure for amending the Constitution illustrate overlapping powers of the federal and state governments?
4. List two civil liberties that are specifically mentioned in the Bill of Rights. What other civil liberties do you think are important?
5. What are some of the powers that the Constitution has granted to the President?
   a. Compare the powers and functions of the President with those of the chief executive of your country.
   b. How are the powers of the President limited? Are the powers of the chief executive of your country limited? If so, how?

6. What do you know about the President's official residence? Describe the residence of the chief executive of your country.
7. How long is the President's term of office? How long can your chief executive remain in power?
8. a. What is the Cabinet? What are department heads called?
   b. Who advises your chief executive?
9. Do you think a civil service system assures that government employees are well qualified for their jobs? Explain your opinion.

Discussion and Composition Topics

1. The presidency has often been described as one of the most difficult jobs in the world. We can almost see each President grow older under the strains and pressures of his work. Why do you think people want to be President? Would you like to be President? Why or why not?
2. The text describes the President as "the voice of the people." How is this role related to the fact that he and the Vice-President are the only officials chosen in a nationwide election?
3. The text also states that an effective President must present an image of authority, honesty, and leadership.
   a. What qualities do you think the chief executive of a country should have?
   b. Give your opinion of the importance of qualifications such as education, military experience, public-speaking ability, political experience, ability to understand several languages, age, economic and social background.
4. At a press conference in June 1962, President John Kennedy said, "I know that when things don't go well, the President gets the blame, and that is one of the things the President is paid for." How does this statement fit with any impressions you may have about the presidency? Do you think the chief executive of any country usually takes the blame when things don't go well, or is this particularly characteristic of the President of the United States?

Library Assignment

Make a list of all the civil liberties that are specifically guaranteed in the Bill of Rights.

Departments of the Executive Branch

For your general information here is a brief description of the departments of the executive branch and some agencies and government corporations. They are all operated under the authority of the President.

Department	Chief Functions
Department	**Chief Functions**
Agriculture	Provides technical assistance to farmers, conducts research on methods of farming and food processing, and makes subsidy payments for certain crops.
Commerce	Promotes foreign and domestic trade, tests the quality of certain manufactured products, issues patents, maintains commerce statistics, and conducts a national census every ten years, also issues official weather reports.
Defense	Supervises the armed forces, buys weapons, and conducts military research.
Health, Education and Welfare	Administers social security benefits for old people, children, and other dependents; finances research on mental and physical health; makes educational grants and loans; sets standards to improve education, including adult and vocational education and programs for the handicapped.
Housing and Urban Development	Encourages private home building, finances low-income public housing, and supplies money and technical assistance to help cities with slum clearance and other improvements.
Interior	Is responsible for American Indians living on reservations; develops and regulates national resources, including power plants and national parks.
Justice	Gives legal advice to the President, represents the government in court, and assists in carrying out judicial orders, including those concerned with civil rights. [The Federal Bureau of Investigation (FBI) is a branch of this department, as is the Immigration and Naturalization Service. The department head is the Attorney General.]
Labor	Administers laws covering wages, hours, working conditions, and unemployment insurance and tries to prevent or to settle strikes; also publishes statistical data on employment, wages, and the cost of living.
State	Conducts diplomatic relations with foreign governments, runs the consular service abroad, and assists the President's office in developing foreign policy.

Transportation	Tries to find safer, faster, cheaper ways to move people and freight throughout the country.
Treasury	Collects taxes, prints money, manages the public debt, and maintains relations with foreign governments on international monetary matters.

Agencies That Are Part of the President's Office

Council of Economic Advisers	Advises the President on matters relating to the national economy, such as taxes and prices.
National Security Council	Advises the President on foreign policy and on defense policy; supervises the Central Intelligence Agency (CIA).
Office of Management and Budget	Assists the President in the preparation of the budget for the entire executive branch, which he must present to Congress for approval; also supervises departments and agencies in spending the money they receive from Congress.

Independent Regulatory Agencies of the Executive Branch

Federal Communications Commission (FCC)	Regulates communications by wire, radio, and television (see Section III).
Interstate Commerce Commission (ICC)	Regulates rail, motor, inland, and coastal shipping.
National Labor Relations Board (NLRB)	Investigates complaints of unfair labor practices and holds elections to determine labor union representation.

Government Corporations of the Executive Branch

Postal Service	Handles all mail as a public business organization.

Administrative Agencies of the Executive Branch

Veterans Administration	Administers benefits and services, including insurance, medical care and hospitalization, education allowances, and home loans to war veterans and their dependents.

(These lists are not complete but offer examples of different kinds of agencies and corporations of the executive branch.)

Listening Exercises for Chapter 3 begin on p. 246.

The Legislature

Congress is the legislative branch of the federal government. There are two houses of Congress: the Senate and the House of Representatives. The Senate is composed of 100 voting members, two from each of the fifty states. They may be elected for an unlimited number of six-year **terms.** A senator must be at least thirty years old and must have been a U.S. citizen for at least nine years. The House has 435 voting members plus non-voting representatives from Puerto Rico and the District of Columbia. The members of the House are called representatives or congressmen. They must be at least twenty-five years of age and must have been U.S. citizens for not less than seven years. They may be elected to an unlimited number of two-year terms.

Many senators and congressmen are reelected term after term. It is not unusual for some to serve for more than twenty years. The legislators who have served for the longest time have the greatest seniority. Regardless of their age they are known as the senior members of Congress.

Senators and representatives are residents of the states from which they are elected. A senator is chosen by voters from the entire state. Representatives are elected by the voters from geographic areas within each state. These areas are called congressional districts. The districts are supposed to have approximately equal numbers of people, and each district elects one congressman.

The number of congressmen from each state varies depending on the size of the population of the state. Every ten years the U.S. Census reports the **distribution** of the population of the entire country. The 435 congressional positions, called seats, are then distributed among the states according to a plan **based on** changes that may have

The Capitol, Washington, D.C.   *Courtesy American Airlines*

The House of Representatives.   *Wide World Photos*

occurred during that ten-year period. If the population of a state has risen sharply, that state is allowed more congressional districts and therefore more representatives. If the population of another state has declined greatly, the number of congressional districts and repre- sentatives is reduced. However, each state must have at least one congressman. At present California has the largest population of any state, and so it has the greatest number of representatives (forty- three). New York ranks second with thirty-nine. Six states have only one representative each. They are Alaska, Delaware, Nevada, South Dakota, Vermont, and Wyoming.

Each senator and representative earns an annual salary of $42,- 500. In addition, he receives extra allowances. Because he must main- tain a home in his state, as well as in Washington, D.C., he gets a $3,000 tax deduction. He has a liberal travel allowance and receives additional money for office and staff requirements, and is also entitled to free postage, known as the franking privilege, for official mail. Senators and congressmen maintain offices in the capital. They must also have fully staffed offices in their home districts in order to keep in touch with their constituents, who are all the people in the area that they represent. Such contact is essential in performing their represen- tative duties, as well as in building support for reelection. To assure complete freedom, every member of both houses is guaranteed pro- tection from libel suits in connection with anything he may say while performing his congressional duties. A libel suit is action in a court of law to protest personal remarks that may unjustly injure someone's reputation.

The U.S. Congress is primarily a man's world. There have been only five women senators since women won the right to vote in 1920. In 1975 there were nineteen congresswomen and no women senators.[1]

Congressional party caucuses select the majority and minority party leaders of each house of the legislature. These men play key roles in the legislative process, organizing support for or opposition to legislation on important issues. The word caucus may come from the Algonquin Indian word caucauasu, which means "someone who ad- vises, urges, and encourages." A caucus is a private political meeting held to select candidates for office or to plan political party activities. To caucus means to hold such a meeting.

A **bill,** or legislative **proposal,** may be introduced by a member of either house, and sometimes supporters of important legislation offer their bills in both houses **simultaneously.** Approximately ten thousand

1. There have been two female members of presidential cabinets and no women judges on the Supreme Court, the highest federal court. Only men have held the offices of Presi- dent and Vice-President.

bills are introduced during each session of Congress. Many bills request action on behalf of an individual or group of individuals from the area that a congressman or senator represents. These are called "private bills." The most important public bills are often introduced at the request of the President or involve major issues with which one or more legislators are especially concerned.

All bills are immediately referred to an appropriate legislative committee. These committees are organized by special subjects such as education, agriculture, and foreign affairs. Each committee is made up of representatives of both parties. The chairmanship is usually held by the committee member of the majority party who has the greatest seniority. Each committee has a special staff. The Library of Congress (see Chapter 1) supplies experts to do research and analysis.

The committee that is responsible for a particular bill holds hearings on it. Experts and other interested individuals appear before the committee and offer suggestions and opinions about the bill. After the hearings, the committee reports its recommendations to the house. These recommendations may include suggested changes in the bill, or the committee may propose an entirely new one. Committee recommendations are of great importance because, when the legislators vote on a bill, they usually follow the committee report. If a committee chooses not to consider a bill, the bill dies. A relatively small number of all bills receive committee attention.

Following the committee action the bill is **debated** on the **floor** of each house. Then a vote is taken. A voice vote, the most common and the quickest, involves a general chorus of Yeas or Nays. The leader or chairman decides which side has the majority. In a **roll-call vote,** each congressman's vote is recorded separately. If a bill is **defeated** in either house, it dies.

If the House of Representatives and the Senate **approve** similar bills with some different provisions, both bills go to a conference committee, in which selected senators and congressmen work to adjust the differences. On rare occasions the committee does not reach an agreement, and the bill is "lost in conference." Usually an agreement is reached, however, and after majority approval by both houses of Congress, the proposed law is sent to the White House for presidential action.

The bill becomes law following one of several steps by the President. He may approve the bill and sign it; he may sign the bill with a statement expressing his disapproval; or he may simply not sign the bill, in which case it automatically becomes a law after ten days. On the other hand, if he hopes to prevent the bill from becoming law, the President **vetoes** it. This means that he expresses his disapproval and refuses to sign it. The proposal may still become law if two-thirds of each house of Congress then votes for it, thus overriding, or defeating, the President's veto. This does not happen often. The President may also use the "pocket veto": If he does not sign a bill within ten days and Congress **adjourns** during that period, the bill does not become law.

Related to the lawmaking power of Congress is its **function** of **investigation,** which involves examination of government activities to determine if the executive branch is performing its duties properly and if new legislation is needed. Investigations also help to inform the public on such different and important subjects as crime and space exploration. The most widely publicized Senate investigation in recent years has been the "Watergate hearings." A special Senate committee investigated charges of criminal activities by members of the White House staff during President Nixon's administration and of a closely related political group called the Committee to Re-elect the President. The first round of hearings was televised and was watched by millions of viewers in the United States and abroad.

VOCABULARY

to adjourn	to break off or end a meeting
an adjournment	The congressional session ended in June. The Congress **adjourned** in June. **Adjournment** had been scheduled for May, but Congress delayed **adjournment** in order to finish certain legislative business.
to approve *(of)*	to agree with something; to judge favorably
approval	The congressional committee reported the bill favorably. It recommended that Congress pass the bill. The committee **approved** the bill. Committee **approval** led to favorable congressional action.
to base on	to found on or build on
a basis (of)	The writers of the Constitution **based** the Bill of
basic (to)	Rights **on** the belief in civil liberties for all citizens. The Bill of Rights is **based on** the belief in civil liberties for all citizens. Many people believe that these liberties form the **basis of** an effective democracy. They believe these civil liberties are fundamental and **basic to** an effective democratic system. (The plural of **basis** is **bases.)**

*a bill   a legislative proposal

The House and Senate passed the **bill** by voice vote. Then it was sent to the President for his signature.

to debate   to discuss and argue
   a debate

The bill was important, and many congressmen disagreed with each other about it. They argued for a long time. They **debated** the bill for many hours. After a long **debate,** Congress passed the bill.

*to defeat   to cause to fail (by voting against); to beat
   a defeat

A majority of the Congress voted against the bill. They **defeated** the bill. Most people had expected Congress to pass the bill. They were surprised by its **defeat.**

*to distribute   to spread out over a large area
   distribution

The Census Bureau gathers statistics on the population, including where people live and how many people live in a particular area. The Bureau reports on population **distribution.** It reports on how the population is **distributed** throughout the country.

*the floor   the part of the hall, or the room, where legislators sit and from which they speak

The bill was debated on **the floor** of the Senate. Senator Jones was called on by the chairman. He had **the floor** and spoke at length against the bill.

a function   a special activity or purpose
   to function

The key **function** of the Congress is to legislate. The most important activity of Congress is to make laws. It also **functions** as an investigating body.

to investigate   to examine; to make a thorough, careful inquiry
   an investigation

Congress functions as an **investigating** body. It **investigates** the operations of the executive branch. It also conducts **investigations** of major current issues. It looks into these matters thoroughly.

*to propose   to offer or put forward for consideration, as a
   a proposal   piece of legislation

The congressman offered a bill to lower income taxes. He **proposed** legislation to lower income taxes. He made a **proposal** to lower income taxes.

a roll-call vote	a vote in which the name of each voter is read aloud and his vote is officially recorded
	The voice vote was so close that a **roll-call vote** was necessary to determine if the bill had passed. The vote of each person was recorded separately.
simultaneous	at the same time
simultaneously	We use both eyes at the same time. We have **simultaneous** use of both eyes. Both eyes see **simultaneously.**
*a term	a limited period of time
	A senator's **term** in office is six years. A representative's **term** is two years. Each may be re-elected for an unlimited number of **terms.** The President's **term** is four years. A Constitutional amendment provides that a President cannot be elected for more than two **terms.**
to veto	to reject or forbid something
a veto	The President may **veto** a bill of which he disapproves.
	The Congress may override or defeat the President's **veto** by a two-thirds vote in each house.

Vocabulary Review

Use the following pairs of words in sentences. You may make a word plural, and you may change the tense of any verb.

EXAMPLE   approve, bill
Congress **approved** the **bill** in a voice vote.

1. function, investigate
2. debate, floor
3. bill, simultaneously
4. propose, adjourn
5. defeat, roll-call vote

Comprehension and Thought Questions

1. a. What are the names of the two houses of Congress?
   b. How many voting members are there in each house?

c. How long are their terms?

d. Which office would you rather have? Why?

2. a. On what basis are congressional districts established?

b. If you have an elected legislature in your country, how is it organized? How many houses are there? How long are the legislators' terms? Does each legislator represent the people in a specific geographic area? If so, how are such areas determined? If not, whom are the legislators supposed to represent?

3. What extra kinds of income do senators and representatives receive? What kinds of extra income do legislators in your country receive?

4. a. What is the possible origin of the word *caucus*?

b. What does *caucus* mean?

5. a. How does the President's veto power illustrate the system of checks and balances between the President and Congress?

b. Is the President's signature necessary for a bill to become a law? Must your chief executive approve legislation in order for it to become law officially?

c. If your country has a legislature, can your chief executive declare laws without prior action by the legislature?

6. a. Do you have hearings on proposed legislation in your country? If so, describe the procedure. Are the hearings open to the public? Are they televised? Are they reported in the newspapers? Who is allowed to testify?

b. How does the investigating function of Congress illustrate checks and balances?

Discussion and Composition Topics

1. At a press conference in July 1959, President Dwight D. Eisenhower said: "When it comes to the relations of any President with a Congress controlled by the opposite party, I just say this: it is no bed of roses."

"Bed of roses" is an idiomatic expression meaning extremely comfortable. What situations can you think of in which the position of the President might be made difficult by a Congress controlled by the opposite party?

2. Here is the kind of moral issue that legislators often have to deal with: Should a senator oppose a bill that might hurt some of his constituents even if it would help many people throughout the country? For example:

Senator Smith comes from a farm state where many people raise cattle that are sold for meat. Meat prices are high, and the farmers in the Senator's state are making a lot of money. Prices are so high, however, that many people throughout the country cannot afford to buy meat.

Senator Barnes comes from an industrial state and has proposed a bill to encourage the purchase of less expensive meat from Argentina and Australia. The purchase of a large amount of this meat would probably bring down meat prices in the United States generally. As a result, Senator Smith's constituents would make less money. On the other hand, more people could buy meat at lower prices.

How should Senator Smith vote on Senator Barnes's bill? (By the way, Senator Smith has served three terms as Senator, and he does not plan to run for reelection when his present term ends next year. Do these facts affect your opinion? Would your opinion be the same if Senator Smith were serving his first term and planned to run for reelection next year?)

a. Pretend that you are Senator Barnes. Another student is Senator Smith. Try to persuade Senator Smith to vote in favor of the bill to encourage the purchase of meat from Argentina and Australia.

b. Pretend that you are a cattle rancher from Senator Smith's state. You have supported Senator Smith since he first entered politics. Try to persuade Senator Smith to vote against the Barnes meat bill.

Listening Exercises for Chapter 4 begin on p. 247.

The Judicial Branch

The Constitution creates a Supreme Court of the United States and leaves to Congress the creation of all lower federal courts. The President, with Senate approval, appoints all federal judges for life terms. These judges receive annual salaries ranging from $40,000 in the lowest court to $62,500 for the Chief Justice of the United States, who heads the Supreme Court.

Federal courts have the power to rule on both criminal and civil cases. Criminal action under federal **jurisdiction** includes such behavior as treason, destruction of government property, counterfeiting, hijacking, and narcotics **violations.** In civil cases a person may be accused of interfering with the rights of another in various ways, such as damaging property, violating a contract, or making libelous statements. If he is found guilty, he may be required to pay a certain amount of money, called damages, but he is never sent to jail. A convicted criminal, on the other hand, may be imprisoned. The Bill of Rights guarantees a trial by jury in all criminal cases. A jury is a group of citizens—usually 12 persons—who make the decision on a case.

The lowest federal court is the district court. Each state has at least one district court, and many states with large populations have several. Cases from such a court may be **reviewed** by the next higher court, the U.S. Court of Appeals. Decisions are final, except for those which are reviewed by the Supreme Court. (Some cases, including those involving the constitutionality of laws passed by Congress, may be brought directly from the district court to the Supreme Court.) In addition to the power to review district court decisions, a court of appeals may also review and enforce orders of federal agencies such

An official portrait of the Justices of the Supreme Court.   *U.P.I.*

as the Federal Communications Commission and the National Labor Relations Board.[1]

In addition to the district and appeals courts, there are special federal courts, such as the Court of Tax Claims and the Court of Military Appeals.

The Supreme Court, composed of nine judges, who are called justices, is the highest court in the nation. As it decides individual cases, it **interprets** the laws or executive actions that each case involves. At the same time, the Court reviews these laws and actions to determine whether they **conform** to the U.S. Constitution. Justices have different political philosophies, and they often disagree in their interpretations of the Constitution. Court decisions are determined by the opinions of the majority of the judges. If the majority rule that the law in question violates the Constitution, the law is declared unconstitutional and becomes **invalid.** This process is known as judicial review. All lower courts follow the rulings of the Supreme Court. Its decisions are final unless the Constitution is amended or the Court

1. See the section listing government agencies at the end of Chapter 3.

later changes its opinion. The Court has established that the Constitution is the supreme law of the land.

Because interpretation of the Constitution, as well as other decisions by the Supreme Court, often involves serious questions of public policy and political philosophy, the Court cannot avoid being a political body as it carries out its judicial functions. Supreme Court decisions have involved almost every major issue that has arisen in the United States. For the first seventy-five years of Supreme Court history, the most important cases involved **conflicts** over the authority of the national government and the state governments. From the middle 1800s until the late 1930s the major decisions of the Court concerned economic regulation—control of business activities and setting economic policy by the federal government. During the past thirty years the most important Supreme Court cases have concerned civil rights and issues of criminal law. Recently cases involving **environment** and **consumer** law have been gaining importance. Cases argued before the Supreme Court in the past few years have raised questions such as:

1 Does the death penalty for convicted criminals violate the Eighth Amendment, which prohibits "cruel and unusual punishment"?
2 Does an unwed father have as much right as an unwed mother for the care of and responsibility for their child?
3 Can one state sue another state (or a city in another state), in order to stop **pollution** that affects them both?
4 Can a landlord remove tenants who, in order to force the landlord to make reasonable repairs, refuse to pay their rent?

All federal judges are expected to be of high character and ability. After they are appointed, they are supposed to withdraw from all political activities, to avoid public positions on controversial issues, and never to permit personal interests to influence their official behavior.

Every state has its own constitution, which provides a plan of state government. Like the federal system, each state follows the three-branches-of-government structure. State chief executives are called governors, and state legislators are usually known as representatives and senators. Unlike federal judges, who are appointed for life, most state judges are elected for limited terms. State courts handle criminal and civil cases that do not come under federal jurisdiction.

Although the U.S. Constitution gives to the states those powers not granted to the federal government, the line between state and federal authority is often **ambiguous.** This ambiguity has resulted in **recurring** conflicts between federal and state officials throughout American history. The issue is known as "states' rights." Over a hundred years ago the long and bloody Civil War between the federal government and the southern states was fought, largely because of this question. Recent disagreement over this division of power has been **reflected** in conflicts about **integration** of black and white school-children[2] and other policies to reduce racial **segregation.** A special presidential commission, which was appointed to investigate several race riots that occurred in the late 1960s, listed as one cause of the outbreaks "the open **defiance** of federal law and federal authority by state and local officials resisting desegregation."[3]

In spite of such conflicts over the jurisdiction of state and federal authority, and in spite of outspoken disapproval by numbers of citizens of such government policies as recent American military action in Southeast Asia, the U.S. governmental system is a stable one. In 1827 an Englishwoman, Frances Trollope, visited the United States and wrote, "There [is one point] on which all Americans agree—namely, that the American government is the best in the world." Over 125 years later another English observer, Denis Brogan, wrote, "No government has less reason to worry about the loyalty of its people than the government of the United States."[4] In the 1970s we may question whether all Americans agree that their government is the best, but certainly it seems that strong support of the governmental system continues throughout the nation.

VOCABULARY

ambiguous *an ambiguity*	of uncertain meaning; having more than one possible meaning
	The instructor gave the homework assignment. The students were not sure whether he told them to read chapters 36 through 38 or chapters 36 to 38. The assignment was **ambiguous.** The students were confused by the **ambiguity.**

2. See Section V, Chapter 15.
3. *Report of the National Advisory Commission on Civil Disorders,* Washington, D.C., U.S. Government Printing Office, 1968, p. 92. In 1954 the Supreme Court ruled that school segregation was illegal (see Section V, Chapter 15), and in 1964 Congress passed the Civil Rights Act, which forbids segregation in hotels, restaurants, gas stations, theaters, and elsewhere.
4. Denis Brogan, *American Aspects,* London, Hamish Hamilton, 1964, p. 4. For further comments about the United States by Mrs. Trollope and Mr. Brogan see Section VII, Chapters 20 and 21.

to conflict (with) *a conflict*	to be in opposition or disagreement Their description of the accident was totally different from ours. Their description **conflicted with** ours. There is often a **conflict** between duty and desire. We want to do one thing, but we ought to do something else.
to conform (to) *conformity*	to be in agreement Young Americans like to dress in similar fashion. They want to **conform to** the style of other young people. **Conformity** seems to give them a sense of belonging to a distinct age group. There is a saying, "When in Rome, do as the Romans do." It means that when you are visiting another country, you should try to **conform** to the customs of the people who live in that country.
a consumer	a person who buys and uses goods such as food and clothing The U.S. Department of Labor publishes monthly statistics on the cost of living. This is known as the **Consumer** Price Index. It measures the prices that people must pay for various items such as housing, food, clothing, and health care.
to defy *defiance*	to refuse to obey; to resist openly The Americans **defied** British authority and declared their independence from British rule. Their **defiance** led to the American Revolution.
environment *environmental*	the surroundings People are increasingly concerned about their physical **environment.** They want to breathe clean air, and they want their city streets to be clean and safe. Industrial cities often have **environmental** problems such as noise, smoke, and dirt.
*to integrate *integration*	to combine into one group Racial **integration** of schools involves black and white children attending the same schools. In 1954 the U.S. Supreme Court ordered all schools to **integrate.**
*to interpret *an interpretation*	to make the meaning clear A good critic **interprets** the artist. The critic's **interpretation** helps the public to understand and appreciate the artist's work.

*invalid	not having the force of law
*valid	having the force of law

The Supreme Court may rule that a law that violates or conflicts with the Constitution is not legal. The Court declares that the law is not **valid.** It is **invalid.** People cannot legally be forced to obey it.

a jurisdiction

tho oxtent or area of legal authority

The courts may make legal decisions affecting foreigners and American citizens. The courts have **jurisdiction** not only over United States citizens but also over foreigners who live in the United States.

to pollute
pollution

to make dirty

People all over the world are concerned about the industrial filth that is ruining the environment. Water is **polluted.** Industrial dirt **pollutes** the air, and it is sometimes not safe to breathe. This problem of **pollution** is steadily increasing.

to recur
a recurrence

to happen again

There was a serious fuel shortage in 1974. Many people feared there would be another. Many people feared the fuel shortage would **recur.** They feared a **recurrence** of the fuel shortage.

*to reflect
a reflection

to express the quality or character of something

The book **reflected** his political philosophy. It expressed how the author felt about major issues of the day. It was a **reflection** of the author's political values and beliefs.

*to review
a review

to consider

A Court of Appeals **reviews** decisions of lower courts and may reverse these decisions.

Judicial **review** by the Supreme Court involves examination of laws and executive acts to determine whether they conform to the provisions of the Constitution.

*to segregate
segregation

to keep apart in separate groups

Racial **segregation** is separation based on race. When black children were not permitted to attend school with white children, they were legally **segregated.** The Supreme Court has outlawed legal **segregation,** but in fact racial **segregation** still exists and remains an issue.

*to violate   to act against or to break a law, regulation, or
   a violation   agreement

A law that **violates** the Constitution does not conform to the provisions of that document. A law that is in **violation** of the Constitution is invalid.

Vocabulary Review

A. Match each verb in list I with one in list II that has a similar meaning.

I	II
EXAMPLE 1. to recur (c) to happen again	a. to consider carefully
2. to interpret _____	b. to disagree sharply
3. to defy _____	c. to happen again
4. to pollute _____	d. to combine or mix
5. to review _____	e. to buy and use goods
6. to conflict _____	f. to explain the meaning
7. to consume _____	g. to dirty
8. to integrate _____	h. to separate
9. to segregate _____	i. to agree with
10. to violate _____	j. to break (a law)
	k. to refuse to obey

B. The words in heavy type in the following sentences are from the vocabulary list. Read each sentence aloud, and indicate whether the vocabulary word is used correctly. If it is wrong, give a brief definition of the word to show why it does not fit the meaning of the sentence.

EXAMPLE   If something never happened before, it **recurred.**
           The vocabulary word is not correct. **Recurred** means happened again.

1. The child always obeyed his parents because he was **defiant.**
2. When boys and girls attend separate schools, their schools are **segregated** by sex.

3. The directions were so clear and **ambiguous** that we found our way easily.
4. The judge **reviewed** the problem carefully.
5. Don't drink that water! It is **polluted.**
6. Our views on the matter **conflicted.** We agreed on every point.
7. His poetry **reflected** the way he felt about life.
8. Supreme Court justices **interpret** the Constitution.
9. The speed limit on the highway was sixty miles an hour. He **violated** the limit when he drove fifty miles an hour.
10. When we try to be different from other people in the way we dress, we are **conforming.**

Comprehension Quiz

Are the following statements correct or incorrect, according to the text? If a statement is incorrect, change it so that it is accurate.

EXAMPLE   The President must have the approval of the Senate only when he appoints judges to the Supreme Court.
This statement is incorrect. The President must have the approval of the Senate when he appoints all federal judges.

1. The Bill of Rights guarantees a trial by jury in all criminal cases.
2. The Supreme Court decisions are based on majority rule. There are nine justices. A majority of those voting must agree in order for the Court to rule on a case.
3. If the Supreme Court rules that a law conflicts with the Constitution, the law is declared invalid. This process is known as judicial review.
4. In recent years the Supreme Court has heard only cases involving issues of the environment and consumer law.
5. The issue of states' rights involves the question of the jurisdiction of state and federal authority. This issue was finally settled in the Civil War.
6. The author believes that the U.S. governmental system is unstable.
7. The chief executive of a state is the governor.
8. The U.S. Supreme Court's function of judicial review illustrates the system of checks and balances between the judicial and the legislative or executive branches.

Discussion and Composition Topics

1. The text states that the U.S. Supreme Court cannot avoid being a political body. In what ways do you think judicial decisions may be political?
2. a. Is there a high, or supreme, court in your country? If so, what kinds of cases does it decide?
   b. How are judges chosen in your country?

3. If you have a constitution, what official authority interprets it?
4. Several questions that have been asked in recent Supreme Court cases are summarized in Chapter 5. Two such questions are:
   a. Does an unwed father have as much right as an unwed mother for the care of and responsibility for their child?
   b. Can a landlord remove tenants who, in order to force the landlord to make reasonable repairs, refuse to pay their rent?

   What are your answers to these questions? Explain your reasons.
   c. Another question involved the death penalty for convicted criminals. The death penalty is known as *capital punishment*. What is your opinion of capital punishment?

Listening Exercises for Chapter 5 begin on p. 248.

General Dicussion and Composition Topics
for Section II

Below are statements by several famous Americans. Choose one and prepare a short paragraph discussing the meaning of the statement and your opinion of it. Notice when the statement was made. The time may affect your opinion. Where possible, analyze these statements as they apply to your own country. If you do not have a president, analyze statements 2, 4, and 5 in terms of your own chief executive.

1. It is not the function of our government to keep the citizen from falling into error; it is the function of the citizen to keep the government from falling into error.
   Robert Jackson, associate Supreme Court justice, court decision, 1950.

2. I would rather be right than President.
   Henry Clay, legislator and cabinet member, speech, 1850.

3. The happiness of society is the end [goal] of government.
   John Adams, President: 1797–1801, *Writings,* 1776.

4. Being a President is like riding a tiger. A man has to keep riding or be swallowed.
   Harry S. Truman, President: 1945–1953, *Memoirs,* Vol. 2, New York, Doubleday, 1956, p. 1.

5. To be President of the United States is to be lonely, very lonely at times of great decisions.
   Ibid., Vol. 1, 1955, p. 14.

VOCABULARY EXERCISES FOR SECTION II

Exercise I

A. More compounds (review of Section I, vocabulary exercise I)
Read the following compounds from the text with your instructor to review stress patterns.

1. a congressman
2. a congresswoman
3. a two-year term
4. a ten-year period
5. an outbreak
6. to overlap
7. to override

B. More nouns that modify other nouns (review of Section I, vocabulary exercise V)
Change the following phrases so that one noun modifies the other.

EXAMPLE   the head of a department   the department head

(*Note:* When an article is used, it modifies the main noun: **the** department **head.**)

1. a trial by jury   _____

2. a court of a district   _____

3. a policy of the government _____

4. a vote by voice   _____

5. property of the government _____

6. approval by the Senate   _____

7. the legislators of a state   _____

C. More words that keep the *same* stress when used as different parts of speech
The following words appeared in Section II. Read them aloud with your instructor to review their pronunciation. Indicate whether each word can be used as a noun, verb, adjective, or any combination.

EXAMPLE   executive   noun and adjective

1. review   _____

2. branch   _____

3. guarantee   _____

4. veto   _____

5. representative _____

6. debate   _____

7. function   _____

8. defeat   _____

9. check   _____

10. balance   _____

Exercise II More Suffixes

The suffix **-(at)ion** is added to some verbs to form nouns. The stress moves to the next to the last syllable of the noun. Note that the pronunciation of **t** changes to **sh.**

EXAMPLE   administer   administration

Change the following verbs from Section II to nouns by adding the suffix **-(at)ion.** Review the pronunciation and spelling of each noun with your instructor.

1. violate	7. interpret
2. represent	8. legislate
3. distribute	9. segregate
4. regulate	10. elect
5. integrate	11. reflect
6. pollute	12. investigate

Exercise III More Prefixes

The following words have negative prefixes. Your instructor will pronounce each word. Repeat the words, giving careful attention to the stress of each. Then remove the negative prefix, and pronounce the resulting word. The stress does not change. Use five of the new words in sentences.

EXAMPLE   invalid   valid
                The law conforms to the Constitution. It is _valid._

1. desegregated	6. unambiguous
2. unspecific	7. to misinterpret
3. unchecked	8. unrepresentative
4. to disapprove	9. unconstitutional
5. unstable	10. misadministered

Exercise IV

Fill in the blanks in the following paragraph, using words from the list. You may make nouns or verbs plural, and you may change verb tenses. The same word may be used more than once.

a. amendment	e. review
b. amend	f. specific
c. guarantee	g. valid
d. civil liberty	

EXAMPLE   The Constitution has been (b) **amended** twenty-six times.

The first ten _____, known as the Bill of Rights,

_____ several _____ freedoms to all

citizens. These freedoms are known as _____

_____. The Supreme Court has often _____

cases involving issues affecting _____ _____

like freedom of speech and freedom of the press.

III
THE NEWS MEDIA

Newspapers

The several means of communication that reach large numbers of people are called mass **media.** These include newspapers and magazines, books, films, radio, and television. This section deals with news media—the means by which people in the United States find out what is happening in their communities, as well as all over the world. More than two-thirds of all Americans get their national and international news from television and radio. The majority depend on local newspapers for local news, and a large number also read news magazines regularly. Most news media are privately owned. Some nonprofit public or educational television and radio stations receive financial assistance from the government and private sources.

The Constitution guarantees freedom of speech and the **press,** and this guarantee applies to all media. It has been established that a publisher has the right to print what he wishes, within certain limits set by the courts, and that the reader has the right to receive information. Newspapers are free **to editorialize, to take stands** on issues, and to decide what news should be printed.

On the other hand, radio and television communication is regulated by a federal law, the Federal Communications Act. This law specifically guarantees the right of free speech, but it states that only radio and television stations with federal licenses or permits may **broadcast.** The Federal Communications Commission (FCC) grants licenses to stations that conform to Commission policy and operate "in the public interest"—for the good of the people. They may editorialize only if all sides of an issue are presented. In political campaigns opposing candidates must be given equal amounts of time to present their opinions. Radio and television stations are expected to devote a certain amount of broadcasting time to public-affairs programs such as news and discussion programs. In newspapers **emphasis** is on the publisher's right to print; in broadcasting it is on the listener's right to hear.

From the very beginning, American newspapers have taken stands on controversial political issues. The first newspaper, *Publick Occurrences,* appeared in Boston in 1690, but publication was quickly forbidden by the British colonial governor, who was angered by its anti-British position. Before the American Revolution four-page weeklies were published in most of the colonies. They contained news reports, letters to the editor, and much local **advertising.** These papers were often read aloud in coffeehouses to people who did not know how to read themselves. As relations between Great Britain and the American colonies grew worse, the **journals** became more and more political and **took** increasingly strong anti-British **positions.** The best known political journalist of that time was Thomas Paine. He wrote these still famous lines in a Pennsylvania newspaper:

> These are the times that try men's souls. The summer soldier and the sunshine patriot will, in this crisis, shrink from the service of their country; but he that stands it now, deserves the love and thanks of man and woman. Tyranny, like hell, is not easily conquered; yet we have this consolation with us, that the harder the conflict, the more glorious the triumph.

After the victorious end of the Revolutionary War, the number of news publications increased rapidly. By 1800 there were more than 450 newspapers in the United States. Country readers often paid for their papers with local produce: corn, wheat, whiskey, or ham. Dailies cost between $6 and $10 a year; weeklies cost between $1.50 and $5 a year. They continued to take strong positions on political issues, and editorial **columns** were important features.

The people welcomed the new constitutional guarantees of free speech and free press. Thomas Jefferson, the third President of the United States, stated, "Where the press is free and every man is able to read, all is safe." But unrestricted freedom led to serious problems during the early nineteenth century. Many newspapers made cruel personal attacks on people with whom the editors disagreed. Although these statements were often made without any proof, they frequently ruined the reputations of innocent people. Fortunately the courts established strong rules regarding libel, this kind of untrue and abusive reporting. Newspapers found guilty of libel suffered heavy financial penalties. The papers soon became more responsible, although occasional libel cases still occur in the courts.

In the early decades of the nineteenth century, most city newspapers were published for educated, upper-class readers, but in the
years between 1830 and 1860 great changes occurred. Improvements
in printing and paper manufacturing sharply reduced production costs,
and "penny papers" were introduced. These newspapers were designed for a new group of readers—the growing working class—and
they were sold for one cent apiece. They **featured sensational** news
reports of scandals, murders, fires, and robberies, and proved both
popular and financially successful.

Some papers followed a more dignified style of journalism. In
1851 the first copy of the *New York Times* appeared, carrying the
slogan that is still printed on its front page: "All the news that's fit to
print."

Ten years earlier, Horace Greeley had founded a well-edited
penny paper. Greeley, one of the giants in the history of American
journalism, also published a weekly that was outstanding for its statements on social, economic, and political affairs. He took a strong
stand against slavery and enthusiastically supported westward expansion.

For many years there had been a slow but steady movement of
people away from the east coast toward the West. By the end of the
1850s, people could travel west by train for over one thousand miles.
Beyond that, some families moved in covered wagons across the
Great Plains and the Rocky Mountains to the Pacific coast. As pioneer
towns appeared along the various railroad routes, so did newspapers.
Villages of only a few hundred people often had two papers with
different points of view. In the West, eastern papers, which were
shipped on monthly steamboats, supplemented the local press.

To speed slow and irregular mail and newspaper deliveries from
the East, the government established an "express post." Express
riders, traveling on small horses called ponies, could cover two thousand miles in eight days. They rode through wild, dangerous country
filled with hostile Indians and changed ponies at special stations located ten miles apart. Although the pony express lasted only from
1860 to 1862, it remains a colorful part of American history.

The Civil War began in 1861 and continued for four painful years,
but those years and the postwar period saw important developments
in American journalism. The war brought increased use of **eyewitness**
reporters, who introduced direct **interviews** with famous people. War
maps and **cartoons** were used as newspaper illustrations. In addition,
many immigrants came from Europe to work in factories, and they
created a demand for foreign-language papers. By 1870 there were
4500 newspapers, plus weekly journals of opinion and monthly politi-

cal magazines. Famous authors such as Mark Twain contributed frequent columns to these newspapers and journals. By then trains were crossing the entire continent. These transcontinental trains and the telegraph introduced rapid news delivery and news service to the postwar country.

During the next thirty years further technical advances contributed to the development of newspapers and magazines. These improvements included extensive cabled and telegraphed news **coverage,** mechanical presses, the cheap manufacture of paper, telephones, typewriters, efficient Linotype machines, and new engraving processes for illustrations.

Journalism had become a recognized profession, and publishing was often big business. Emphasis shifted from politics to wider fields of news and human-interest stories.

Joseph Pulitzer, an important newspaper publisher in the last decades of the nineteenth century, set many of the patterns still followed in modern journalism. He emphasized excellent world news coverage; employed a large, alert staff to report city news; used unusual **eye-catching headlines;** published a high-quality editorial page; introduced a sports section; and made extensive use of pictures, cartoons, and special features. In 1889 he introduced the first regular Sunday comic section.

New groups of readers were an important part of the expanding press audience. With large-scale department-store advertising directed to women at home, newspapers had to appeal to women readers. This interest led to special women's features and to the employment of women reporters to write news from the feminine point of view.

Even more important were the numbers of relatively uneducated people who needed papers written in simple words and with lots of pictures. To attract this group of readers, the "yellow press" was developed. This type of journalism featured very large headlines that screamed excitement, extensive use of illustrations, Sunday supplements with colored comics, sensational articles, false, or made-up, interviews, and a few worthwhile campaigns against abuses suffered by poor, working-class people. The worst example of the "yellow press" was William Randolph Hearst's *Journal,* which emphasized sex and sensationalism.

Competition for sales led to irresponsible and false news coverage of Cuban-Spanish relations at the end of the nineteenth century and actually contributed to United States involvement in the Spanish-American War in 1898. A strong reaction against this type of sensational and irresponsible journalism resulted in a sharp decline of the

Newsboy
selling the
New York
Journal
in 1905.
*Culver
Pictures, Inc.*

"yellow press" by 1916, but certain features can still be found in newspapers today. They include large headlines in heavy type, the extensive use of pictures, and weekly comics; many papers still emphasize sensational stories of sex and crime to attract readers.

VOCABULARY

*to advertise
*advertising
an advertisement

to make known to the people by paid announcement

Grocery stores often **advertise** food sales in local newspapers. They hope to increase their sales by letting people know about special food prices.

Newspapers in the United States earn approximately two-thirds of their income from **advertising.** Most newspaper **advertisements** are run by local merchants.

*to broadcast   to send sounds and pictures through the air

    broadcasting   Radio and television communication to the general public is known as **broadcasting**. News is **broadcast** every day by radio and television. Newscasts are news **broadcasts** sent by television and radio stations.

    a broadcast

*a cartoon   an amusing and often critical drawing about a current event

Political **cartoons** appear on the editorial pages of most newspapers.

*a column   a narrow division of a printed page, usually separated by vertical lines

    a columnist   The most important news is usually printed in the right-hand **column** of the front page of a newspaper.

Newspaper **columnists** write regularly on specific subjects such as politics, sports, and business.

coverage   information about and description of something

    to cover   Complete news **coverage** of an event must include all information about that event. When a newspaper writer **covers** a news event, he must get all the information that is available, and then he must include the important material in his story.

an editor   a manager of a publication

    to edit   A newspaper **editor** plans ands directs the operation of a newspaper. He decides what news should be printed and where it should appear in the paper. An **editor** also **edits** newspaper articles. He revises and corrects them. In addition, an **editor** expresses his personal point of view on current issues in **editorials** that appear on the **editorial** page of the paper.

    an editorial

to emphasize   to place special importance on something

    an emphasis   A pronunciation teacher pays special attention to the ways in which students speak. He **emphasizes** the use of the correct sounds of the language. He puts his **emphasis** on teaching correct pronunciation. (The plural of **emphasis** is **emphases**.)

eye-catching   attracting attention

A cleverly planned newspaper advertisement will cause the reader to stop and read it. It catches the reader's eye. It is an **eye-catching** ad.

an eyewitness	an observer who sees something happen

The reporter happened to be there when the accident occurred. He saw everything that happened. He was an **eyewitness.** He wrote an **eyewitness** account of the accident.

*a feature
    to feature

a special article that appears in a newspaper or magazine

The magazine is presenting the work of a famous poet as its most important article this month. The **feature** this month is the work of a famous poet. This month the magazine is **featuring** the work of a well-known poet.

a headline

a brief summary of a news story, printed in large letters and appearing at the top of the news article

The front page of a newspaper always has several **headlines** which are printed in various sizes of type.

a by-line

A **by-line** is the printed name of the reporter who has written a special news article. The **by-line** usually appears at the top of the article under the **headline.**

a dateline

A **dateline** gives the date when and the city where the news article was written. The **dateline** appears at the beginning of the article.

*an interview
    to interview

an exchange of questions and answers, often between a representative of the press and somebody whose opinion the newsman wants to report

The reporter **interviewed** the President about the proposed budget for the executive branch. He asked the President several questions, which the President answered. The President gave the reporter an **interview.**

a journal
    a journalist
    journalism

a newspaper or periodical

More than 8000 newspapers and over 1600 periodicals are published in the United States every week. Over 2400 weekly **journals** are published.

The work of a **journalist** involves editing or writing for a newspaper or magazine. This kind of work is called **journalism.**

*a medium	the means by which something is done Radio is a **medium** of communication. (The plural of **medium** is **media**.)
*the press	printed materials, especially magazines and newspapers; also the people such as editors and reporters, who work on these publications Freedom of **the press** is the right of newspapers to report events and express opinions. Recently television and radio have been included in a broad definition of **the press**. They are called the electronic **press**.
sensational *sensationalism*	appealing to the emotions, not to the intellect; exciting **Sensational** journalism presents news in a way that tries to cause emotional reactions rather than careful thought. Responsible newspapers try to avoid **sensationalism.**
to take a stand to take a position	to express one's opinion firmly on a specific issue In this country newspapers are expected to express their editors' opinions on political issues. Readers expect a newspaper **to take a stand** for or against particular political candidates. They expect a newspaper **to take a position** on controversial questions.

Vocabulary Review

A. Bring a newspaper to class for use in the following review and use it to answer the following questions.

1. How many **columns** are there on the first page? the second page? the **editorial** page?
2. Is there a **cartoon** in your newspaper? a comic strip? What is the difference between a newspaper **cartoon** and a comic strip?
3. Where does the TV schedule appear? What time is the first evening TV **newscast?** How long does it last?
4. Find an **eye-catching advertisement** if you can.
5. Read aloud the **headline** of the most important article on the first page.
6. How much **coverage** of national, international, and local news appears on the first page?
7. Point out one **feature** that appears on the women's page.
8. Name one **columnist** who writes special articles on sports in your paper.
9. Look at the **editorials.** Name one issue on which the **editor has taken a stand.**
10. How many letters to the **editor** are printed in your copy of the paper?

B. Pretend that you are a reporter who is covering a bank robbery. You were not at the scene when the robbery occurred, but you have found an **eyewitness** who has agreed to be **interviewed.** What are the first two questions you will ask?

Comprehension and Thought Questions

1. Using the paper you brought to class for the vocabulary review, comment on the following:
   a. how much space is devoted to local, national, and international news
   b. the amount and kinds of advertising
   c. the subjects of the editorials
   d. the subjects of the letters to the editor that appear on the editorial page
   e. special features
2. What are mass media? news media?
3. Read the following statements aloud, and indicate which of them are not correct according to what you have read in the text. Change the inaccurate statements (if any) so that they are correct.
   a. Over two-thirds of all Americans get their international, national, and local news from television and the radio.
   b. American newspapers have traditionally taken stands on controversial issues.
   c. By the middle of the nineteenth century many small towns had two newspapers with different points of view.
   d. By the end of the nineteenth century journalism had become a recognized profession.
   e. The yellow press was an example of conservative, responsible journalism.
4. Nineteenth century newspapers reflected the social and economic composition of the population. Give examples from the text that illustrate this statement.
5. Write a headline for a newspaper that was published in 1862. The headline should announce the end of the pony express.

Discussion and Composition Topics

1. a. Thomas Jefferson said, "Where the press is free and every man is able to read, all is safe." Do you agree? Explain your answer.
   b. Jefferson also said, "If it were left to me to decide whether we should have a government without newspapers or newspapers without a government, I should not hesitate to prefer the latter." What is your opinion of this statement?
2. Choose a major news story that interests you. Compare the way in which two different American newspapers treated the story. You will find several newspapers in the periodical room of your library.
   a. On what page does the story appear in each paper?

    b. What do the headlines say?

    c. Does one paper present the story in a more sensational way?

    d. If either paper has an editorial about the news story, summarize the editor's position.

3. Prepare a brief summary of a newspaper or magazine article. Give the printed article to your instructor so that he can compare your summary with the original.

4. Bring a political cartoon to class. (Cartoons usually appear on the editorial page.) Discuss with your classmates what the cartoon is about. What point is the cartoonist trying to make?

5. Pretend that you are a reporter for a student newspaper. Interview one of your classmates for an article to be entitled "A Foreign Student in the United States." Ask about the student's family, education, initial reactions to the United States, future plans, and any other points that you think will bring forth interesting information.

6. Tom Paine was considered a political radical by many people, even those who supported the Revolution. If he were alive today, what issues do you think he would write about? What do you think his stand on those issues might be? If he were living in your country, what issues might he write about?

Listening Exercises for Chapter 6 begin on p. 250.

The News Media Before Television

One of the most important developments in newspaper organization during the first part of the twentieth century was the growth of telegraph services, which are known as wire services. Wire-service companies employed staffs of reporters, who covered stories all over the world. Their news reports, as well as columns, pictures, and cartoons, were sent to papers throughout the country by telegraph. The papers paid an annual fee for this service. Wire services continue to play an important role in newspaper operations. Today the major wire services are the Associated Press (AP) and United Press International (UPI). You will frequently find AP or UPI at the beginning of a news story, showing that the source of the story is the particular wire service, rather than a reporter who is employed directly by the paper.

Newspaper chains and mergers began to appear in the early 1900s. A chain consists of two or more newspapers owned by a single person or organization. A merger involves combining two or more papers into one. During the nineteenth century many cities had more than one **competitive** independent paper. Today in most cities there are only one or two newspapers, and they are usually operated by a single owner. Often newspapers in several cities belong to one chain. Papers have combined in order to survive under the pressure of rising costs. Chains and mergers have cut down production costs and brought the advantages of big-business methods to the newspaper industry. On the other hand, they have reduced the number of small independent newspapers that were once an important part of American journalism.

The modern newspaper, as we know it, began to appear at the outbreak of World War I in 1914. Numbers of **foreign** correspondents went to various European capitals and war fronts. Foreign-news coverage by eyewitness reporters, who represented individual news-papers, chains, and wire services, became a feature of American journalism. In addition, a large **press corps** developed in Washington, where it continues to provide reports and **analyses** of important news developments.

The twentieth century has also witnessed the introduction of the daily tabloid and the weekly news magazine. A tabloid is a newspaper with small-size pages, a **terse** and simple **style,** and many pictures. Tabloids frequently present highly sensational news stories. Today more than two million people read the *New York Daily News,* a tabloid that has the largest **circulation** of any American newspaper. The next two leading newspapers are the *Los Angeles Times,* which has a cir-culation of 950,000, and the *New York Times,* with a circulation of 895,000.

Time, Newsweek, and *U.S. News & World Report* are popular news magazines. They present national and international news, stories of **human interest,** and reports on new books, movies, and plays. The articles are written in an informal style, and they are illustrated with photographs. More than nine million people read news magazines regularly. Two picture magazines, *Life* and *Look,* enjoyed popularity for many years. They presented the news with simple texts and many photographs, and they remained among the most widely read maga-zines until the late 1960s. Some people think these picture magazines were forced out of business because they could not compete success-fully with the live pictures on televised news programs.

Today there are approximately 1750 daily newspapers, with a total circulation of over 62 million, and more than 580 Sunday papers, with a circulation of almost 60 million. The typical daily paper contains more than forty pages of local, national, and foreign news; editorials; cartoons; and information about sports, art, music, books, and general entertainment, including radio and television schedules. It usually in-cludes special features, such as columns of news analysis by well-known writers, business news, a women's page, comics, general ad-vertising, and real-estate and employment advertisements, which are known as classified ads. Approximately two-thirds of the income of the average daily newspaper comes from advertising. The rest comes from sales.

There are also about 10,000 weekly, biweekly, and triweekly news-papers. Biweekly papers are published every two weeks; triweekly papers appear every three weeks. Most of these papers are **special-interest** publications, such as labor-union papers; papers for black readers; industrial, farm, trade, religious, and educational journals; and foreign-language editions.

By far the most important news development of the twentieth century has been the introduction and expansion of radio and television newscasting. In 1920 the results of the presidential election were broadcast for the first time, and that event began a remarkable expansion in the radio industry. There were only twelve radio stations in existence that year. Within two years the number had increased to over six hundred. Manufacturers could not keep up with the demand for radios. The first **sponsored programs** were broadcast in 1922. Advertisers bought program time to advertise their products, and within a few years the development of radio networks brought nationwide programing and advertising.

A network is a group of broadcasting stations that are linked or joined in their operations so that each station can use the same program. This program is not available to non-network stations. Sponsors of network programs buy nationwide broadcasting time. Network programs are supplemented by **local** broadcasts produced by the individual local stations. For unusual events, such as presidential speeches and press conferences, there is no advertising. Broadcast costs for these programs are paid for by the networks. Today the major radio and TV networks are the Columbia Broadcasting System (CBS), the National Broadcasting System (NBC), and the American Broadcasting System (ABC).

Approximately 75 percent of all **commercial** radio stations and 12 percent of all commercial television stations are not affiliated with any network. They supplement their broadcasts of local news with **domestic** and foreign news from the wire services and from newspapers.

In the early years of radio, stations gave occasional news reports based on information supplied by newspapers and the wire services without charge. At first, newspaper publishers assumed that news broadcasting would result in an increase in newspaper reading. The first nationwide Election Day newscasts in 1932 were highly successful, however, and the publishers quickly recognized that the radio offered serious competition to newspapers as a news medium. Advertisers, as well as readers, were turning to the radio, and the publishers became alarmed and angry.

In 1933 the American Newspaper Publishers Association, the wire services, and the radio networks reached an agreement on the regulation of news broadcasting. Broadcasters were supplied with short news items by the wire services for two daily newscasts. These items were to be presented in the late morning and the late evening in order to avoid competition with newspapers. Radio **commentators** were forbidden to use news that was less than twelve hours old, and they were allowed to give only broad **generalizations** and summaries.

Many radio stations quickly rejected this arrangement, and soon several independent news services were formed to provide news to these stations. The programs were immediately successful and were often sponsored commercially. Newspaper publishers, recognizing that news broadcasting was becoming increasingly dangerous competition, soon changed their attitude. They began to purchase radio stations and to apply for radio licenses to establish new stations. By 1940 newspapers owned or controlled more than one third of all radio stations, and this pattern continues. Today newspapers own, completely or partially, more than half of all radio and TV stations.

Analysis and factual reporting were important features of newscasting in the 1930s. As the pre-World War II situation in Europe grew more tense, direct reporting from abroad became a regular part of radio news programs. By 1938 CBS had a team of reporters in Europe; they sent on-the-spot newscasts to the United States, which meant that the reporters broadcast from the places where the events were happening. Two years later all the major networks were making daily reports from abroad.

President Franklin D. Roosevelt making a "fireside chat."   *U.P.I.*

Radio was also playing an important role in political developments within the United States. Franklin D. Roosevelt, who was President from 1933 until his death in 1945, was the first President to use
the radio with great effect. His frequent talks to the American people,
known as "fireside chats," always began "My friends. . . ." He created
the impression that the radio listeners were members of his family
with whom he was discussing problems that they all shared. He also
used the radio successfully in political campaigns.

During World War II (1941–1945) radio stations and newspapers
followed a voluntary **censorship** plan, with suggestions and directions
from the government. Within these limits, radio newscasts gave wide
and immediate coverage of war developments. The growing importance of radio during this period was reflected in a survey conducted
by the government in 1942. People were asked, "Do you have more
confidence in the war news on the radio or the war news in the newspapers?" Forty-six percent said, "Radio." Eighteen percent answered,
"Newspapers." However, newspapers remained the most popular
source of all news until 1963, when, for the first time, the majority of
Americans reported that television was their favorite news medium.

VOCABULARY

an analysis *to analyze*	a careful study or examination of all parts of something **Analysis** of a news item involves examination of all aspects of the issue. The newscaster **analyzed** the news. (The plural of **analysis** is **analyses.**)

to censor
    censorship
    a censor
	to forbid the publication of items that the authorities consider undesirable
	
	The Constitution guarantees freedom of the press. The news cannot be **censored.** Official **censorship** is unconstitutional.
	
	A **censor** has the authority to forbid the publication of items that he considers undesirable.

a circulation	the number of copies of a newspaper or periodical that are sold to the public The *New York Daily News* has the largest **circulation** of any newspaper in the United States. More copies of the *New York Daily News* are sold than of any other newspaper.

*a commentator
  to comment
  a comment

a person who broadcasts his opinion of something

The news **commentator** discussed the provisions of the treaty. He **commented** on the treaty. He made some **comments** on the treaty.

commercial
  a commercial

related to trade or finance; operated to make a profit

United States radio and television are businesses. They are **commercial** operations. Their major function is to make money.

Advertisements on radio and television are known as **commercials.**

to compete
  competitive
  competition

to take part in a contest or race

Each television network tries to earn the most money from advertising. The networks **compete** with one another to make the highest profits from advertising. Television is a **competitive** business.

"**Competition** may be sometimes hard for the individual, but it is best for the race because it insures the survival of the fittest. . . ."

> Andrew Carnegie, American industrialist,
> in *North American Review,* 1889.

*domestic

referring to one's own country

Domestic news refers to events that happen in the United States.

The first sentence of the Constitution calls for **domestic** tranquility—peace throughout the nation.

*foreign

referring to other countries, not one's own

The *New York Times* carries a large amount of **foreign** news. *New York Times* reporters are located all over the world. They are **foreign** correspondents.

to generalize
  a generalization

to make a broad, unspecific statement

It is not wise to **generalize** about human behavior. Each person is different. Therefore, don't make **generalizations** about people unless you have adequate proof.

of human interest

attracting the attention of people because of a particularly amusing, sad, or unusual quality

A **human-interest** news story has been described as follows: When a dog bites a man, that's not news; but, when a man bites a dog, that's news. It is a story **of human interest.**

in the public interest	for the good of the people
	The FCC says radio and television stations must operate for the good of the people. They must operate **in the public interest.** They must offer **public-interest** programs.
of special interest	attracting the attention of a particular group
	Ebony is a magazine published by Blacks for black readers. It is a magazine **of special interest** to Blacks. It is a **special-interest** magazine.
*local	of a place or district
	Local news refers to events that happen in a particular town or city and nearby areas.
a press corps	a group of newsmen and newswomen
	The Washington **press corps** is composed of news reporters, columnists, and news analysts who work in Washington, D.C. They represent the news media all over the United States and some foreign news media as well.
*a program *to program*	a show or event that is broadcast on radio or television
	Comedies and mysteries are among the most popular television **programs.**
	To **program** television time, TV officials must know what shows will attract large audiences. They plan popular **programs** that advertisers will buy.
*a sponsor *to sponsor*	a person or company that pays for a radio or television program
	There is no **sponsor** for presidential broadcasts. Advertising is not permitted on that kind of public-affairs program.
	Drug and soap advertisers **sponsor** more than half of all television shows.
*a style	a manner of writing or speaking
	Editorials are often more informal than news stories. The editor frequently seems to be talking directly to the reader. News stories are written in a different **style.** They are more formal and factual.
terse *tersely*	brief and to the point
	He never uses more words than necessary to describe an event. His writing is **terse.** He writes **tersely.**

Vocabulary Review

In class write five questions that can be used to analyze a radio or television newscast. Include as many words from the vocabulary list of Chapter 7 as possible.

EXAMPLE   What time was the **program broadcast?** How long did it last?

If you can listen to a radio or television newscast this evening, analyze the program, using the questions as a guide. Bring your report to class tomorrow, so that you can compare the analyses.

If you can't listen to a radio or TV program, prepare some questions for use in analyzing a newspaper. Include as many vocabulary words as possible. Bring the newspaper and your analysis to class for general discussion.

EXAMPLE   Is it a **special-interest paper,** or is it read by the **general** public?

Vocabulary Quiz

Your instructor will read a short listening comprehension exercise using several words from the vocabulary list of Chapter 7. Take notes and answer the following questions about the paragraph. Then *read* Listening Comprehension I, pp. 251–252.
1. What purpose are broadcasting stations expected to serve?
2. What has happened to broadcasting over the years?
3. What kind of advertising accounts for over half of radio stations' income?
4. From what kind of shows does television receive most of its income?

Comprehension and Thought Questions

1. What are wire services? What kinds of services do they provide? What wire services (if any) supply news to newspapers in your country?
2. a. What advantages and disadvantages have newspaper chains and mergers brought to the business organization of newspapers in the United States? to American newspaper readers?
   b. Discuss the ownership pattern of newspapers in your native country. Describe some of the major competitive newspapers (if any) in your country and the extent to which different papers present different points of view on controversial issues.
3. What kind of news is covered by the Washington press corps? Is there a foreign newspaper correspondent from your country who writes from the United States? If so, is he widely read in your country? What do you think of his reporting?
4. When was the first important political news broadcast in the United States?

5. a. What is a broadcasting network?
   b. How did network broadcasting affect advertising?
6. What was the early reaction of newspaper publishers to radio news? Describe what happened after the 1932 Election Day broadcast?
7. How did the pre-World War II situation in Europe affect American radio news coverage?
8. How extensive is the coverage of foreign news on television in your country? on the radio? in newspapers? Is there on-the-spot coverage by foreign correspondents? Compare foreign news coverage in your country with what you have observed about foreign news coverage by the United States news media.

Discussion and Composition Topics

1. Several speeches by Presidents Roosevelt, Truman, Eisenhower, Kennedy, Johnson, and Nixon have been recorded. If any of these records is available in your library, listen to part or all of one.

   If you were a news reporter, what would you write about the speech? Include information about when and where the speech was made, whether it was originally delivered on radio or on television, and some of the important points of the speech.

2. One dictionary[1] defines **news** as reports of unusual or notable recent events.

   Frank L. Mott, the author of *News in America*,[2] gives two other definitions of newspaper news:
   a. News is whatever newspaper readers want to know about.
   b. News is whatever a good editor chooses to print.

   Pick a news item (not on the first page) from a recent edition of a newspaper. In your opinion, which definition or definitions describe the article most accurately. Why?

Library Assignment 1

On October 30, 1938, a radio play, based on the novel *War of the Worlds* by the English writer H. G. Wells, was broadcast by CBS. The story dealt with an attack on Earth by creatures from the planet Mars. There were reports that seemed to be eyewitness accounts of the frightening events. Actors spoke as if they were delivering real newscasts. Hundreds of terrified listeners believed that hostile Martians actually had arrived.

Read an account of this event in a newspaper or magazine from your library. Then, if your library has the records, listen to the recorded broadcast of the play. (The first half of the recording is the part that is particularly relevant to this assignment.)

1. *The American Heritage Dictionary,* Boston, American Heritage, 1971, pp. 884–885.
2. Frank L. Mott, *News in America,* Cambridge, Harvard University Press, 1952, p. 26.

You will find references to the broadcast in the *Readers' Guide* for 1938 under the classification Radio Broadcasting: Social Aspects and in the *New York Times Index* for 1938 under Radio: United States—Dramatizations.

It will be helpful if you are familiar with the following words that are used in the recording:

astronomer	a scientist who studies the sun, moon, stars, and planets
calamity	a great misfortune or disaster
cordon	a line or ring of persons acting as guards
cylinder	a solid or hollow body shaped like this:
diameter	the distance across a circle or a cylinder passing through the center
disc	a thin round object
earthquake	a sudden violent shaking of the earth's surface
evacuate	withdraw from and leave empty
gravity	the force that attracts objects toward the center of the earth
incandescence	a very bright and intense light
meteorology	the study of the weather and the earth's atmosphere
observatory	a building from which the sun, stars, moon, and planets may be observed
telescope	an instrument that makes distant objects appear nearer and larger
vanguard	the foremost or leading position
velocity	speed
vibration	a continuing rapid movement back and forth or up and down

If the records are available, give your opinion of the news coverage in the play. Why did people believe it?

The FCC later prohibited this kind of fictitious newscasting. Do you agree with this ruling? Why or why not?

Library Assignment 2

Look at a current issue of an American news magazine (*Time, Newsweek, U.S. News & World Report*) in the periodical room. Report on the organization of the magazine: the kinds of news stories, the amount of domestic news, the amount of foreign news, the use of pictures, and the amount of advertising.

Listening Exercises for Chapter 7 begin on p. 251.

Television, Radio, and the Press

Television made its first public appearance just before the outbreak of World War II, but it did not gain real importance until a few years after the end of **hostilities.** By 1950 ninety-eight TV stations were broadcasting programs to Americans, who watched them on more than four million sets. Two years later the number of sets had risen to more than 15 million.

The television networks followed the newscasting **procedures** that had been established for radio, with one important difference. Radio news had always been "live." Broadcasts had not been recorded or taped for later presentation; broadcasters had always spoken directly to their listeners. At first television newscasts used news films that had been made by movie producing companies. These companies made short news films that were presented in most movie theaters as part of the regular programs. Each film, which usually lasted from fifteen to thirty minutes, presented pictures of events of the preceding week. In the days of silent films, printed explanations accompanied the pictures. After the introduction of sound films, or "talkies," the recorded voice of a narrator commented on each filmed event. Early TV news films followed the same procedure.

In addition to these movies, TV network camera crews in a few cities took pictures of events that had been planned in advance, and the film was flown to the broadcasting station. This system did not provide coverage for unexpected events, however, and newscasters made up for these limitations by reading a few news summaries at the end of each show. Television also presented documentaries: detailed studies of current issues, each lasting an hour or more. TV public affairs shows included presidential speeches, interviews, and discus-

The Kennedy-Nixon debates. *NBC-TV*

sions of current issues, as well as important congressional hearings.

The presidential election was the major domestic news event in 1952. Although radio still had a larger audience than television, campaigners gave TV their main attention. Each network found sponsors for the political conventions and the coverage of election returns. In addition to televised speeches by the candidates, this election introduced paid election "spot" advertising. The spots were very short ads that appeared on the screen to "sell" a candidate to the viewers. Television had become a very important **influence** on the political scene. In the presidential campaign eight years later, the two candidates, Richard M. Nixon and John F. Kennedy, participated in several televised debates. Approximately 75 million people watched them. This number is almost 6 million greater than the total number of people who voted that year. Many observers believe that John Kennedy won the election in large part because of the favorable impression he created in those television appearances. The debates can be heard on records, which may be available in your library.

Presidents now frequently deliver major speeches to television audiences, and in recent years many presidential press conferences have been televised. Presidential press conferences began almost seventy years ago. These question-and-answer sessions between the President and reporters have continued on an irregular basis ever since. For many years the conferences were printed in the newspapers along with news stories and analyses of the important points made at the conferences. In 1955 President Eisenhower permitted the filming of a press conference for the first time, but the films were edited before they were **released** for television. In the 1960s and 1970s Presidents Kennedy, Johnson, Nixon, and Ford permitted occasional "live" telecasts of press conferences, as well as televised interviews with newspaper and television reporters.

In addition, the President and other government officials often hold news **briefings** and **background** press conferences. These sessions are supposed to help reporters understand complex issues and government policies. Frequently they are "off the record," which means that the reporters cannot quote the information in their news stories. The White House press secretary serves as the President's official representative to the press. He often holds press conferences and briefings on presidential policies.

Newspapers in the United States have always been highly political. Readers expect newspapers to take political stands and to **endorse** political candidates on the editorial pages. At the same time, they expect factual news to be reported honestly and **objectively.** Approximately half of all daily newspapers classify themselves as Independent. Another quarter call themselves Independent-Democrat or Independent-Republican. The rest are clearly identified with one or the other of the two major parties. Two-thirds of all newspapers usually support the Republican presidential candidate, probably because most newspaper publishers are Republicans.

Unlike newspapers, radio and television stations are traditionally **neutral** in politics. They rarely endorse political candidates or take stands on controversial political issues. Network spokesmen have stated repeatedly that broadcasters must present the news and public issues objectively, without **offending** listeners or advertisers. The Federal Communications Commission permits editorializing but requires radio and television stations to present all sides of a controversial issue and to offer political opponents equal amounts of time to present their opinions.

In recent years, however, both the press and the broadcasting networks were sharply criticized by government officials who **complained** that the media did not present the news objectively. During the early 1970s Vice-President Spiro Agnew repeatedly **charged** that the networks were hostile to President Nixon and his administration. Other government officials said that this criticism should be extended to newspapers as well. One of the strongest criticisms was made by President Nixon at a press conference in 1973. He described television news reporting as "outrageous, vicious, [and] distorted. . . ."[1] Representatives of the media have expressed deep concern about these criticisms. They insist that they have presented the news objectively and honestly.

There are other critics of the media. Some people believe that **violence** in the United States can be traced in part to the influence of TV entertainment programs that feature killings, fighting, and other violent action. Many studies of the influence of violence shown on television find that these programs have a harmful effect on the attitudes and behavior of young people.

A different criticism came from a special commission appointed to investigate race riots that occurred in the late 1960s. The commission criticized the media's "failure to report adequately on race relations and racial problems and failure to bring more Negroes into journalism. In . . . explaining [race] relations in the United States the communications media . . . failed to communicate."[2] The commission pointed out that few Blacks were employed by the news media, and it **urged** newspapers to hire black journalists.

Probably the most widespread criticism has been directed against general television programing. Many people complain about the low quality of television shows and the large amounts of advertising that appear on the screen. Network officials, however, insist that they do not believe commercial television should try to raise the **standards** or tastes of TV audiences. Instead, they say, television should satisfy the largest number of viewers. Big audiences attract advertisers, and advertising is the key to the success of commercial television.

Commercial television is totally financed by advertising. Eight minutes of an average television hour are used for ads; six of these minutes are for network ads and two for local ads. These minutes are divided into several short advertising "breaks," or "spots," which appear frequently during the hour.

Commercial networks present approximately thirty minutes of sponsored national and international news every evening, in addition to frequent daytime newscasts and coverage of special events of national interest. Local television and radio stations carry local news broadcasts and supplement network news (if they are network members) with information from the wire services.

Basically, however, television is an entertainment medium. The advertiser buys commercials on the shows that attract the largest audiences. These shows include those that feature well-known stars,

1. President Nixon's press conference, October 26, 1973.
2. *Report of the National Advisory Commission on Civil Disorders,* Washington, D.C., U.S. Government Printing Office, 1968, p. 210.

and westerns, comedies, movies, spy shows, quiz shows, and soap operas. On most quiz shows members of the audience are asked questions; if they give the correct answers, they receive valuable prizes. Soap operas are plays that continue their story from day to day. They began on the radio and are now regular features of afternoon television. Originally they were sponsored by soap advertisers. They are called "operas" because they present highly emotional situations like many European operas of the nineteenth century.

Some people look to public, or noncommercial, television for better programing because it emphasizes cultural, informational, and educational programs. Approximately one-third of public television's prime time programs are devoted to news and public affairs. "Prime time" refers to the evening hours when the greatest number of viewers watch television. Today there are more than two hundred noncommercial TV stations. In addition, there are more than five hundred public radio stations that feature music, educational, and public-affairs programs. Several noncommercial networks provide live and recorded programs to their member stations. These programs include news and coverage of special events such as lectures, conferences, and congressional hearings.

Financial support for public broadcasting comes from listeners' contributions, foundations, and federal, state, and local governments. The Corporation for Public Broadcasting (CPB), which was established by Congress in 1967, finances a number of programs. CPB also works closely with the Public Broadcasting System, a government-sponsored service that plans and **distributes** programs to noncommercial TV stations. A poll conducted in the early 1970s reported that public television had a weekly audience of more than 51 million people and that the number of viewers was increasing steadily.

Cable television may be another answer to the commercial programing problem. Viewers subscribe to a cable service, paying for special wiring that enables them to receive programs such as sports events and concerts that are not available on regular television channels. The cable TV audience is still very small, and it is too early to tell how important it will be.

Today over 95 percent of all American homes have television sets. More than 25 percent have two or more sets. The sets are on between four and five hours a day. One FCC commissioner estimated that the average viewer will watch 3000 days' worth of television between his second and sixty-fifth years—an amount of time equal to nine years of his life.[3]

3. Nicholas Johnson, "TV and Violence," *Television Quarterly*, Winter 1969, **8**, p. 31.

Although television is primarily an entertainment medium, more than two-thirds of all Americans receive their national and international news from the TV screen. They have seen U.S. soldiers fighting in a war on the other side of the world. They have seen and heard men on the moon. Television has changed their view of the world in which they live, as well as their lives at home.

VOCABULARY

*background	information that gives the reporter more complete knowledge and understanding of a specific subject or situation
	During the Vietnam war military authorities held many **background** news conferences on the situation. These conferences were supposed to give the reporters information they could not get from other sources. Often the **background** information was off the record; the reporters could not use the specific data in their news reports.
*a briefing *to brief*	a press conference in which news reporters learn detailed facts on a particular subject
	The White House press secretary gave a **briefing** on the proposed legislation. He explained the bill in detail. He **briefed** the reporters on the legislative proposal.
*to charge *a charge*	to say that someone has done something wrong
	The prisoner was accused of murder. He was **charged** with having committed murder. The policeman made a **charge** against the prisoner. He **charged** that the prisoner had committed murder.
to complain *a complaint*	to express dissatisfaction
	Many television viewers **complain** about the poor quality of television programs. Their **complaints** are against the poor quality of television programs.
*to distribute *a distribution*	to give or to send out to a number of persons or places
	Government departments and agencies regularly **distribute** printed news announcements to reporters. These statements often describe new government policies. **Distribution** of these an-

nouncements helps to inform the reporters about developments in the government.

*to endorse
  an endorsement

to support or approve

The members of the committee approved the statement of their chairman. They all **endorsed** it. They gave the statement a unanimous **endorsement.**

hostilities
  hostility
  hostile

acts of war

After the peace treaty was signed in 1973, **hostilities** continued in Vietnam.

He seemed very unfriendly. His attitude was **hostile.** His attitude was one of extreme unfriendliness. He was filled with **hostility.**

to influence
  an influence

to affect beliefs or actions

Many things affect the way someone votes. These include the personality of the candidate and his stand on important issues. They may also include the voter's ethnic origin and the social and economic group to which he belongs. These are some of the factors that **influence** the voter. His family voting pattern is another important **influence.**

*neutral
  neutrality

not favoring any position on a controversial issue

For many years Switzerland has been officially **neutral** in European wars. It has not been involved in the hostilities. It has not supported any of the warring countries. It has followed a policy of **neutrality.**

*objective
  objectivity
  objectively

not influenced by personal beliefs or feelings

A good reporter should be **objective** in his treatment of the news. He should not let his personal beliefs affect his account of the news. He must keep his **objectivity** when he reports the news. He must report the news **objectively.**

to offend
  an offense
  offensive

to displease or annoy

Many viewers are highly annoyed by the amount and the quality of advertising on television. Television commercials **offend** them. Viewers find the advertising **offensive.** Television advertising gives **offense** to many viewers.

a procedure

a way of doing something

The way in which radio and television stations get their licenses to broadcast is established by law. The Federal Communications Act describes the **procedures** that broadcasting stations must follow in order to receive their licenses.

to release
  a release

to allow to go

After a war, war prisoners are usually **released** and permitted to return to their homes.

Government officials regularly distribute printed statements about government programs to newsmen. These statements are official news **releases,** or press **releases.**

*a standard

a specified degree of excellence

The National Citizens' Committee for Broadcasting wants to improve the quality of children's television programs. Its members believe that the FCC should set high moral and artistic **standards** for children's programs. They say that programs that do not meet these **standards** should not be broadcast.

to urge

to try to persuade or to request earnestly

The National Citizens' Committee for Broadcasting is earnestly requesting the FCC to raise the standards of television programs. It **is urging** the FCC to improve the quality of television programs.

violence
  violent

rough action involving force

This committee is especially concerned about the large number of programs featuring fighting, shooting, murder, and other acts of **violence.** It claims that children see five **violent** acts during every hour that they watch television.

Vocabulary Review

The following imaginary situations use words from the vocabulary list of Chapter 8. Read each situation and then describe what you would do. Your instructor will tell you which answers should be given orally.

1. You are in an expensive restaurant, and you discover a fly in your soup! You immediately decide to **complain.** What **procedure** will you follow when you make your **complaint?**
2. You have accidentally **offended** a friend. You said something unkind about his brother, and his reaction was extremely **hostile.** He **charges** you with rudeness and says that he no longer wants to be your friend. You believe that what you said is true, but you want to keep his friendship. What will you do now?

3. You are a White House reporter for an **influential** newspaper. You have just attended a news **briefing** at which you were told that the President is about to announce the nomination of Mr. Barton for an appointment to the Supreme Court. You personally do not approve of this choice. You believe that Mr. Barton does not meet the intellectual or moral **standards** proper for a Supreme Court justice. You hope that the Senate will not **endorse** this appointment. However, you must try to write an **objective** news story.
   a. Write the first two or three sentences of your article.
   b. Then write a short note to your editor expressing your opinion of Mr. Barton.
4. You are a member of the White House staff. You have to prepare a brief press **release** for **distribution** to members of the press corps. It deals with the outbreak of **hostilities** between two countries in Africa. The **release** must contain a summary of a statement by the President that the United States will remain **neutral** in the conflict but that he will **urge** the United Nations to take steps that may prevent widespread **violence.** Write the press **release.**

Comprehension and Thought Questions

1. Underline the phrase or clause that correctly completes the following sentences. Sometimes both choices are correct; sometimes neither choice is correct.
   a. Early television newscasts were (1) usually live; (2) usually films made by movie producing companies.
   b. In the 1952 presidential election campaign, (1) paid political "spot" advertising was introduced on television; (2) speeches of the candidates were televised for the first time.
   c. Presidential press conferences (1) are held on a regular weekly basis; (2) are sometimes televised.
   d. Newspapers and television stations (1) are traditionally neutral in politics; (2) must present all sides of a controversial issue.
   e. Some critics of television complain about (1) the extensive use of violence on TV programs; (2) the poor quality of the shows and the large amount of advertising.
   f. Some people look to public television for improved programs because (1) it is regulated by the government; (2) it emphasizes cultural and educational programs.
   g. More than two-thirds of all Americans (1) own television sets; (2) get their national and international news from television.
2. a. At presidential press conferences, the President is often asked difficult questions by critical and sometimes hostile reporters. Why do you think a President holds press conferences?
   b. Do you think presidential press conferences should be televised? Why or why not?

   c. Does the chief executive of your country hold press conferences? If so, how often? Are they televised?

3. How do you think the methods of financing public and commercial television affect the quality of the programs?

4. a. Compare U.S. government regulation of newspapers, radio, and television with the official regulation of the news media in your country.

   b. Describe any government-sponsored newspaper or radio or television station existing in your country.

   c. Do you think newspapers, radio, and television should have identical regulations? For example, if a broadcasting station must be licensed by the FCC, should newspapers and magazines also be licensed by a federal agency? Explain your answer.

   d. If newspapers are free to take a stand on controversial issues, should broadcasting stations be required to present all sides of such issues? Explain your answer.

Discussion and Composition Topics

1. Ask a student in your class to describe television in his or her country. Is it commercial or noncommercial? Does the government regulate it? What kinds of programs are most popular?

2. Compare television news programs in your country with American programs. How often are they broadcast? Do they emphasize national or international news? Do you depend mostly on television, radio, or newspapers for news in your country? Why?

3. Some countries, like Great Britain, have government television and radio networks and competitive commercial networks as well. Do you think broadcasting should be sponsored commercially or by the government, or should it combine both kinds of operations? Explain your opinion.

4. Marshall McLuhan, a well-known philosopher and analyst of television, says that the *process* of television, the way in which television works and relates to the viewer, is at least as important as what is on the screen. He points out that newspapers and radio involve only one sense each: sight or hearing. Television involves two senses, which distribute the incoming information. As a result, he believes that television involves the viewer much more deeply and completely than the other communications media. Is it easier for you to stop reading a paper or book or listening to a radio program than it is to turn off a television program? Which medium seems to involve you the most? What reasons can you give for your answer? How does this answer fit with McLuhan's analysis?

5. "One picture is worth a thousand words." Discuss this old Chinese proverb in relation to television, radio, and newspaper news coverage.

6. How do the quantity and quality of television advertising in the United States compare with those of television advertising in your country, if you have commercial television?

Special Assignment I

Prepare a public-opinion poll about television. Ask five people (not classmates) whether or not they watch TV: how much time each day, the kinds of programs they like the most, the kinds of programs they like the least, how they feel about television programing in general, and how they feel about commercials.

Identify the people you interview by age, sex, and education. If you cannot interview five people, make up interviews with fictitious people. Write a summary of what you find.

Special Assignment II

Watch an evening television network news show. Take notes on the news items that were covered and how much time was given to each item. The next morning examine the front page of a newspaper.
1. How many of the same items were reported in both media? Compare the television and newspaper coverage of these stories.
2. a. What items appeared on TV that did not appear on the front page of the newspaper? What stories were printed on the first page that did not appear on TV?
   b. Do you think television is a better medium for some kinds of news and that newspapers are better for other kinds? Explain your opinion.
3. Which medium do you prefer for news? Why?

Listening Exercises for Chapter 8 begin on p. 253.

VOCABULARY EXERCISES FOR SECTION III

Exercise I   More Suffixes

The suffix **-ist** may be added to some words to form nouns that describe persons in a specific field of work or who have special beliefs or attitudes. The stress does not change.

Add the suffix **-ist** to the following words from the text. Then use each new word in a sentence.

EXAMPLE   art   artist
A great television performer is often called a television **artist.**

1. integration _____   5. machine   _____

2. segregation _____   6. journal   _____

3. column   _____   7. cartoon   _____

4. conform   _____   8. humor   _____

Exercise II   More Prefixes

Here is a list of prefixes used in Section III.

a. pro-   in favor of
b. anti-   against
c. pre-   before
d. post-   after
e. non-   not
f. bi-   two
g. tri-   three
h. trans-   across

Using these prefixes, construct words or phrases that mean:

EXAMPLE   1. in favor of slavery   _____proslavery_____

2. a paper published every three weeks _____

3. against slavery   _____

4. before the war   _____

5. a train that travels across the
   continent   _____

6. not commercial   _____

7. after the war   _____

8. a paper published every two weeks   _____

Exercise III

Many verbs end in **-ize** or **-ise.**

The following verbs that end in **-ize** or **-ise** are used in the text of Section III or are constructed from words in the text. Pronounce each verb. Then give a noun or adjective based on the same root as the verb.

EXAMPLE   criticize   <u>critic</u> (noun)

1. advertise   _____

2. commercialize _____

3. emphasize   _____

4. editorialize   _____

5. generalize   _____

6. localize   _____

7. publicize   _____

8. televise   _____

Exercise IV

Substitute the appropriate two- or three-word verb from the following list for the words in heavy type in each sentence. You may change the tense if necessary. All these verbs were used in Section III.

a. make up   f. cut down
b. find out   g. point out
c. lead to   h. keep up with
d. look to   i. make up for
e. turn to

EXAMPLE   He did not have a good excuse for being late, so he **invented** one **that was not true.**
          He did not have a good excuse for being late, so he **(a) made** one **up.**

1. You must **reduce** the number of cigarettes you smoke.
2. The scientists tried to **learn** what the moon is made of.

3. The teacher **showed** the mistake to the student.
4. In the early days of radio, manufacturers could not **meet** the demand for new radio sets.
5. Such hard work will **result in** good grades.
6. Many people **rely on** the President for strong leadership.
7. He behaved very politely to **compensate for** his earlier rudeness.

Exercise V

Substitute one word from the following list for the word or words in heavy type in each sentence. Choose words that are closest in meaning to the words in heavy type. You may change the tense and make words plural.

a. emphasize	e. objective
b. analysis	f. influence
c. style	g. feature
d. hostile	

EXAMPLE   The editor **placed great importance on** the accuracy of every news story.

The editor **(a) emphasized** the accuracy of every news story.

1. His **manner of writing** was simple and easy to understand.
2. Many people are worried about the **effect** that television may have on children.
3. A **detailed examination** of the situation may help him to understand what is wrong.
4. There is a **special article** in today's newspaper about unemployment.
5. A reporter should **not** be **influenced by his personal feelings and opinions** when he is writing a news story.

IV
THE ARTS

American Painting

Until several years after the American Revolution the most important works of art in America were family **portraits.** A few of these pictures were painted by skilled and gifted artists who had studied in London, but most of the painters were self-taught craftsmen—sign painters, housepainters, and carriage painters. After the end of the war in 1781 many artists turned to **landscape** painting. They painted their country's natural beauties—the grandeur of the mountains, the wildness of the forests, and the brilliant colors of the autumn leaves. These pictures reflected the new nationalism, the belief that the United States was one of the greatest countries in the world.

The first American professional **school** of landscape artists, the Hudson River school, painted scenes of the East: the Hudson River valley and the eastern mountains. Artists also accompanied expeditions that were exploring the unknown country. As they traveled westward, these artists painted pictures of Yosemite Valley, the Grand Canyon, and the Rocky Mountains. One of them, George Catlin, drew pictures not only of the country but also of Indians in their colorful native dress. These illustrations have become valuable historical records. James Audubon, a scientist and artist, painted watercolor pictures of native birds with remarkable **precision** and beauty.

The early and mid-nineteenth century saw the development of art that portrayed the life of ordinary people. Country life was a favorite subject. Artists did not present the actual hard daily existence of the farmer, however. Instead, they pictured a simple, happy **rural** world. There was little reference to growing industrialization or to crowded, dirty cities. Still-life painting of inanimate subjects like flowers and fruit was also popular.

Painting by James Audubon. *NAS Photo from National Audubon Society*

The last third of the nineteenth century was a time of tremendous expansion in industry, private wealth, and cultural interests, especially art. Two leading painters of the time were Winslow Homer and Thomas Eakins. Homer painted the outdoor life of America, particularly the drama and beauty of the sea. Eakins presented a realistic picture of the ordinary, middle-class, city life of his time.

While these painters were creating pictures of American life, European and Japanese art was influencing other American artists. James Whistler, who spent most of his life abroad, was deeply affected

Mandan War Chief with His Favorite Wife, George Catlin. *National Gallery of Art, Washington, Collection of Mr. and Mrs. Paul Mellon*

by Spanish and Japanese painting. He was interested in color and spatial patterns, and his work contributed to later developments in **abstract** art. American-born Mary Cassatt lived in France, and her work reflects the French impressionists' treatment of light and color. By the turn of the century, impressionism had become a major influence on American painting. It introduced new **techniques** for handling light and color, air and sunshine.

In the years that followed there emerged a group of young painters, known as the "Ash Can" school. These artists turned to the city for subjects of their work. With realism, warmth, and humor they painted ordinary **urban** scenes—people, streets, restaurants, and dance halls as they really were. An ash can is a large container in which wood and coal ashes are stored, and this name was given to these painters by people who did not approve of these subjects. Edward Hopper, another city realist, portrayed the loneliness of the city. Later he painted the eastern countryside and its highways, gas stations, and railroad tracks, always with honesty and deep emotion.

Meanwhile revolutionary changes were taking place in the post-impressionist European art world, and young American artists brought these new developments home from the Old World. In 1913 they presented a view of the Paris art scene at the New York Armory Show.[1] This exhibition introduced abstract art to a surprised and largely hostile American public. Abstract artists were trying to **express** what they felt was important about a particular object—without attempting to present that object in its realistic form. Pictures at the Armory Show included examples of fauvism, which is painting in extremely vivid colors, and cubism, which reduces natural forms to geometric patterns. The show created excited controversy in the American art world. Although there was a great deal of unfavorable criticism of this modern painting, the exhibition had an important influence on the techniques and philosophies of many young artists. Abstract art did not become important in the United States until many years later, however.

During the years that followed the Armory Show, the United States was entering a great expansion of the machine age. Much American painting of the period reflected the precise, geometric patterns of **skyscrapers,** factories, railroads, and machine-made objects, all of which were becoming increasingly important in American life. Some artists, such as John Marin, caught the electric vitality of the city in semiabstract landscapes. Marin also painted **seascapes** with skillful use of color. At the same time artists continued to be

---

1. An armory is a large building originally constructed for the indoor training of military groups.

interested in what was happening in the European art world.

By the mid-1920s, however, many Americans were becoming political isolationists. They were turning away from involvement with
other countries. This shift marked a sharp change from the international spirit that had existed during the period of World War I. Isola-
tionism extended to many American artists, too. They were no longer
deeply interested in developments in Europe and in European art.
Instead, they were renewing their interest in the United States. **Regionalism,** a concern with special parts of the country, particularly
the Midwest, became the dominant theme in American art. Regional
artists painted the land as they saw it—industrial towns, dreary
streets, and huge mansions. Regional painters, such as Thomas Hart
Benton and Grant Wood, portrayed rural society—farmers, folksingers,[2] religious meetings—with humor and affection.

Regionalism was encouraged by federal art programs that were
designed to give work to unemployed artists during the great depression of the 1930s. Artists were employed to paint pictures of the
American scene, and they frequently introduced social and political
messages into their work. They painted unemployed workers and poor
farmers. Their subjects often reflected their feelings about poverty
and social and economic injustice. Through their painting they expressed their support of labor unionism, and they attacked fascism
and militarism. Until that time social and political comment in pictures
had appeared only in cartoons. The Depression brought a new movement of "social art."

Meanwhile some painters were searching for new means of expression through their art. Realism did not express what they wanted
to say. Abstract art, which had appeared briefly at the time of the
famous Armory Show, began to gain importance. The development
was immensely strengthened by the influence of many abstract artists
who came to America as refugees from the Nazis in Europe.

By the 1950s several different styles of abstract painting domi-
nated the American art world. Many artists were no longer concerned
with presenting objects in abstract forms. Instead their interests centered on colors and the patterns of paint that could be produced on
canvases. They expressed themselves with freedom of style and brilliant colors, emphasizing movement and space. Even their canvases
were often of tremendous size. Jackson Pollock replaced carefully
planned patterns with **improvised** dripping of paint. Described as
"action painting," his technique involved dropping paint on the canvas
with regular, wide-swinging armstrokes. Mark Rothko's canvases fea-

2. Folk are ordinary, common people. Folksongs are the simple songs of the ordinary
people, usually of a particular region. Folksingers are the people who sing these songs.

THE FOG WARNING,
Winslow Homer.
*Courtesy Museum of Fine Arts,
Boston, Otis Norcross Fund*

MOTHER AND CHILD,
Mary Cassatt.
*National Gallery of Art,
Washington,
Chester Dale Collection*

CONVERGENCE,
Jackson Pollock.
*Albright-Knox Art Gallery,
Buffalo, New York,
Gift of Seymour Knox*

tured great floating areas of color. In their own ways abstract artists were expressing characteristics of the modern world and the United States: love of action, speed, and energy.

The 1960s and early 1970s have seen some reaction against this free-form abstract painting. There is more emphasis on precision, with attention to brilliant colors and large, simple forms. Other recent developments have been op art and pop art. Op, or optical art, is a purely abstract art based on the precise, scientific treatment of line and color. Op artists create extraordinary visual effects with unusual uses of color and design. Pop art is in many ways the complete opposite of abstract art. It portrays the most ordinary features of daily life in the United States: comics, canned goods, soft drinks such as Coca-Cola, and automobiles. Through these subjects, pop artists are offering **satirical** comments on **contemporary** American life in a prosperous, materialistic society. **Representational** art also holds an important place in today's art world. Andrew Wyeth, one of the most popular contemporary painters, is a leading painter of representational works.

A significant characteristic of contemporary American art is its **diversity.** A visit to a contemporary art museum or group of galleries in any large city will clearly demonstrate that American art today includes individual painters and whole schools with different techniques, subjects, and points of view. This diversity has been encouraged by the National Endowment for the Arts, which was recently established by the federal government to give financial assistance to the arts, including support for artists, museums, and art-school programs. Although financial aid has been relatively small, many people are hopeful that the program will be expanded and that it will make an important contribution to American artists and their work.

The contemporary art world reflects aspects of the entire American society. In spite of pressures for uniformity, art remains free and changing and offers wide opportunities for individualism.

VOCABULARY

*abstract

nonrealistic; representing the artist's feelings, rather than exact realistic images

There are different kinds of **abstract** art. Some **abstract** paintings express what the artist feels about a particular object, rather than presenting that object in its realistic form. Other **abstract** paintings are not based on physical objects at all. Instead they present the artist's emotions and ideas through the use of color and design.

Some people are puzzled by **abstract** art. They do not find familiar, recognizable forms. They prefer representational painting.

*a canvas

a cloth on which pictures are painted; also a synonym for a painting.

"I like to tack my **canvas** to the wall or the floor. On the floor I am more at ease. I feel nearer, more a part of my painting since I can walk around it, work from four sides. . . ."

Jackson Pollock, in Barbara Rose, ed.,
Readings in American Art Since 1900,
New York, Praeger, 1966, p. 152

contemporary
  a contemporary

existing now; existing or happening at the same time as someone or something else

Who is your favorite artist who is living today? Who is your favorite **contemporary** artist?

Audubon and Catlin were **contemporaries.** They lived at the same time.

diverse
  (a) diversity

different; various

He was interested in many things. He had **diverse** interests.

Diversity is the opposite of uniformity and sameness.

to express
  an expression

to make known by words, looks, or actions

An artist speaks to the world through his painting. He makes his feelings known through his painting. He **expresses** his feelings through his art. His painting is an **expression** of his feelings.

A smile **expresses** happiness. Tears are an **expression** of sadness.

to improvise
  an improvisation

to prepare or perform without planning in advance

If an actor forgets his words, he has to make them up. He has to **improvise.** If he is very skillful, the audience may not be aware of his **improvisation.**

a landscape

a picture of land; a view of land

a seascape

a picture of the sea

Pictures of outdoor scenery can be of the land or the sea. They are **landscapes** or **seascapes.**

a portrait
   to portray

a picture of a person or an animal

Many artists paint pictures of themselves. They paint **self-portraits.** They **portray** themselves in their pictures.

precise
   precision

exact

He drew the map with great accuracy. He drew it with **precision.** The map was **precise.**

a region
   regional

a particular area

Many painters of the 1920s and 1930s painted local scenes, such as small towns, farms, and wheat fields. They were interested in **regional** landscapes. Their paintings represented American life, especially in **regions** of the Midwest.

*to represent
   a representation
   representational

to portray or make a picture of something

A picture of buildings, sidewalks, and streets **represents** a scene in a city. It is a **representation** of a city scene.

A **representational** painting is the realistic picture of a subject as it actually is.

"I believe that the **representation** of objective forms and the presentation of abstract ideas of form to be of equal artistic value."

Thomas Hart Benton, in Rose, p. 108

rural

referring to the country or farm areas

According to the 1970 Census, slightly more than 2 percent of the American people lived in **rural** communities of less than 1000 persons.

a satire
   to satirize
   satirical

a sharp criticism expressed with humor

Political cartoons are often excellent examples of political **satire.** Political cartoons often **satirize** important government officials. They are **satirical** drawings.

*a school

a group of artists who use similar methods and deal with similar subjects

Two famous **schools** of American art are the Hudson River **school** and the Ash Can **school.**

a skyscraper

a very tall building

The Empire State Building is a famous New York **skyscraper.**

a technique

a manner or method of doing something

This chapter on American painting emphasizes the subjects that artists paint, rather than the

techniques with which they put paint on their canvases.

". . . any artist—painter, poet, dancer, or singer—should have something to say before bothering about his **technique**."

John Graham, cubist painter, in Rose, p. 122

urban

referring to the city

The growth of big industrial cities has brought serious **urban** problems, such as poor housing, crowded schools, and pollution.

Vocabulary Review

A. Place a plus sign (+) in front of the word in list II if it has a meaning that is the same as or similar to the corresponding word in list I. Put a minus sign (−) in front of the word if the word in list I has a different meaning.

I	II
EXAMPLE 1. to satirize	_−_ a. to praise
2. to express	_____ b. to reflect
3. abstract	_____ c. representational
4. diverse	_____ d. uniform
5. contemporary	_____ e. future
6. to improvise	_____ f. to plan
7. precise	_____ g. inexact
8. to represent	_____ h. to portray
9. rural	_____ i. urban
10. technique	_____ j. method
11. canvas	_____ k. painting

B. The words in heavy type in the following sentences are from the vocabulary list. Read each sentence aloud and tell whether the word is used correctly. If it is not, explain why it does not fit the meaning of the sentence.

EXAMPLE   1. If you praise someone, you **satirize** him.
Satirize is not used correctly. **Satirize** means criticize with humor.

2. The poet **expresses** his feelings about the world through his poetry.
3. **Abstract** paintings are realistic.
4. If we have **diverse** opinions about something, we agree.
5. A painter who is living now is a **contemporary** artist.
6. Paintings of **urban** scenes portray country landscapes.
7. His answers to the questions were often careless and incorrect. They were **precise.**

8. The Mona Lisa is a famous **portrait** by Leonardo da Vinci. It is the picture of a smiling woman.
9. Pollock's **technique** involved dripping paint on the canvas.
10. When you plan carefully, you **improvise.**

Comprehension and Thought Questions

A. Read the following statements aloud, and indicate whether each is correct or incorrect, based on the information in the text. If any are incorrect, change them so that they are accurate.

1. The landscape paintings of the late 1700s and early 1800s reflected the feeling of nationalism that followed the American Revolution.
2. Still-life painting portrays peaceful rural scenes.
3. Audubon was a scientist and artist who painted beautiful pictures of birds with imprecision.
4. Early and mid-nineteenth-century painters accurately represented farm life as simple and happy.
5. The Ash Can school consisted of a group of young artists who painted realistic urban scenes.
6. The Armory Show introduced abstract art to a surprised and largely hostile American public.
7. American regional art of the late 1920s concentrated on particular areas of the United States.
8. The depression of the 1930s resulted in a new movement of "social art," which expressed criticism of social and economic injustice.
9. Pop art is a satirical commentary on contemporary life.
10. Jackson Pollock's action painting involved placing paint on the canvas in carefully planned patterns.

B. Some of the American paintings of the 1930s and some pop art of the 1960s and 1970s have offered messages and comments about American society. What are some of these messages and comments? Do you think artists should use their work to convey social and political ideas? Why?

C. How did European art influence developments in American art? Give some examples.

D. The text of this chapter concludes with the statement that contemporary American art is diverse. What does this statement mean? In what ways does diversity in American art—subjects and techniques—reflect diversity in American society?

Discussion and Composition Topics

1. Here is an adaptation of an interview with Jackson Pollock by William Wright, from Francis V. O'Connor, *Jackson Pollock,* New York, Museum of Modern Art, 1967, p. 79.

Q. Mr. Pollock, in your opinion what is the meaning of modern art?

A. Modern art to me is nothing more than the expression of contemporary aims of the age that we're living in.

Q. The classical artists had a world to express and they did so by representing the objects in the world. Why doesn't the modern artist do the same thing?

A. The modern artist is living in a mechanical age, and we have mechanical means of representing objects in nature, such as the camera and photograph. The modern artist, it seems to me, is working and expressing an inner world—in other words the energy, the motion, and other inner forces.

   a. In your own words, summarize the questions and answers of this interview.

   b. Do you agree with Mr. Pollock?

   c. What other questions would you have asked if you had been the interviewer?

   d. What answers do you think Mr. Pollock might have given?

2. Who is your favorite painter, if you have one? Why do you like his or her work? Describe one of his or her paintings.

3. Do you prefer to visit art museums or galleries? Why?

4. If a museum is conveniently located, arrange a visit. Inquire about the museum's collection of American paintings. Look for examples of the art that was referred to in the text. Report on your visit.

Library Assignment

Find books in the library that contain illustrations of paintings by some of the artists who are mentioned in the text. Bring one or two of these books to class, and discuss the illustrations with your fellow students.

Two books that present illustrated surveys of American art are Oliver Larkin, *Art and Life in America,* New York, Holt, Rinehart & Winston, 1949; and William H. Pierson and Martha Davidson, *Arts of the United States,* New York, McGraw-Hill, 1960. Consult the catalog for others.

Listening Exercises for Chapter 9 begin on p. 255.

American Theater

Theater in the United States has been strongly influenced by European **drama,** but the "musical" is of truly American origin. The musical is a play with spoken lines, songs, and dances. In the 1920s and 1930s these plays were called "musical comedies." They told simple stories with happy endings: "Boy meets girl, boy loses girl, boy gets girl." One important exception to this pattern was *Showboat*. Written in the 1920s, this musical play introduced a sad and serious **theme,** the problem of an interracial love affair between a white man and a black woman.

It was not until the 1940s and the production of *Oklahoma* that musicals began to change in style and content. Although the basic plot of *Oklahoma* presented an **uncomplicated** love story, the characters in the play seemed more like real people, and, instead of the routine dancing, ballet was introduced. Since *Oklahoma* many successful musical plays have appeared on the American stage. No longer just light and amusing, they often deal with serious themes, accompanied by **sophisticated** music and dancing. One example is *West Side Story,* a modern **version** of Shakespeare's *Romeo and Juliet,* the story of young lovers who die tragically. Set in New York City, it portrays tense and hostile relationships between Puerto Ricans and native New Yorkers. The music was written by Leonard Bernstein, an outstanding composer and conductor of the New York Philharmonic Symphony Orchestra.

Another highly successful musical play was *My Fair Lady,* the musical version of a play by the Irish **playwright** George Bernard Shaw. It tells the story of a poor London girl who wants to change her working-class accent. The scene in which she studies vowel sounds

A scene from the play *Oklahoma.* Culver Pictures, Inc.

A scene from the play *Death of a Salesman.*
Culver Pictures, Inc.

is particularly popular with students who are studying English pronunciation.[1]

The first important American playwright of serious, nonmusical drama was Eugene O'Neill, who wrote deep and sensitive analyses of human relationships. Although he died more than twenty years ago, O'Neill remains this country's most important dramatist, and his plays are **performed** frequently. Other notable modern American playwrights include Thornton Wilder, Lillian Hellman, Tennessee Williams, Edward Albee, and Arthur Miller. These names are only a few from the long list of contributors to the contemporary stage. Wilder's best known play, *Our Town,* portrays the lives of people in a small New England town. Albee, the author of *Who's Afraid of Virginia Woolf?,* is concerned with the difficulties of human communication. Williams and Hellman write about relationships in the South. The American playwright who is most widely known today is Arthur Miller. His play *Death of a Salesman* has been performed in countries throughout the world. This work captures with sympathy and understanding the heartbreak of an unsuccessful man who cannot manage the forces in his life.

Two important developments in recent years are the "theater of the **absurd**" and the "black theater." There are also some controversial **experiments** with electronic music and lighting, body movements to replace spoken words in expressing ideas, and even **spontaneous audience** participation in some performances. The theater of the absurd has been largely influenced by such European writers as the Rumanian Eugène Ionesco and the Irish playwright Samuel Beckett. These plays satirize some of the more ridiculous aspects of contemporary society. They portray a world in which life and human action seem meaningless and beyond understanding.

Black theater presents plays about black people, written by black playwrights, and performed by black **casts.** Originally dramas about Blacks carried messages of protest against racial prejudice. Today, although this theme of protest is still present, black theater is increasingly concerned with Blacks as individual human beings and with their problems as ordinary people. In 1970 for the first time the Pulitzer Prize[2] was awarded to a black playwright, Charles Gordone.

New York City is the theater center of the United States. Most

1. The musical numbers from these four plays have been recorded, and these recordings may be available in your library.
2. In 1903 Joseph Pulitzer (See Section III, Chapter 6), a newspaper publisher, gave money to be used for prizes for achievements in various fields, including American literature. A special committee makes an annual award to the author of the best American play. Although there is often widespread disagreement on the choice, the winners have been among the most famous in American stage history. All the American playwrights mentioned here have won the Pulitzer Prize. Eugene O'Neill received the award four times, a record unequaled by any other playwright.

important new plays are produced there. For years young actors, actresses, and playwrights have gone to New York, hoping to find success.

The New York theater world is divided into two parts. One centers around Broadway, which is one of the city's most important streets. Almost all the large commercial theaters are located on or near Broadway in the midtown area. Plays performed in these theaters are known as Broadway **productions.** Because rents are very high, these plays must attract large audiences willing to buy expensive tickets. Experimental plays have not been successful on Broadway. Most Broadway theatergoers seem to prefer musicals and sophisticated dramas or comedies featuring one or two highly paid **stars.**

The other New York theater division, off-Broadway, has no definite geographic location. Off-Broadway theaters are found throughout the city in buildings once used as garages, offices, and stores. Rents are low, and there is just space enough for small audiences. Sometimes there is no raised stage. Then the cast performs in the center of the room, surrounded on all sides by the audience. This arrangement is known as "theater-in-the-round."

Off-Broadway productions were begun in the late 1940s and early 1950s by young actors and playwrights who were unable to find employment on Broadway. Often they wanted to perform in new and experimental plays. By keeping production costs down and by using unknown casts instead of star performers, producers have been able to offer interesting theater at low prices.

Many theater groups are active outside New York. In the early 1970s there were more than fifty professional companies in major cities. Some of them follow repertory schedules: Different plays are performed several times by the same group of actors within a period of a few weeks or months. There are also traveling acting companies that tour throughout the country. In addition, there are nonprofessional university and community theater groups.

Unlike many other countries, there is no nationally **subsidized** theater in the United States. Some acting companies receive a little financial help from the National Endowment for the Arts, foundations,[3] and a few communities. However, many theater groups suffer from lack of adequate financing. Frequently commercial theaters must charge very high prices for tickets in order to pay production costs and make some profit. As a result, many people who love the theater cannot afford to go very often.

3. Foundations are nongovernmental, tax-free organizations established to subsidize or support approved projects. The best known are the Ford, Rockefeller, and Carnegie foundations.

Theater critics write **reviews** of plays. A review summarizes the **plot** and comments on the quality of the writing and the acting. Theatergoers are often guided by a reviewer's opinion when they are deciding whether or not to see a particular production. Local newspapers are the best sources of information on theater activities. Plays are usually advertised in the Saturday or Sunday paper.

Usually there are two ways to buy theater tickets. Tickets can be ordered by mail or purchased at the theater **box office.** When buying tickets by mail, you must specify the date of the performance you wish to see and indicate whether you want to attend the matinee (afternoon) or evening performance. You should also indicate the location of the seats you want—orchestra, mezzanine, or balcony. Orchestra seats are on the ground floor and are the most expensive. Mezzanine seats are above and behind the orchestra. Balcony seats, the cheapest, are on higher floors above the orchestra. Price lists are usually given in the newspaper ads. A mail request should include a check or money order and a stamped, self-addressed envelope.

If you buy tickets at the theater, you get them at the box office, which is located in the theater lobby or at the entrance to the theater. You should be prepared with information about the date of the performance you want to see and the desired location of seats, and you must pay cash. If a play has a "rave" review, all tickets may be sold quickly. Then sometimes standing-room tickets are available. This is indicated by a sign reading "S.R.O." (Standing Room Only). For a reduced price, the theatergoer is allowed to stand in the back of the theater, behind the orchestra seats, and watch the performance. Sometimes student "rush" tickets are available just before the performance begins. These tickets are sold at reduced prices to students with identication (I.D.) cards.

VOCABULARY

absurd	very foolish; not reasonable or sensible
	His statement was silly and foolish. It was **absurd.**
	It is **absurd** to think that you will live forever.
*an audience	a gathering of people to see a play (or hear a concert) at a theater
	Some members of the **audience** did not like the play, and they left before it was finished.
	"Tomorrow I appear for the first time before a Boston **audience**—4000 critics."
	Mark Twain, American writer, in a letter, 1869

a box office — the place in a theater where tickets can be bought

The play was a "sell-out." There were no more tickets available at the **box office.**

*a cast
to cast — the actors in a play

The players in a musical include singers and dancers, as well as actors and actresses. The **cast** in a musical is composed of singers, dancers, actors, and actresses.

The director selected the actors and actresses for the play. He **cast** the play.

complicated — difficult to understand; made up of several parts

Many students think that English is a difficult language. They find it very **complicated.**

*(a) drama
dramatic — a play for the theater; the composition and performance of plays for the theater

Death of a Salesman is a major contemporary American **drama.**

A good theater critic must be interested in **drama.**

"To many people **dramatic** criticism must seem like an attempt to paint soap bubbles."

Adapted from John Mason Brown, drama critic, 1940, in Bartlett, *Familiar Quotations,* 14th ed., Boston, Little Brown, 1968, p. 1047a

*an experiment
to experiment
experimental — something new and untried, using unusual methods in writing and acting

The Living Theater and the Open Theater are American theater companies that have introduced many theatrical **experiments.** They use unusual acting techniques in original plays. Their plays are **experimental.** These companies **experiment** with completely new methods. **Experimental** theater has not been popular with Broadway audiences. It has been more successful with off-Broadway and university audiences.

*to perform
a performer
a performance — to act in a play

Laurence Olivier, the famous English actor, has **performed** in many plays by Shakespeare. He is a great Shakespearian **performer.** His **performances** are usually excellent.

If you want to know what time the play will begin, you should look at the newspaper ad. It tells the time of the matinee and evening **performances.**

a playwright	a person who writes a play Arthur Miller is a famous American **playwright.**
*a plot	the plan or outline of a story, especially of a novel or drama In the theater of the absurd there is often no clear **plot.** There is no development of an easily understood story. 　Shakespeare's plays often have one main **plot** and several sub**plots,** or less important stories.
*a production 　to produce 　a producer	the organization of a play and putting it on stage A **producer** raises the money to finance a play and arranges for it to be performed. Although he does not write the play or act in it, he is responsible for its entire **production.** He **produces** the play.
*a review 　to review 　a reviewer	a summary, commentary, and analysis of a play (or movie, book, or musical performance), usually published in a newspaper or magazine The *New York Times* drama critic writes **reviews** of Broadway and off-Broadway theater productions. He is the theater **reviewer.** He **reviews** new plays. 　　Nature fits all her children with 　　　　something to do, 　He who wants to write and can't write, 　　　　can surely *review.* James Russell Lowell, nineteenth century American poet, adapted from *A Fable for Critics,* 1848
sophisticated	wise in the ways of the world; worldly "We considered ourselves very **sophisticated** and talked of sex and morality in a superior way." 　　Jawaharlal Nehru (1889–1964), Prime Minister 　　of India, in *American Heritage Dictionary,* 　　New York, McGraw-Hill, p. 1232
spontaneous 　spontaneously	done voluntarily and naturally without having been planned The actor spoke his lines so well that the audience applauded **spontaneously.** When he finished his speech, the applause was loud and **spontaneous.**
*a star 　to star 　stellar	a famous actor or actress Charlie Chaplin is an internationally famous movie **star.** He has **starred** in many movies.

The cast was composed of many **stars**. It was a **stellar** cast.

to subsidize *a subsidy*	to give financial support (private or governmental)

Do you think the government should give financial assistance to playwrights? Do you think the government should **subsidize** playwrights? Do you think playwrights should receive financial **subsidies**?

*a theme — the subject of a talk or piece of writing, such as a play

"To produce a mighty book you must choose a mighty **theme**."
> Herman Melville, nineteenth-century American author, in *Moby Dick*

*a version — an adaptation or change of a work of art or literature into another style

Charles Lamb rewrote Shakespeare's plays as children's stories. Lamb's **version** of Shakespeare's plays is called *Tales from Shakespeare*.

Vocabulary Review

A. Use the following pairs of words from the vocabulary list in sentences.

EXAMPLE   playwright, version

The **playwright** wrote a modern **version** of an ancient Greek tragedy.

1. sophisticated, dramas
2. audience, spontaneously
3. complicated, theme
4. performance, subsidized
5. experimental, productions
6. absurd, plot
7. cast, stars

B. Write a short paragraph about the theater in your country, using at least five of the following words from the vocabulary lists of Chapters 9 and 10. You may make these words plural and use them in any form: noun, verb, adjective, or adverb.

1. theme	5. perform
2. plot	6. production
3. review	7. sophisticated
4. contemporary	8. technique

Comprehension and Thought Questions

1. a. The text mentioned four musical plays. What are they?
   b. Describe the theme of *Showboat*. In what way was this musical "ahead of its time"?
2. What is the Pulitzer Prize for drama? Name some of the playwrights who have won this award. Are prizes given in your country to outstanding authors? If so, describe one of the winners and the prize.
3. What is the theater of the absurd? Have you ever seen or read an example of the theater of the absurd? If so, describe it.
4. a. How is American theater financed? How is theater financed in your country?
   b. Do you think the government should subsidize the theater? Explain your answer. Discuss what you know about government theater subsidies in your own country or in other countries.
5. a. If you were a New York theatergoer, would you prefer Broadway or off-Broadway plays? Why?
   b. Is one city the theater center in your country? If so, which city? Describe the role of university theater in your country. Is a stellar cast important for a production's success in your country? How popular are experimental productions? If you have ever seen an experimental play, describe it.
6. a. How can you order theater tickets by mail? What must you do if you want to buy them at the theater?
   b. How do you obtain theater tickets in your country? How expensive are they?
7. What do "social art," pop art (Chapter 9), and the theater of the absurd have in common?

Discussion and Composition Topics

A number of American plays are available on records. Libraries will often arrange to obtain records not available in their collections. Listed below are some recommended records. Most of these plays also appear in inexpensive paperback editions. These are indicated by an asterisk before the title. Students of English usually find it interesting and instructive to follow these three steps:

1. Read the text of a play.
2. Listen to the record, and read the text at the same time.
3. Listen to the record without the text.

A. Read (and, if possible, listen to) one of these plays:

1. Albee, Edward	*Who's Afraid of Virginia Woolf?*
	The Zoo Story
2. Benét, Stephen Vincent	John Brown's Body
3. Duberman, Martin	*In White America*

4. Hansberry, Lorraine	*Raisin in the Sun
	*To Be Young, Gifted, and Black
5. Kipphardt, Heinar	*In the Matter of J. Robert Oppenheimer
	This play was not written by an American, but it deals with an American subject and is performed by an American cast.
6. Lowell, Robert	*Old Glory
	Benito Cereno
7. MacLeish, Archibald	Scratch
8. Miller, Arthur	*After the Fall
	*The Crucible
	*Death of a Salesman
	*Incident at Vichy
	*A View from the Bridge
9. O'Neill, Eugene	*Ah, Wilderness
	*The Emperor Jones
	*Long Day's Journey Into Night
	*A Moon for the Misbegotten
	*More Stately Mansions
10. Williams, Tennessee	*The Glass Menagerie
	*The Rose Tattoo

B. Pretend that you are a theater critic for a newspaper. Write a review of the play that you read for the preceding exercise. Summarize the story and discuss the playwright's theme and the characters. If you can listen to a recording of the play, comment on the acting.

C. Library Assignment: The printed text of the play you have chosen should indicate the date on which the play was first produced in New York. Locate the original review in the *New York Times Index*. (A review usually appears on the day after the first performance.) Read the original review and prepare a brief summary of the reviewer's comments. Be sure to note the name of the reviewer, the date of the newspaper, and the number of the page on which the review appeared.

D. Discuss a play you have seen recently. Summarize the plot and comment on the acting. (If you have not seen a play, discuss a recent movie.)

E. Do you prefer plays or movies? Why?

Listening Exercises for Chapter 10 begin on p. 256.

11 A History of American Architecture

Before European settlers arrived in America, the American Indians had developed their own **indigenous** architecture. In the eastern regions of the country the Indians lived in wigwams. "Wigwam" is an Indian word meaning dwelling or place to live. These dwellings, or houses, were made of poles tied together to form conical △ , rectangular ☐ , or loaf-shaped ⌐⌐ frames. The frame was covered with materials such as bark, which is the outer covering of a tree trunk, or animal skins, with a hole at the top to release smoke from the fire used for cooking or heating. Some wigwams housed just one family. Others were big enough for several families to live in together.

In the region of the Great Plains (flat lands that now include the states of North and South Dakota, Montana, Wyoming, Oklahoma, Nebraska, Kansas, and parts of Colorado and Texas) lived nomadic, or wandering, Indian tribes such as the Sioux, the Crow, and the Blackfeet. They needed dwellings that were easy to put up, take down, and carry with them. The tepee, a portable, conical tent, met these requirements. "Tepee" is a Sioux word that means dwelling or place to live. The frame of the tepee was made of poles, which were tied together with split wood or strips of leather. Over these poles were hung highly decorated bark and animal skins with an opening at the top which served as a smoke escape. The skins were processed so that the **interior** remained dry, even in heavy rainstorms. The tepee was roomy enough for a family to live comfortably.

A completely different kind of housing was constructed by Indians in the Southwest. The Spanish explorers called these dwellings "pueblos." They were built of stone or adobe bricks made of clay and

130

straw. A pueblo housed the families of an entire community. Like a large apartment house, it consisted of hundreds of rooms, built on five or six floors. Each floor was set back from the floor below in an irregular pattern. Ground-floor rooms were used for storage, and rooms on the upper floors were used for everyday living. Cooking was done in fire pits built against the walls, and the smoke went out through holes in the roof. Outside ladders served as stairs from floor to floor. The pueblos were built around open courtyards, which were used for dances and other public ceremonies.

As a general rule **settlers** in a new country try to **reproduce** the buildings they knew in their home countries. This was certainly true of the early settlers who came to America from Europe. They did not adopt Indian-style housing. Instead, they **adapted** familiar styles from home to meet their needs. As a result, colonial architecture was as diverse as the countries from which these people came.

The English in New England built simple wood houses with low ceilings and small windows to make heating easier. Later, well-to-do people constructed larger and more splendid brick houses, which were often copied from pictures and **designs** brought from England. Early southern homes also followed English styles but had long central halls to keep air circulating during the summer heat. By the mid-eighteenth century gentleman farmers in Virginia and the Carolinas

A camp of Indian buffalo hunters. *The New York Public Library Picture Collection*

lived in mansions that were often modeled after British country houses but had separate kitchens and slave quarters.

The Dutch, who settled in New York and New Jersey, built with wood, brick, and stone, using variously shaped bricks and decorative tiles. German farmers constructed great wood-and-stone barns in Pennsylvania. Roman Catholic priests from Spain, who went to the Southwest to christianize the Indians, adapted Italian and Spanish architecture, using native stone and adobe to build their missions. French settlers in New Orleans built charming houses, whose balconies were decorated with **elaborate** designs in iron. This ironwork is called "wrought iron."

In the early 1600s Scandinavians introduced log cabins, the kind of housing they knew best. By the time of the American Revolution settlers all along the western **frontier** were living in these small, sturdy houses. Log cabins were well suited to the difficult life of the frontier. They required few tools for construction, and wood was readily available. Tree trunks were fitted on top of one another **horizontally,** and the cracks were filled with dry grass, clay, or mud. The roof was covered with bark; dried plant stems called thatch; or shingles, which are thin pieces of wood laid in overlapping rows. Because glass was expensive, windows were covered with animal skins or paper. Most cabins were one story high and had one or two rooms. Abraham Lincoln, the sixteenth President of the United States, was born in a log cabin (in 1809), and so the log cabin has become the **symbol** of a lowly beginning from which, according to the American dream, anyone can rise to fame and fortune.

During the American Revolution there was little building, and, when the war ended, attention turned to the construction of official buildings for the new nation. Charles Bulfinch, a native architect who had studied abroad, designed the Massachusetts State House, where the state legislature and the governor carried on their business. Throughout the nineteenth century its great copper dome was a model for many state capitols and city halls all over the country. Bulfinch, who was influenced by English architecture, also designed gracious private residences in Boston. They remain important examples of the architecture of what is known as the federal period, which lasted from approximately 1790 to 1820.

Although this period was a time of growing nationalism, of pride in the new country and in everything American, European influence on architecture remained strong. The nation's new capital city, Washington, D.C., was planned by a Frenchman, Pierre L'Enfant. The residence of the President was designed by an Irishman, James Hoban, and the Capitol building was originally planned by English-born Ben-

The White House.
Courtesy The White House

The Palace,
Williamsburg,
Virginia.
American Airlines

A typical log cabin.
*The New York
Public Library
Picture Collection*

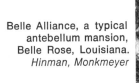

Belle Alliance, a typical
antebellum mansion,
Belle Rose, Louisiana.
Hinman, Monkmeyer

jamin Latrobe, although it was finally completed under the direction of Bulfinch.

In large part these choices reflect the **taste** of Thomas Jefferson, the third President of the United States. Jefferson was not only a **skillful** politician but was also a remarkable artist and intellectual with a wide variety of interests.[1] He had spent much time abroad and was especially impressed by the architecture of Rome. To him the buildings of the republic of Rome symbolized democracy combined with good taste. As a result of Jefferson's influence, many of the public buildings of this period were reproductions of classic Roman styles.

The classical influence continued well into the mid-nineteenth century, but by the 1820s ancient Greek architectural forms were replacing Roman forms in houses, as well as in public buildings. Simple wood houses were often painted white with Greek Revival columned **porches** added to their basic rectangular form. Many banks, state capitols, and churches followed the classic Greek styles. Perhaps the most romantic examples of Greek Revival architecture were the mansions on the plantations of the antebellum (pre-Civil War) South. As sugar and cotton fortunes grew, these splendid columned houses, modeled after Greek temples, looked down on the cabins that housed the slaves.

As the population expanded westward in the early and mid-nineteenth century, new towns were established. Here the most functional kind of house for the ordinary man followed the simple New England style. Rectangular in shape with a slanted roof to shed snow and rain, this wooden house was inexpensive and could be built easily without a trained architect.

By the end of the Civil War in 1865 classical architecture was replaced by a wild "battle of styles," even including elaborate adaptations of ancient Egyptian and Byzantine buildings. There was free borrowing and combining of many architectural designs, and much of the building of the late nineteenth and the early twentieth centuries reflected great wealth, rather than good taste. H. H. Richardson was one of the few architects who rejected this trend and looked for functionalism combined with a sense of **aesthetics.** From the mid-1860s to the mid-1880s, he designed churches, railroad stations, libraries, and college buildings that showed strength and simplicity and influenced many younger architects.

---

1. At a White House dinner honoring some of America's leading scientists, artists, and writers in 1962, President Kennedy said, "I think this is the most extraordinary collection of talent, of human knowledge, that has ever been gathered together at the White House, with the possible exception of when Thomas Jefferson dined here alone."

VOCABULARY

to adapt
   an adaptation
	to change in order to be suitable for a new need or new use
	The novel was rewritten for use as a television play. The novel was **adapted** for television. The television play was an **adaptation** of a novel.
	  Many foreigners find it difficult to get used to the food in this country. **Adapting** to unfamiliar food takes time and effort.

aesthetics
  (also spelled esthetics)
  aesthetic
  aesthetically
	the philosophy of what is beautiful, especially in art and literature
	Thomas Jefferson had great respect for **aesthetics.** He recognized and appreciated beauty. He had a great **aesthetic** sense. Roman architecture pleased him **aesthetically,** intellectually, and spiritually.
	  "Painting isn't just an **aesthetic** process; it's a form of magic. . . ."
	    Pablo Picasso, in Françoise Gilot, *Life With Picasso,* New York, McGraw-Hill, 1946, p. 266

*a design *to design*	a plan; a general arrangement or pattern of something (a building, a machine, a piece of furniture, etc.) The early settler constructed his house with much more attention to practical, functional **design** than to aesthetics. He **designed** a practical, functional house.
elaborate	worked out with great attention to complicated details Indian tepees were often richly decorated with **elaborate,** colorful paintings.
*a frontier	An undeveloped region just beyond a populated one Frederick Turner was a famous American historian who wrote about the movement of American people westward into undeveloped land during the nineteenth century. He believed that certain American characteristics developed as the result of the experience of conquering the western **frontier.** He thought **frontier** life encouraged individualism and independence.

horizontal
vertical

flat across; parallel to the horizon
straight up and down

This figure is a square. Lines *a* and *b* are **horizontal.** Lines *c* and *d* are **vertical.**

indigenous

native to a particular land or region

Maize, a kind of corn, was not originally grown in Europe or Asia. It was native to the New World (North and South America). It was **indigenous** to the New World and was brought to Europe by early explorers. Tobacco was also **indigenous** to the New World and was introduced to Europe by Spanish and Portuguese explorers.

interior
exterior

inside
outside

Interior decorators decorate the inside of a building. They choose the furniture, curtains, and colors of paint for the **interior** of the building.

During the first half of the nineteenth century the **exterior** design of many American buildings followed the form of Greek temples. The **exteriors** of many buildings were modeled after Greek temples.

a porch

an open area with a floor and a roof, attached to the outside of a building, usually a house

Many older people like to sit on their **porches** in the summertime and watch people walking past their houses.

*to reproduce
    a reproduction

to make a copy of something

Many late-nineteenth-century American residences are **reproductions** of Paris townhouses. Architects followed pictures and designs of Paris houses in order to **reproduce** them as exactly as possible.

*to settle
    a settler

to make one's home in a new place

A person who makes his home in a new region is a **settler.** People from many European countries established homes in the New World. They **settled** in the New World.

(a) skill | the ability to do something expertly and well

skillful
skilled

A surgeon must have great **skill** to perform successful operations. A good surgeon must be **skillful.** He must be **skilled.**

"Good literature is not an abstract science. It is an art, the success of which depends on the author's **skill** to give and on our ability to receive."

> Sir Arthur Thomas Quiller-Couch, British educator,
> in a lecture at Cambridge University, 1913,
> in Bartlett, *Familiar Quotations,* 14th ed.,
> Boston, Little Brown, 1968, p. 866b

a symbol
  to symbolize

something that stands for, or represents, something else

The dove frequently represents peace. It is a **symbol** of peace. It **symbolizes** peace.

*(a)taste
  tasteful

the ability to appreciate beauty, especially in art and literature

The house was elegantly decorated. It was decorated in elegant **taste.** The decoration was **tasteful.**

Vocabulary Review

The words in heavy type in the following sentences are from the vocabulary list of Chapter 11. Substitute a synonym for each word, or give a brief definition of it.

EXAMPLE   Someone who has **taste** in the arts may be described as having a fine sense of aesthetics.

Someone who appreciates excellence and beauty in the arts may be described as having a fine sense of aesthetics.

1. The only truly **indigenous** Americans are the Indians.
2. Museums sell inexpensive **reproductions** of pictures that are in their collections.
3. They moved to a new city and **settled** there.
4. The dancer performed with great **skill.**
5. The eagle is a bird that **symbolizes** the United States.
6. Early American settlers kept moving to new **frontiers.**
7. Good architects **design** buildings that are beautiful and functional.
8. **Elaborate** designs do not always reflect good taste.
9. The **exterior** of the house was painted white.
10. The difficult book was **adapted** to the reading abilities of the children.

Comprehension and Thought Questions

1. Three kinds of Indian housing are discussed in the text. They are the wigwam, the tepee, and the pueblo. Describe them. Can you think of housing in other parts of the world that is similar to any of these three? If so, describe it.
2. The text states that colonial architecture was as diverse as the countries from which the early settlers came. Explain this statement, and give examples of different kinds of colonial architecture. Why do you think that settlers usually try to reproduce the buildings they knew in their home countries?
3. What did the log cabin and the New England style house have in common? How did these types of houses meet the special needs of the people who built them and lived in them?
4. What does the log cabin symbolize today? Are there any particular styles of buildings (houses, palaces, churches) in your country that have special symbolic meaning? If so, describe them and explain the symbolism.
5. Identify
   a. Charles Bulfinch
   b. James Hoban
   c. Pierre L'Enfant
   d. Benjamin Latrobe
6. What is meant by Greek Revival architecture?
7. Who was H. H. Richardson? Why were his attitudes toward architectural styles unusual for his time?

Discussion and Composition Topics

A. Here are three statements about architecture.

1. I call architecture music in space.

Johann Wolfgang von Goethe, letter, 1829

2. The great architect is necessarily a great poet.

Frank Lloyd Wright, contemporary American architect, in Seldman Rodman, *Conversations with Artists,* New York, Devin-Adair, 1957, p. 47

3. It is much better to be good than to be original.

Mies van der Rohe, contemporary American architect, in Rodman, *ibid.*

Give your opinion of each of these statements. Do you agree or disagree and why?

B. In 1847 Walter Prescott, an American historian, wrote in *The Conquest of Peru:*

The surest test of the civilization of a people—at least as sure as any
. . . is to be found in their architecture, which presents so noble a

field for the display of the grand and the beautiful and which, at the same time, is so intimately connected with the essential comforts of life.

1. Choose a building with which you are familiar. It can be located anywhere and can have been built at any time. (For example, you may wish to choose a school building, a church, a bank, a house, or the like.) Describe it. Then analyze it in Prescott's terms—as a "test of the civilization of a people."

2. If you were to come here in 2975 A.D. and examine the building in which this class is held, what conclusions might you draw about the civilization of the people who used it in 1975? For example, what might you conclude about their attitudes toward education, physical comforts, and their aesthetic values?

C. 1. Landscape architecture, also known as landscape designing, is a field of professional designing. It involves changing and improving the appearance of land by planting flowers, bushes, and trees, especially around buildings.

   Describe an example of landscape architecture or landscaping that you have seen recently. It may be on the campus of your school, around a city building, around a private home, and the like. How does it relate to the building? How does it affect the exterior appearance of the building? Do you think the landscape architect conferred with the building architect? Explain your opinion.

2. Interior decorating is another field of professional designing. It involves planning the colors and furnishings of the interior of a building.

   Describe the interior of a building that you think has been professionally decorated. It may be a private home, a dormitory, a library, an office building, a theater, etc. Did you find it aesthetically pleasing? Why or why not?

D. There are several American magazines that deal with architecture. Some, like *Better Homes and Gardens,* are written for nonprofessional readers. Others, like *Architectural Forum,* are professional publications. Make a list of as many examples of such magazines as you can find in your library and, if possible, on a newsstand. Prepare a report on one of these magazines. Describe the kinds of articles: who wrote them? what are they about? what kind of reader do you think they are written for?

Listening Exercises for Chapter 11 begin on p. 258.

Modern American Architecture

In 1883 a Chicago architect, W. L. B. Jenney, was asked to design an office building. Twenty-six years earlier the first American elevator had been installed in a New York building. **Taking advantage** of elevator transportation, Jenney designed the first skyscraper. It was originally ten stories high; two more stories were added later. Other tall elevator buildings soon followed.

In Jenney's office worked a young architect, Louis Sullivan, who became a leader of the opposition to the use of **traditional** styles in American architecture. Sullivan was not only a great architect but also a great philosopher. His building designs contributed to the development of modern architecture, and his writing influenced many young architects. He was deeply moved by the **potential** beauty of the skyscraper, which, he said, must be "a proud and soaring thing." Sullivan believed that the function of a building must determine its form and that practical needs must be the basis of an architect's planning and design.

In the years after 1900 Frank Lloyd Wright, a student of Sullivan, continued his teacher's **rejection** of traditional design. He had a deep belief in simplicity and in the importance of the **unity** of form and function. During his sixty-six-year career, which lasted until his death in 1959, Wright designed houses, churches, museums, skyscrapers, and factories. His low, one-story houses established many features of contemporary house design, including the "carport," which he invented and named. The carport is a roofed area, attached to the house and used as a shelter for an automobile. Wright was probably the most original and creative architect of his time.

The important new architecture of the early twentieth century was

The Guggenheim Museum
designed by Frank Lloyd Wright.
Wide World

the modern skyscraper. By the 1930s these **towering** buildings reached their greatest height in the Empire State Building, which rises 102 stories and 1250 feet. Skyscrapers seemed particularly suitable for large cities, where land was expensive and tall buildings offered the most efficient use of space. Some cities, however, have limited the number of floors that a building may have. Washington, D.C., for example, prohibits the construction of buildings more than thirteen stories high. It is felt that skyscrapers would spoil the appearance of the city and the government buildings. In recent years architects have designed somewhat lower structures and have given attention to light and open space. Many post-World War II skyscrapers feature what have been called glass-curtain walls. Entire walls of these tall buildings are made of panes of glass. However, with the increasing concern over the declining supply of energy sources, many architects are turning away from this emphasis on glass. They are looking for building materials and designs that will require less air conditioning in hot weather and less artificial heat in cold weather.

The last several years have seen renewed interest in the construction of very tall skyscrapers. The World Trade Center in New York, which was completed in the early 1970s, is the second tallest building in the world. It consists of twin towers, each 1350 feet high, with lobbies seven stories high and fifty-five passenger elevators. The Sears Tower, a new Chicago skyscraper, is 100 feet higher. There

141

is considerable debate in the architectural world about the future of such towering buildings. Many critics reject them as uneconomical and inefficient. Others reject skyscrapers devoted only to office space. They think that future skyscrapers should also provide living areas for those who work in the city.

Many modern urban and **suburban** apartment houses have adapted skyscraper architecture to contemporary living. Known as "high-rise" buildings, they house many families in single buildings or groups of buildings. Apartments in these buildings are often equipped with such **conveniences** as air conditioning and various electric kitchen appliances such as clothes washing and drying machines and automatic waste disposers. Some expensive apartment houses even contain small grocery stores for convenient shopping.

Urban architecture and problems of city living have received increasing attention in recent years. In large industrial cities many people have lived in crowded, poorly heated, and badly **ventilated** tenement houses. A tenement is a very run-down apartment building. During the waves of European migration of the late 1800s and early 1900s tenements were occupied by poorly paid immigrants and in recent years many Blacks who have moved from the South to northern industrial centers have occupied them. The result has been **slum** ghettos, areas of racially segregated, substandard housing in the oldest sections of the cities.

To some extent, the government has tried to improve the housing of the poor. During the depression years the Roosevelt administration sponsored some housing projects—low-rent housing for numbers of poor families. A few private organizations, including some labor unions, have also constructed low-rent buildings. In 1965 the federal government established the Department of Housing and Urban Development. Programs of this department have granted money to encourage construction of housing for medium-income and low-income families. Special attention has been given to urban-renewal programs. These programs involve the improvement of existing buildings or the construction of new buildings in what were urban slum areas. It is too soon, however, to measure the long-term effects of these programs, and housing of the nation's poor remains a major problem.

In addition to urban-renewal programs for slum areas, architects and urban planners are turning their attention to the needs of entire communities, rather than to individual buildings. Taking advantage of such technical advances as new building materials, air conditioning, and improved lighting methods, architects are designing modern hospitals, schools, airports, libraries, and museums. Poorly lit city factories are being replaced by industrial buildings that are often con-

The Sears Tower in Chicago, Illinois.
Courtesy Sears, Roebuck and Co.

The Empire State Building.
Courtesy New York Convention and Visitors Bureau

A view of the towers of the World Trade Center in New York City during construction.
Wide World

structed on the outskirts of the city or in the suburbs in pleasant park-like surroundings. One popular suburban **innovation** is the shopping center, a group of many stores with adequate parking facilities and sometimes a concert hall, theater, and community meeting place.

With the increased **complexity** and diversity of modern architectural planning has come the "umbrella" organization. Working together, architects, engineers, scientists, and landscape and interior designers combine their knowledge and skills in commercial, industrial, and other complex projects. This type of group activity is not so important for private residences, which a single architect can design.

Many Americans dream of owning their own homes on small plots of land in pleasant suburban areas, but an individual house designed by an architect is too expensive for the average homeowner. To meet this demand, builders have constructed housing developments in suburban areas all over the United States. A development is a large group of similar houses, built by one company at a cost that middle-income families can afford. Some of these developments offer handsome examples of good design, with variations in each house to give it some **individuality.** Others, often constructed by builders who have not employed architects, frequently reflect poor taste and little planning.

In recent years prefabricated houses have been introduced in an attempt to provide moderately priced, attractive housing on a **mass scale.** Prefabrication is a process of construction. Houses are designed by architects and separate parts are **mass-produced** in factories. Such a prebuilt house can be quickly put up on the **site.** The advantage can be a well-designed house at a relatively low cost. In 1973 the country's largest producer of factory-built housing announced that it had arranged for the Frank Lloyd Wright Foundation to design all of its "pre-fab" houses. Architects who were trained by Wright designed houses of different prices, but most of them cost between $20,000 and $30,000, which was the most popular price range for houses at that time. Although the number of prefabricated houses currently manufactured is very small (and the prices go up as costs increase), this method is an interesting example of the relatively economical, experimental building techniques that are being used all over the world.

The past thirty years have seen the development of modern architecture, which combines American styles with diverse forms introduced from Europe and Asia and adapted to meet American tastes and needs. There are too many important modern architects in the United States to list, but it is interesting to note a few who came as refugees from Hitler's Europe and who have influenced the contemporary American scene. They include Walter Gropius and Ludwig Mies van der Rohe (Germany) and Marcel Breuer (Hungary). In addition, other architects, such as I. M. Pei (Chinese), Minoru Yamasaki (Japanese), Richard Neutra (Austrian), Pietro Belluschi (Italian), and Eero Saarinen (Finnish), have reflected the influence of their foreign **heritages.**

It is impossible to give a precise definition or description of contemporary American architecture. It is constantly changing, and there is great diversity and experimentation. It is characterized by new styles, new uses of space, new materials, and new building techniques. To some it seems cold and **austere.** To others it seems exciting and alive. Lewis Mumford, a widely known architectural critic, says, "Modern architecture . . . gives expression to the best aspects of our civilization; it also gives full representation to its worst elements. . . . Architecture is the expression of our society."[1]

VOCABULARY

*austere *austerity*	simple and plain, without ornament or comfort The houses of the early settlers were quite **austere.** The settlers were more concerned with survival than with comfortable living. Their houses were furnished with **austerity.**

complex
   (a) complexity
   a complex
	made up of many parts
	The Indian tepee was not a **complex** structure. Its design was simple, and it was easy to construct.
	   The modern hospital, on the other hand, is an example of architectural **complexity.** Scientists, engineers, and interior designers must work with the architects to design **a complex** of medical buildings that can meet many needs.

convenient
   (a) convenience
	well suited to and helpful for one's purposes and needs
	The Indian tepee was a **convenient** kind of dwelling for nomadic tribes. It was easy to put up and take down and provided comfortable housing.
	   The electrical dishwasher is a modern **convenience** for housewives. It saves them time and trouble. It offers great **convenience.**

---

1. Lewis Mumford, *Roots of Contemporary American Architecture*, New York, Grove Press, 1959, pp. xiii *ff.*

a heritage

something other than property or money that is passed down from previous generations

"Liberty is the **heritage** of all men in all lands everywhere."

Abraham Lincoln, President, 1861–1865, speech, 1858

individual

individuality

single, separate, and distinct

In some student dormitories each person has his own **individual** room. He does not share his room with another student. Because such rooms are usually furnished in the same way, they do not reflect the students' **individuality.** They do not reflect how the students differ from one another.

to innovate

an innovation
an innovator
innovative

to make changes by introducing something new

Benjamin Franklin had an original, creative mind. He introduced many new ideas. For example, he established the first public subscription library. He also designed a highly efficient stove for cooking and heating. He was an **innovator.** He had an **innovative** mind. He liked to **innovate.**

Central heating was an important **innovation** of the late nineteenth century. Before the introduction of central heating, people depended on stoves or fireplaces in each room.

mass-produced
mass scale

manufactured in big quantities from one design
a very large amount

Henry Ford introduced **mass-production** methods in the manufacturing of automobiles. His first auto, the Model T, was manufactured in large numbers and was sold at relatively low cost. Between 1909 and 1928 more than 15 million Model T cars were manufactured and sold. These cars were **mass-produced.** They were manufactured and sold on a **mass scale.**

Ford's **mass-production** method was an innovation in manufacturing techniques.

potential

a potentiality
a potential

possible; may come into existence

Although we know Mozart was a musical genius, we cannot know if he fully reached his **potential** creativity. He died when he was only 35. We do not know if he achieved his full **potentiality.**

"Most people live, whether physically, morally or intellectually, in a very restricted circle of their **potential** being. They make use of a very

small portion of their possible . . . resources . . .
and **potentials.**"

Henry James, novelist, letter, 1906

to reject
a rejection

to refuse to accept

Frank Lloyd Wright **rejected** the elaborate historic styles of nineteenth-century architecture. He refused to use those styles in his designs.

His philosophy of architecture was strongly influenced by Louis Sullivan's **rejection** of these styles.

a site
to site

a place where something (usually a building) is located

Greek temples often seem to be part of the ground on which they are built. They seem to grow naturally out of their **sites.**

The old school was torn down, and a new one was built exactly where the old one had been. The new school was constructed on the same **site.** It was **sited** where the old one had been.

a slum
the slums
slummy

an area of run-down housing and general poverty

Slum-clearance projects are attempts to get rid of **slums** and rehouse the people in more suitable dwellings.

The slums are the areas in towns or cities where run-down housing and poverty are found. The housing there is **slummy.**

a suburb
suburban
the suburbs

a residential area outside a town or city

In the last ten years there has been a considerable increase in the number of people who have moved from cities to **suburbs.** They have found city living difficult and prefer **suburban** life. They often continue to work in the city and travel to and from their jobs by bus or car.

The suburbs is a general term referring to all outlying residential districts.

to take advantage of

to use for benefit or gain

He was fifteen minutes early for his plane. He **took advantage of** that extra time to buy a newspaper to read on the trip.

to tower
a tower

to rise to great height, usually when compared to the height of the surroundings

In the 1950s Frank Lloyd Wright built a skyscraper in a small town in Oklahoma. The population of the town was only 25,000, and all the other buildings were relatively low. Wright's structure **towered** above the other buildings.

The **Tower** of Pisa in Italy is 180 feet high. It is called "the leaning **tower**" because it does not stand straight.

a tradition
traditional

an attitude, belief, or custom that is handed down from generation to generation

For many years drinking afternoon tea has been a British **tradition.** In Great Britain it is **traditional** to drink tea in the afternoon.

unity
to unite

the state or condition of being one

The Revolutionary War patriot John Dickinson called for **unity** of all Americans in their opposition to Britain. In his *Liberty Song* (1768) he wrote:

> Then join hand in hand, brave
> Americans all,
> By **uniting** we stand, by dividing
> we fall.

*to ventilate
ventilation

to cause air to move in and out freely

When a building is heated and there is no change of air, the air becomes unhealthy. In designing a heating system attention must be given to the **ventilation.** A well-constructed building must be properly **ventilated.**

Vocabulary Review

The following words appear in the glossed vocabulary of Chapter 12. From this list choose words that mean the opposite of the words in list I. Then choose words with meanings similar to the words or phrases in list II.

Vocabulary

a. austere   g. ventilated
b. innovation   h. individual
c. potential   i. suburb
d. heritage   j. unite
e. mass-produced   k. convenient
f. site   l. reject

	I		**II**	
EXAMPLE	1. elaborate	a. austere	1. possible	c. potential
	2. general	_____	2. new change	_____
	3. inner city	_____	3. location	_____

4. accept   _____   4. aired   _____

5. separate   _____   5. manufactured in large
quantities   _____

Comprehension and Thought Questions

1. How does the skyscraper take advantage of elevator transportation?
2. The text states that Sullivan was deeply moved by the potential beauty of the skyscraper. What do you think this statement means?
3. Explain the meaning of "the unity of form and function." Find something in your classroom that illustrates this concept. (For example, a pen or a pencil?)
4. Why do skyscrapers seem particularly suitable in cities where land is expensive and space is limited? Are there skyscrapers in large cities in your country? If so, are they used as hotels? office buildings? residential buildings? How tall are they? Are they specially adapted to the climate? If so, how?
5. The text refers to the problem of slums in American cities. Do urban or rural slums exist in your country? If so, how serious is the problem, and what efforts have been made to improve the situation?
6. Explain the meaning of the following:
   a. slum ghettos
   b. urban renewal
   c. housing development
   d. shopping center
7. Reread the quotation from Mumford that appears at the end of the text of this chapter, and comment on it. Indicate whether you agree or disagree and why. Even if you have not seen them, comment on how the World Trade Building and the Sears Tower might illustrate Mumford's opinion of the "best and the worst."

Discussion and Composition Topics

A. Eero Saarinen, an important American architect who died a few years ago, wrote that the interest of many architects is primarily aesthetic. Saarinen believed that buildings should also express what they are. "A church must have the expression of a church. An airport should be an expression related to flight. It should make one feel the excitement of arrival and departure and the pleasures and adventures of travel. . . ."

Eero Saarinen in William A. Coles and Herman Hope Reed Jr., (eds.), *Architecture in America*, New York, Appleton, 1961, p. 126.

What contemporary building have you seen recently? an airport? a church? a new office building? a house? Do you think this building "expresses what it is" in Saarinen's terms? Explain your opinion.

B. 1. Describe the building in which you now live. Is it an apartment house, dormitory, private home? How adequately does it meet your living requirements? your aesthetic standards?
   2. Describe the building in which you grew up.

C. What modern or historic building in your country has impressed you? Describe it.

D. 1. If there is an interesting contemporary or historic building (library, city hall, office building, etc.) conveniently located, plan a visit. Examine the exterior and interior of the building. Then write a description of it, including your personal opinion of it in aesthetic and functional terms.
   2. Discuss your school library in terms of aesthetics and function.

E. What is your opinion about "mixing" architectural styles? Specifically, how do you feel about introducing contemporary architecture, including skyscrapers, into cities that are famous for their beautiful old buildings?

F. A dialogue between a "client" and an "architect" (to follow Listening Comprehension I, pp. 259–260).

   One student should act as the client who is discussing plans for a new home with an architect. Another student should act as the architect. The client has not yet definitely decided whether he will choose this architect. The architect does not yet know anything about the client.
   1. The client asks the architect whether he builds traditional- or contemporary-style homes.
   2. The architect asks what style the client prefers.
   Continue the discussion until the client is ready to decide whether or not he wants this architect to design his home. You should include a description of the client's life style and needs, of his current house, a discussion of cost, of desired site, of plans for interior design and landscape design. You may vary this interview by introducing a husband and wife who are clients. They should present their program together. The architect should try to describe the house he would design to satisfy the clients' needs and taste.

Library Assignment

Marcus Whiffen has compiled in *American Architecture Since 1780*, Cambridge, MIT Press, 1969, the following list of guidebooks on local and regional architecture. You may wish to refer to some of these books if you live in one of the areas that is described.

American Institute of Architects (Philadelphia chapter), *Philadelphia Architecture*, New York, Reinhold, 1961.
Ballinger, B., *A Guide to the Architecture of Frank Lloyd Wright in Oak Park and River Forest, Illinois*, Oak Park Public Library, 1966.

Gebhard, D., and Winter, R., *A Guide to Architecture in Southern California,* Los Angeles County Museum of Art, 1965.

Hitchcock, H. R., *A Guide to Boston Architecture, 1637–1954,* New York, Reinhold, 1954.

Huxtable A. L., *Four Walking Tours of Modern Architecture in New York City,* Garden City, Doubleday, 1961.

Jacobsen, H. N., ed., *A Guide to the Architecture of Washington, D.C.,* New York, Praeger, 1965.

McClure, H. E., *Twin Cities Architecture: Minneapolis and St. Paul, 1820–1955,* New York, Reinhold, 1955.

McCue, G., *The Building Art in St. Louis: Two Centuries,* St. Louis, American Institute of Architects, 1964.

Siegel, A., ed., *Chicago's Famous Buildings: A Photographic Guide to the City's Architectural Landmarks and Other Notable Buildings,* Chicago, University of Chicago Press, 1965.

Steinbrueck, V., *Seattle Architecture, 1850–1953,* New York, Reinhold, 1953.

Wilson, S., Jr. *A Guide to Architecture of New Orleans, 1699–1959,* New York, Reinhold, 1959.

Woodbridge, J. M. and S. B., *Buildings of the Bay Area: A Guide to the Architecture of the San Francisco Bay Region,* New York, Grove, 1960.

For general reading on architecture in America, your reference librarian may be able to suggest recent illustrated books. Two that contain fine pictures, as well as interesting written material, are: Ian McCallum, *Architecture: USA,* New York, Reinhold, 1960, which is devoted to contemporary architecture, with biographies of leading architects and pictures of some of their work; and Marcus Whiffen, *American Architecture Since 1780,* Cambridge, MIT Press, 1969, which has photographs of representative architecture and descriptive text on different historic and contemporary styles.

Listening Exercises for Chapter 12 begin on p. 259.

VOCABULARY EXERCISES FOR SECTION IV

Exercise I—Suffixes

A. The suffix **-ism** may be added to some nouns or adjectives to form new nouns. The stress does not change. Add the suffix **-ism** to the following words, which were used in Section IV, and pronounce each new noun.

EXAMPLE   national, nationalism

1. regional
2. international
3. functional
4. isolation
5. real
6. professional
7. symbol
8. impression
9. romantic (note pronunciation change)
10. cube (note spelling change)
11. individual
12. industrial

B. The suffix **-ness** may be added to many adjectives to form nouns. The stress does not change. Add the suffix **-ness** to each of the following adjectives from the text and pronounce the new nouns.

EXAMPLE   sad, sadness

1. spacious
2. gentle
3. lonely (note the spelling change)
4. wild
5. elaborate
6. cold
7. harsh
8. serious
9. foolish

C. The suffix **-ive** may be added to some verbs (especially verbs ending in the t sound) to form adjectives. The stress usually does not change. Add the adjectival suffix **-ive** to the following verbs from Section IV. Pronounce each new adjective.

EXAMPLE   act, active

1. to innovate
2. to reflect
3. to construct
4. to express
5. to create
6. to decorate (note the pronunciation change)
7. to attract

Exercise II

In the following paragraph on American Indian art fill in the blanks with an appropriate word from the following vocabulary list. Use each word only once. Change the word to the correct form (noun, verb, adjective, or adverb).

a. indigenous
b. regional
c. abstract
d. represent
e. potential
f. complex

g. symbol   i. tradition
h. aesthetics   j. function

EXAMPLE   American Indian art is the only (a) <u>indigenous</u> art that this country can claim.

Indian art deserves serious study for historical and _____

reasons. It was neither uniform nor national. Each geographic

_____ had its own art forms, which differed from any

others. Although decoration was important, Indian art was basically

_____. It had a ceremonial or religious purpose, and

_____ designs often _____ religious

ideas. Each tribe had its own _____ designs, which

_____ special meanings to members of that tribe. Early

designs were very simple, but later, improved tools enabled artists to

create designs of greater _____.

Exercise III

Match the words in column I with the words in column II that have opposite meanings.

	I		**II**
EXAMPLE	1. innovative	h. traditional	a. urban
	2. complicated	_____	b. horizontal
	3. vertical	_____	c. sensible
	4. absurd	_____	d. intelligent
	5. precise	_____	e. similar
	6. diverse	_____	f. accepted
	7. rural	_____	g. inexact
	8. rejected	_____	h. traditional
			i. simple

Exercise IV

The following adjectives from Section IV have been made negative by the addition of a negative prefix. Pronounce each word. Then omit the prefix and use each new adjective in a sentence.

EXAMPLE   undecorated, decorated

The beautifully decorated house was filled with valuable antique furniture.

1. imprecise
2. uncomplicated
3. unskilled
4. inconvenient
5. unsubsidized
6. inefficient
7. unsophisticated
8. unspontaneous
9. inexpensive
10. untraditional
11. unventilated
12. undramatic

Exercise V

The following nouns from Section IV are either countable or uncountable, depending on the intended meaning. Use each word in two sentences illustrating its use as a countable noun and then as an uncountable noun. An uncountable noun cannot be made plural.

EXAMPLE   drama

There are not many good contemporary *dramas* (c.).
Drama is her major field of study (unc.).

1. theater
2. painting
3. skill
4. beauty
5. convenience
6. building
7. glass
8. stage
9. space
10. light

Exercise VI

Change the following sentences, using words from the following vocabulary list to replace the words in heavy type. You may change the word order and verb tense and add prepositions and articles when necessary.

a. traditional
b. complicated
c. reject
d. rural
e. portray
f. contemporary
g. experiment
h. express
i. landscapes
j. techniques

EXAMPLE   **Paintings of country scenes** often **picture** farms and farm animals.

(d) **Rural** (i) **landscapes** often (e) **portray** farms and farm animals.

Many artists **refuse to accept** painting **methods that have been used for generations.** They are **trying out** new methods in order to **make known** their feelings about **today's** world, **which is so hard to understand.**

Exercise VII

Here is a list of adjectives from the text that can also be used as nouns. The pronunciation does not change. Use each word as a noun in a sentence.

EXAMPLE   complex

A shopping center is a building **complex** that often includes stores, restaurants, and a movie theater.

1. potential   4. professional
2. individual   5. particular
3. original   6. light

Exercise VIII

The prefix **mis-** may be added to some nouns, verbs, adjectives, and adverbs. It means bad(ly) or wrong(ly). Add the prefix **mis-** to the following words from Section V and pronounce them. The stress does not change.

1. to understand   6. spent
2. to represent   7. used
3. to place   8. guided
4. to cast   9. fortune
5. to lead

V
EDUCATION AND THE FAMILY

The School Years

Soon after the United States was founded, Thomas Jefferson, who was President from 1801 to 1809, wrote, "If a nation expects to be ignorant and free in a state of civilization, it expects what never was and never will be." Jefferson believed that the new republic would be served best by literate, well-informed citizens and that everyone should have a guarantee of some education, with further education for those who wanted it and were qualified. The American system of public education has been built on this philosophy. Public education in this country is expected to offer equal educational **opportunities** to everyone enrolled in **secular** schools, which are publicly controlled and publicly **financed,** with free **tuition,** free books, and **compulsory attendance.**

There is no mention of education in the Constitution, and each state is responsible for its own educational system. Public schools are financed primarily by local and state taxes, and the amount of money spent on public school students varies from state to state. Alabama, for example, spent an average of $716 for each pupil in 1974, the lowest rate of any state. New York, by contrast, had the highest rate, $1809 per pupil. The majority of states spent more than $800 per pupil.

There are great differences in **expenditures** by communities within each state, depending on the amount of local funds available for public education. Often, well-to-do communities spend several hundred dollars more for each child than poorer towns nearby do. These figures reflect differences in expenditures for such items as teachers' salaries, the purchase of books, and school construction and **maintenance.**

Despite these differences, there is general uniformity in the organization and **curricula** of public schools throughout the country. Each state is divided into local school districts. Usually a state department of education sets the general requirements that local communities or school districts must meet. Local school **boards,** usually elected by members of their communities, are responsible for the detailed organization and operation of their schools. This responsibility includes hiring teachers and administrators and setting their salaries.

The twelve years of public school education usually begin when a child is six years old. Some school systems are divided into eight years of primary school and four years of secondary school. Primary schools are often called elementary schools, and secondary schools are called high schools. Many systems combine the last two years of elementary school and the first year of high school in what is known as junior high school. This is followed by three years of senior high school. A large number of school systems also have a kindergarten program that provides one year of preschool training for five-year-old children before they begin the formal school years. The **academic** year lasts nine months, from September to June, with winter and spring vacations. Classes are held five days a week, from Monday through Friday.

Elementary schools are usually organized on a **neighborhood** basis. Children living in the same area attend a school that is close to their homes. High schools, on the other hand, serve children from many different elementary schools, and a single high school often has several thousand students from various parts of the community. Many towns have just one high school. In rural areas one elementary school and one high school frequently serve the children from several communities. When schools are located beyond convenient walking distance, children are transported free of charge in bright yellow school buses. Today more than 40 percent of all American school children are bused to and from school daily.

It took many years for Jefferson's dream of education for everyone to approach reality. In 1870 only slightly more than half of all children of school age attended school. It was not until 1918 that every state had a compulsory school-attendance law. Today most states require the attendance of all children between the ages of six and sixteen. Approximately 99 percent of all American children of elementary school age (six through thirteen) and 94 percent of high school age (fourteen through seventeen) go to school.

The quality of education has changed as much as the record of school attendance. For example, in a typical mid-nineteenth century elementary school class

> Children sat in one place in one position for hours on end, with periodic arm-swinging for exercise and perhaps occasional permission to go to the bathroom. The method of instruction was catechism [questions by the teacher with memorized responses by the students]. . . . The teacher fed the stuff out one day and wanted it back the next, in her own words.[1]

Emphasis was on good behavior and learning what were called "the three Rs"—reading, 'riting, and 'rithmetic. Most of the teachers had no more than elementary school education themselves.

In the modern elementary school, in addition to the study of reading, arithmetic, and language arts (including spelling), children are taught social studies (history, geography, and civics or government), science, art, and music. They are often also taught cooking and manual skills such as carpentry and sewing. Outdoor playgrounds and indoor gymnasiums offer opportunities for lots of physical exercise.

Modern teaching theories and methods vary greatly, but they frequently reflect the influence of John Dewey, an important twentieth-century educator and philosopher. Dewey believed that education should be more concerned with the interests and needs of each child than with the particular subjects that the child is taught. Today many teachers try to give considerable attention to the personal development of each individual student, especially at the elementary school level.

Entrance to high school is **automatic** when a student completes elementary school. No examinations are required. High schools usually offer courses in English literature and composition, the social sciences, mathematics, laboratory sciences, and foreign languages, as well as art, music, and physical education. After completing certain basic requirements, students are often permitted to choose the subjects that best suit their plans for college or for work after graduation.

Extracurricular activities including clubs, school newspapers and magazines, and sports are important features of high-school life. In addition, student representatives, elected by their fellow students, often work with school officials in planning school policies. This arrangement is an effort to encourage students' interest in self-government and in their responsibilities as citizens.

1. Martin Mayer, *The Schools,* New York, Doubleday, 1963, p. 46.

Children in a typical
elementary school.
Paul Conklin, Monkmeyer

Most high schools are organized on what is called a **comprehensive** basis, which means that programs in academic (college preparatory), **vocational,** and general education are offered in the same school. In some large cities specialized high schools concentrate on just one type of program. In addition, many communities provide programs for **handicapped** children (children who are deaf, blind, crippled, emotionally disturbed, or mentally retarded) and children who are specially gifted, intellectually or artistically.

Eligibility requirements for public school teachers vary from school district to school district, but most elementary school teachers must have a bachelor of arts degree with a **major** in education. High school teachers have usually majored in the field of their special interest and, in addition, have a master of arts degree in education.

More than 10 percent of school-age children attend private schools. These include a few secular schools, but most are operated by church groups, especially the Roman Catholic church. Because of the absolute separation of church and state in this country, children are not allowed to receive religious instruction in public schools. Parents who want their children to have a religious education must

send their children to privately financed schools or to church-orga-
nized classes that are held after regular school hours or on weekends.

VOCABULARY

academic	referring to teaching and studying literary or classical subjects; not referring to technical training for occupations such as mechanic or secretary
	Students who plan to go to college study an **academic** program in high school.
	The **academic** life is supposed to be quiet and protected from the world outside the college or university. It is called "life in the ivory tower."
*to attend	to be present at
attendance	Children are required to go to school. They must **attend** school. Their **attendance** is required.
*automatic	self-acting or self-moving without a plan or conscious choice
automatically	If an elementary school student does not fail any subjects, he **automatically** moves up to the next class or grade. His promotion or advancement is **automatic.** When he completes elementary school, he is **automatically** admitted to secondary school. He is not required to take any examinations before he enters high school. His admission is **automatic.**
*a board	a small organized group of administrators
	A local school **board** is composed of men and women who are responsible for the schools in their local school district. A school **board** is also known as a **board** of education.
comprehensive	including a great deal
	The final examination included questions on everything the students had studied that year. It was a **comprehensive** examination.
compulsory	required
to compel	Massachusetts was the first state that had a **compulsory** school-attendance law. It was enacted in 1852 and required children to attend elementary school. The law **compelled** children to attend elementary school.

a curriculum
  extracurricular

a course or program of studies offered by a school

The **curriculum** of an academic high school used to include four years of Latin, but few students study Latin today. (The plural of **curriculum** is **curricula**.)

  Extracurricular activities are school activities outside regular classes. Such activities include organized sports, school newspapers and magazines, and clubs.

an expenditure

an act of spending or using up something, usually money or time

There are differences in the amount of money each state spends per pupil. There are also differences in the **expenditure** per pupil by communities within the same state. Rich communities make larger **expenditures** on their schools than poor communities do.

to finance
  finances
  financial

to provide money for something

State and local taxes pay for most of the cost of public education. Some additional money comes from the federal government. State and local taxes **finance** most of the cost of public education. Some additional **financial** support comes from the federal government. The **finances** of each school district are handled by the school board. The local school board handles all matters relating to money for its district schools.

a handicap
  to handicap

a disability or disadvantage

Poor eyesight is a serious **handicap** to a student who must read a great deal. Poor eyesight **handicaps** a student who must read a great deal.

  There are special school programs for **handicapped** children. Blind children are taught to read Braille with their fingers. Deaf children are taught to communicate in a special sign language.

*maintenance
  to maintain

the action of keeping something in proper condition

Local school districts are responsible for the **maintenance** of their schools. The local school authorities must keep the schools in good condition. The authorities must **maintain** the schools. School buildings must be properly heated and ventilated, and they must be free from the danger of fire.

It is expensive to **maintain** school buildings, but proper **maintenance** is essential.

to major in
a major

to pursue academic studies in a particular field

His special interest was chemistry. He **majored in** chemistry at college. Chemistry was his **major.** Most of his courses were related to chemistry.

a neighborhood
a neighbor

a particular area or district, usually one in which a group of people live

They lived in a pleasant **neighborhood** of large houses and quiet streets.

The children lived in houses located on the same street. They were **neighbors.** They attended a nearby school. They attended a **neighborhood** school.

"We, the peoples of the United Nations, determined to . . . live together in peace with one another as good **neighbors.** . . ."
From the Charter of the United Nations (June 1945)

(an) opportunity

a favorable chance

The free public school was established to give everyone an equal chance to obtain an education. The public school is expected to provide an equal educational **opportunity** to everyone.

secular

of the "world" and not of the church; not related to religion

Schools in colonial days were organized by religious groups. When public schools were established, they were **secular.** The curriculum was not religious, and the schools were controlled by the states, not by church organizations.

tuition

the fee or sum of money that is paid for instruction

Public elementary and secondary schools are free. There is no **tuition.**

vocational
a vocation

referring to an occupation or a trade

A **vocational** school trains students for specific occupations such as secretary, electric-appliance repairman, and automobile mechanic. At this kind of school the students receive training for various **vocations.** There are also special **vocational** training programs for handicapped people so that they will be able to work and support themselves.

Vocabulary Review

Change the following sentences using words from the following vocabulary list to replace the words in heavy type. Change the word order of the sentence, when necessary.

a. vocational   f. curriculum
b. secular   g. compulsory
c. tuition   h. finance
d. neighborhood i. handicap
e. expenditure

EXAMPLE   All children **are required** to attend school.
    School attendance is (g) **compulsory** for all children.

1. The academic **program** of most high schools includes English, mathematics, social science, and laboratory science.
2. A child who is crippled has a physical **disability.**
3. State and local taxes **provide the money for** public education.
4. Most children attend schools **located in areas where they live.**
5. Public schools in the United States are **not related to any church group** and do not provide religious education.
6. Training **for occupations such as secretary and automobile repairman** is provided by certain high school programs.
7. Children who attend public schools do not have to pay **fees for their education.**

Comprehension and Thought Questions

1. How does compulsory school attendance fit the general philosophy on which the American system of public education has been built?
2. a. How does the method of public school financing result in some educational inequalities in the United States?
   b. Do you have public schools in your country? If so, how are they financed?
3. a. What is a school board? What are its responsibilities?
   b. Who is responsible for the educational system in your country? What role, if any, do residents of local communities have?
4. List a few ways in which American elementary school education has changed during the past 125 years, in attendance, curriculum, and teacher qualifications.
5. Why do some American parents send their children to church schools? If children in your country receive religious education in public schools, describe that education. Who teaches classes in religion? How much time is devoted to religious education? Is religious education compulsory?
6. American secondary schools place great emphasis on extracurricular

activities. Are extracurricular activities important in your secondary schools? Describe the kinds of extracurricular activities that are most popular in your country.

Discussion and Composition Topics

1. Compare the elementary school system and the high school system in the United States with the educational systems in your country. Include references to attendance requirements, curricula, tuition (if any), admission standards, and coeducation. Give additional information about schools in your country including size of classes, teacher requirements, public and private schools.
2. Should children be allowed to enter secondary schools automatically after they complete primary school, or should they be required to pass entrance examinations? Why?
3. Do you think *all* children should be *required* to go to school? *allowed* to go to school? from what age and until what age? Explain your opinion.

Listening Exercises for Chapter 13 begin on p. 262.

Colleges and Universities

More than 60 percent of all high school graduates continue their formal education after graduation. Many attend colleges that offer four-year programs leading to a bachelor's degree. College students are called undergraduates, and their four years of study are divided into the freshman, sophomore, junior, and senior years. In most colleges the first two years are designed to provide a broad general education, and during this time the college student is usually required to take courses in general areas of study, such as English, science, foreign languages, and social science. By the junior year the student begins to major in one particular field of study, or **discipline.**

Some institutions of higher learning offer only the four-year college program. A university offers graduate or postcollege programs, as well. Graduate degrees in fields such as English literature, chemistry, and history are granted by graduate schools of arts and sciences. These schools may offer one- or two-year programs leading to a master's degree (M.A.), and programs lasting three years or more that lead to the degree of Doctor of Philosophy (Ph.D.). A candidate for a Ph.D. must meet certain course requirements in his field, pass written and oral examinations, and present a written thesis based on original research. Some universities offer postdoctoral programs that extend study and research beyond the Ph.D.

Many universities also have what are called professional schools for study in such fields as law, medicine, engineering, architecture, social work, business, library science, and education. Professional schools differ widely in their requirements for admission and the lengths of their programs. Medical students, for example, must complete at least three years of premedical studies at an undergraduate school before they can enter the three- or four-year program at a medical school. Engineering and architecture students, on the other hand, can enter a four- or five-year professional school immediately upon completion of secondary school.

The various disciplines, or fields of study, are organized by department. These departments are staffed by faculty members **ranging** from full professors to instructors. A full professor has tenure, which is a permanent appointment with guaranteed employment at the institution until his **retirement.** Ranking below the full professors are the associate professors, who may or may not have tenure, depending on the policy of the particular college or university. Next are the assistant professors, who do not have tenure. At the bottom of this academic ladder are the instructors. They are usually young teachers who have just received their doctorates or will receive them shortly. Sometimes graduate students are employed as part-time teaching assistants while they are completing their graduate work.

Today almost 5 million men and more than 3 million women attend more than 2500 colleges and universities. Approximately 85 percent of these schools are coeducational, which means that both men and women are **enrolled** in the same institutions. Colleges range in size from a few hundred students to many thousands. Several universities have more than 20,000 undergraduate and graduate students on one **campus.** A number of large state institutions maintain branches on several different campuses throughout the state. Classes vary from seminars, or small discussion groups, of fewer than twenty to large lecture courses for hundreds of students.

Approximately one-fourth of all college and university students attend private institutions. The rest study at state or **municipal,** publicly financed colleges and universities. Every state has at least one public university, and in addition there are several hundred state and locally supported colleges. The academic programs of these private and public institutions are very similar. Indeed, there are only a few important differences between public and private colleges. Private colleges are privately organized and privately run; public institutions are operated under the control of state or local officials. The other differences involve admissions policies and the methods by which public and private institutions are financed.

Admission to a state university is usually open to all men and women who have graduated from high schools of the state and who have satisfactory high school records. Many state universities require students to earn high scores on **achievement** and **aptitude** examinations, but the underlying philosophy is that all students who want an education and are qualified should have the opportunity to continue their education at public institutions. Tuition rates are low, compared to private-college costs, and **scholarship** aid and loans are frequently available. A few nonresidents are admitted to state schools, but they must pay much higher tuition fees than residents of the state.

Admission to some private colleges is more **selective** and **rigid** than admission to some public institutions, and frequently the student body is smaller. High school **applicants** to some private colleges must submit detailed application forms, and they must take scholastic aptitude and achievement examinations. College admissions committees decide which students to accept, basing their judgment on these applications, the results of the examinations, high school records, and other factors such as personal interviews with the applicants and letters of recommendation from high school teachers. For certain colleges, such as Harvard, Yale, Princeton, Stanford, and Columbia, applications usually far exceed the number of students who are accepted. In 1975, for example, Harvard received 7620 applications for 1500 available places.

The average private college tuition in the early 1970s was $2161 a year. This figure was approximately four times greater than the average public-college tuition. At Harvard, for example, tuition cost $3200 in 1973–1974. The University of Massachusetts, a publicly supported institution in the same state, charged $300 for a state resident. These tuition figures do not include the costs of room, food, and other everyday living expenses. Some students receive scholarship assistance and loans to help pay for the cost of their education. Many students at private and public colleges work while they are attending school, in order to pay their expenses.

Almost 1500 American colleges and universities are privately organized and financed. More than half the income of these institutions comes from student tuition payments. The rest comes from private gifts, **endowment** earnings, and some federal research grants. Because of steadily rising costs, many private institutions have had to raise tuition rates, reduce scholarship aid, and limit some academic programs. The poor financial condition of most private institutions is a very serious problem in the world of higher education today.

Student fees account for only 15 percent of the income of public colleges and universities. The rest comes from municipal or state and some federal government sources. Although public institutions have also experienced the problem of rising costs, they have often been able to depend on state legislators for financial support. In large part this support may be explained by the legislators' response to the wishes of the people who elected them and to general acceptance of the American tradition that everyone who is qualified should have the opportunity to continue his climb up the educational ladder at publicly financed institutions.

In recent years there has been a considerable increase in the number of publicly financed community or junior colleges. Many of these schools offer two years of a regular four-year college program. Often junior college students transfer to four-year colleges to complete their schooling. Many community colleges also offer two-year programs of technical training for a variety of jobs, ranging from laboratory technician to automobile mechanic.

More than one hundred public and private colleges and universities were originally established for black students. Now many of these schools have some white students as well. Among the best known of these **predominantly** black institutions are Howard and Fisk Universities and Tuskegee Institute.

VOCABULARY

to achieve
    an achievement
	to do or gain something successfully, usually by means of effort and skill
	
	An academic **achievement** test measures skills or accomplishments in various fields of academic study.
	
	"[Do not] be afraid of greatness: some are born great, some **achieve** greatness, and some have greatness thrust upon them."
	        William Shakespeare, *Twelfth Night*
	
	". . . let us . . . do all which may **achieve** a just and lasting peace among ourselves and with all nations."
	        Abraham Lincoln, President, 1861–1865, speech, March 17, 1865

*to apply
    an application
    an applicant
	to request a position or an appointment
	
	More than 7000 students **applied** for admission to Harvard College in 1975. There were 7620 **applicants** for admission to the freshman class. More than 7000 students submitted **applications** for admission to Harvard.

(an) aptitude	a natural ability to learn a skill or to gain knowledge An **aptitude** test measures the ability of a person to develop skills or to gain knowledge.

a campus

the grounds of a school, college, or university

Students frequently live **off campus,** or away from the school grounds, but usually all classroom buildings are located on the school **campus.**

*a discipline

a specific field of knowledge or teaching

Economics and sociology are two **disciplines** in the general area of social science.

*an endowment
   to endow

money that is given to provide a regular income (to a college, for example)

The National **Endowment** for the Arts is a federal agency that receives money from Congress and uses that money to support artists and artistic projects.

Very wealthy graduates (alumni or alumnae) sometimes **endow** their colleges with large gifts of money that serve as a source of income for the schools. Foundations also give **endowments** to colleges and universities.

to enroll
   an enrollment

to place one's name on an official list (for example, on a list of students)

Three hundred young people became members of the freshman class. Three hundred students **enrolled** as freshmen. The freshmen class had an **enrollment** of three hundred students.

In order to **enroll** in college, a student must fill out and sign several forms, and he must pay his tuition.

municipal
   a municipality

of a town or a city

Municipal buses supply transportation within a town or city.

The mayor is the chief **municipal** official. He is the chief executive of the **municipality.**

predominant
   predominantly
   predominance

having the greatest number or importance

Most of the children in urban ghetto schools are black. Children in urban ghetto schools are **predominantly** black. The **predominance** of black students is an important characteristic of urban ghetto schools.

The **predominant** feature of the American public school system is supposed to be its equality of opportunity to children of all racial, religious, social, and economic backgrounds.

*to range
   a range

to vary or to differ within specified limits

The annual salary of most full professors **ranges** from $12,000 to $21,000. The salary **range** of most associate professors is $10,000 to $17,000 a year.

*to retire
   retirement

to give up one's work, usually because of old age

Many universities require professors **to retire** at the age of 65. They must stop teaching at the age of 65. When a professor reaches the age of compulsory **retirement,** he usually receives a pension or **retirement** allowance.

*rigid

stiff and unbending

Most colleges require students to pass a specific number of courses in order to receive the bachelor's degree. No student may be excused from these requirements. These requirements are **rigid.**

a scholar
   scholarship
   a scholarship
   scholastic

a student; a very learned, well-educated person

The professor was a famous Greek **scholar.** He was famous for his Greek **scholarship. Scholarship** refers to learning or knowledge.

A **scholarship** means a financial grant given to a student to pay for school expenses. A fellowship is a **scholarship** given to a graduate student.

A **scholastic** aptitude test measures a person's ability to learn academic subjects.

to select
   a selection
   selective

to choose from among several

Colleges **select** their students from many applicants. The admissions committees make their **selections** on the basis of the students' high school records and the results of special examinations. Some private colleges are more **selective** in their admissions policies than some public institutions. On the other hand, many public institutions are more **selective** than a large number of private colleges.

Vocabulary Review

Match the nouns in column I with the words in column II that have similar meanings.

I		II
EXAMPLE 1. achievement	c. accomplishment	a. special field of knowledge
2. application	_____	b. large gift of money
3. discipline	_____	c. accomplishment
4. endowment	_____	d. school grounds
5. aptitude	_____	e. city or town
6. municipality	_____	f. request
7. campus	_____	g. great majority
8. selection	_____	h. natural ability
		i. choice

Comprehension and Thought Questions

1. a. What is a bachelor's degree (B.A.)? a master's degree (M.A.)? a Doctor of Philosophy degree (Ph.D.)?
   b. What are the requirements for each of these degrees?
   c. Are the same (or different) degrees offered by institutions of higher learning in your country? What are the requirements for each degree in your country?
   d. Can you identify these academic titles: B.S., M.D., LL.B., M.B.A., B.E., M.F.A.?
2. If you were a U.S. citizen, would you apply for admission to a state university or a private university? Why?
3. What steps did you have to take to enroll in this class? List them, from the time when you first heard about this English program. Did you have to take aptitude or achievement tests?
4. Compare the system of higher education in your country with the American system described in the text. Include the following: public or private institutions, tuition costs, availability of scholarships and fellowships (Do students in your country often work their way through college?), admissions policies and competitive examinations, coeducation, professional schools, and college academic programs. In what year do undergraduates in your country begin to major in a specific discipline? Do they take

courses that are unrelated to their major fields of study? If so, what courses? Are there any *required* courses that are not related to their majors?

5. Read each of the following statements aloud, and indicate whether it is true or false. Correct the inaccurate statements.

   a. Every state has at least one publicly financed university.
   b. Tuition rates of private colleges are often higher than those of public colleges.
   c. A postdoctoral program provides for study and research following the master's degree.
   d. Professional schools usually have similar requirements for admission.
   e. An undergraduate is usually expected to major in a particular discipline by his junior year.
   f. Most colleges and universities are segregated by sex. Many colleges are also segregated by race.

Discussion and Composition Topics

1. If you wanted to get a master of science degree in chemistry at the University of California at Berkeley, how would you obtain information about admissions requirements, courses offered in the chemistry department, degree requirements, and tuition? What other information might you need? How would you get it?

2. What proportion of high school graduates go to college in your country?
   In the United States almost 60 percent of all high school graduates go on to college. There is a popular saying that in the United States "There is a college for everyone." Do you think that everyone who wants to go to college should be encouraged to do so, or do you think college admissions should be highly competitive and limited? Explain your opinion.

3. Do you think college students should be allowed to choose their majors, or should their training be restricted to those fields that the government believes are most needed in the country? Explain your opinion.

4. In recent years, especially during the 1960s, there was much discussion about "the brain drain," which involved the departure of students and scholars from their own countries to other countries that offered better opportunities for study, research, and employment. For example, according to U.N. statistics, between 1962 and 1966 more than 50 percent of all engineering graduates of Iran and 14 percent of Iranian scientists left their country for work abroad. Over 30 percent of Chilean engineers and 15 percent of Turkish physicians also went to work in other countries. Probably the greatest brain drain occurred among young scientists who had gone abroad to study. Many of them had previously planned to return to their countries to teach but chose to remain in more industrialized nations where they were able to continue their work and their research in fields in which there were no job opportunities at home. The countries

that attracted most of these scientists were the United States, Great Britain, Germany, France, Canada, and Australia.

Recent studies indicate that the brain drain to the United States may be declining. Many foreign scientists are going home again, and in some cases American scientists are leaving the United States for employment in other countries. The main reasons are that good jobs are becoming scarce here, federal research funds have been sharply cut, and university fellowships and research grants have declined. However, in the field of medicine the drain to the United States still goes on. Today more than one of every five American doctors is foreign-born, and several thousand foreign doctors immigrate to the United States each year. Over eighty countries have asked the State Department to send students who are skilled in essential fields such as medicine back home when their study programs are over.

a. Ask another student in your class if the brain drain has been a problem in his or her country. If so, what fields of specialized training have been involved? How serious has the problem been? Ask about recent developments.
b. Write a short paper answering these questions as they apply to your country.
c. Do you think the government of a country should be able to limit the right of any highly trained citizen (doctor, nurse, engineer, and so forth) to migrate to another country?

Listening Exercises for Chapter 14 begin on p. 263.

The Role of the Government: Issues and Problems in Education Today

In recent years the federal government has played an increasingly important and diverse role in the nation's educational programs. At the college and university level the government provides some scholarships, fellowships, and low-cost loans to students who need financial assistance. It also sponsors work-study programs that provide government-financed part-time employment to students while they attend school. In addition it grants money for research projects to colleges and universities.

More than $40 billion is spent annually on elementary and secondary education. Of this sum approximately 7 percent comes from the federal government. Much of this federal money is used for school construction, supplementing teachers' salaries, and sponsoring programs to train teachers and school administrators. In addition, the government supplies advisory and information services to state departments of education and finances a variety of other programs, such as hot lunches, medical care, and preschool classes for children from poor families. It also finances many vocational training programs.

In addition, the federal government participates in a number of international educational activities. The international teacher-development program brings foreign educators from approximately fifty countries to the United States to study at American educational institutions. The teacher-exchange program provides for American teachers to teach abroad for a year and for foreign teachers to spend a year teaching at schools in the United States. Other federal programs help to finance American scholars who study abroad and provide assistance to foreign countries in curriculum development, teacher training, and the preparation of classroom materials.

The most controversial educational issue in which the federal government has been involved concerns racial segregation in American public schools. After the Civil War southern schools were segregated by state laws. White children attended schools taught by white teachers. Black children were required to attend separate schools that were taught by black teachers. In 1954 the Supreme Court declared that these racially segregated schools were unconstitutional. The Court stated that "in these days, it is doubtful that any child may reasonably be expected to succeed in life if he is denied the opportunity of an education. Such an opportunity . . . is a right which must be made available to all on equal terms." The Court unanimously ordered an end to racial segregation by law in public schools. Since that time southern schools have slowly been desegregated. By 1970, 85 percent of southern black school children were attending racially mixed schools. In some cases children are bused to schools in other neighborhoods in order to achieve racial balance between black and white students.

Schools in the North are not racially segregated by law, but they are often segregated in fact. This situation is particularly common in large cities where inner-city areas are populated predominantly by black families. The student enrollment in the neighborhood schools that the children of these families attend is almost completely black, although the teachers are often white. The legality of this kind of school segregation, which results from ghetto residence patterns, is now being tested in federal courts.

Although only about 3 percent of the 18–20 million children transported to school by bus are actually involved in desegregation programs today, the question of busing to achieve racial integration has become a major issue. Some parents, both black and white, are opposed to busing children away from their neighborhood schools. At the present time, however, it appears impossible to achieve racial balance in schools unless some children are bused out of their white or predominantly black neighborhoods.

Problems related to the education of black children have been given considerable attention, and there is growing concern about difficulties that involve other minority groups. For example, thousands of Spanish-speaking children from Puerto Rican and Mexican-American families need special English-language instruction. A few schools have established bilingual (English and Spanish) programs designed to help these children to learn English and to adjust to English-speaking classes. However, these programs have to be greatly expanded to meet the needs of all these children.

There are many other serious problems. Teachers complain that their salaries are too low. In recent years they have organized major work stoppages, or strikes, demanding increases in pay and greater participation in planning school curricula. School administrators complain about inadequate budgets for school operations. Parents and educators are concerned about reports that children's reading levels are frequently below established standards. Children from urban slums often have poorer academic records than children from middle-class backgrounds. Many people believe that inner-city schools are inferior to other schools and need great improvement.

These complaints are based on the traditional American belief that the quality of teaching and school facilities have the greatest influence on student achievement. But today even this belief is being questioned. A number of recent studies suggest the possibility that social and economic conditions beyond the school's control have a greater effect on a student's academic achievement than the quality of school education does. The author of one study that has received wide attention states that "the sources of inequality of educational opportunity appear to lie first in the home itself and in the cultural influences immediately surrounding the home."[1] Although these findings are certainly not accepted by everyone, they are at the center of the controversies over education in the 1970s.

(There is no vocabulary section for this chapter.)

Comprehension and Thought Questions

1. Describe some of the activities of the federal government
   a. at the college and university level;
   b. at the elementary and high school level;
   c. in international education.
2. What was the 1954 Supreme Court decision on school segregation? Why was this decision particularly important?
3. How are "the busing issue," racially balanced schools, and neighborhood schools interrelated?
4. What problems related to education does the text describe? Do similar problems exist in your country? other problems? If so, describe them. What steps are being taken by your officials to solve these problems?
5. The text refers to work stoppages by teachers in different communities. The American Federation of Teachers (AFL–CIO) and the National Education Association are the two largest organizations of elementary and high school teachers. In the past few years representatives of these two groups have been discussing the possibilities of merging into one large teachers' union that would represent almost all public school teachers throughout the United States. If most teachers belonged to one union, it would be

1. James S. Coleman, "Equal Schools or Equal Students?" *The Public Interest*, No. 4, Summer 1966, pp. 73–74.

possible to hold simultaneous strikes in schools throughout the country.[2]
a. Do you think teachers should be allowed to strike? Why?
b. Do you think a nationwide school strike would be good or bad for students? teachers? the community? Why?
c. Do you think a national teachers' union might help to solve some of the current problems in education? Why?
d. Are teachers unionized in your country? Are they permitted to strike? If not, how are teachers' complaints and problems handled?

Discussion and Composition Topics

1. Academic freedom is the freedom of a teacher to express his opinion without fear of losing his job. It also involves freedom of institutions of higher learning to determine their policies and practices without interference or control by outside forces. What do you think of the importance of academic freedom? Can you think of a situation in which this freedom should be limited? Explain your opinion.
2. Here are some statements about education. Choose one, write a short paper indicating whether or not you agree, and explain your opinion. In the library look up the author of each statement, identify him by nationality and discipline, and give the dates (years) of his birth and death, if they are available.
   a. "An ignorant people can be governed, but only an educated people can govern itself."

   > William T. Harris, 17th Annual Report of the Board of Directors of the St. Louis Schools, quoted in Lawrence Cremin, *Transformation of the School,* New York, Knopf, 1962, p. 16

   b. "Only the educated are free."

   > Epictetus, *Discourses,* Book I

   c. "Educated men are as much superior to uneducated men as the living are to the dead."

   > Aristotle, *Diogenes Laertius,* Book V, Section 17

   d. "It was in making education not only common to all, but in some sense compulsory for all, that the destiny . . . of America was practically settled."

   > James Russell Lowell, *Literary Essays,* Vol. II (1870–1890), *New England Two Centuries Ago*

   e. "Education is the best provision for old age."

   > Aristotle

   f. "Education . . . has produced a vast population which is able to read but unable to distinguish what is worth reading."

   > George Macaulay Trevelyan, in Bartlett, *Familiar Quotations,* 14th ed., Boston, Little, Brown, 1968, p. 941b

Listening Exercises for Chapter 15 begin on p. 265.

---

2. In 1974 it was estimated that the membership of the American Federation of Teachers totalled 400,000 and that the membership of the National Education Association exceeded 1.4 million. There are approximately 2 million public school teachers.

The Family

A remarkable characteristic of American society is its diversity. For example, according to recent census reports, of the population of over 200 million, more than 16 percent were born in other countries or are the children of at least one foreign-born parent. They come from more than seventeen European countries, as well as from Canada and Mexico and other Latin American nations. Almost 1.5 million are of Asian origin, particularly from Japan, China, and the Philippines. Over 22 million are Blacks, and there are more than 700,000 American Indians.

Approximately two-thirds of all Americans belong to a church. Of these, approximately 55 percent are Protestants, who are members of more than seventy different Protestant church groups. Almost 37 percent are Roman Catholic, and over 4 percent are Jewish. The rest are Moslems, Buddhists, Hindus, or members of other Christian churches.

Income distribution ranges widely. More than 22 percent of all American families have annual incomes of $15,000 or more. By contrast, almost 20 percent receive less than $5,000.

Despite social and economic diversity among Americans, many American families have certain characteristics **in common.** Both the husband and wife were born in the United States and are of European **ancestry.** They have completed high school, and they are Protestants. Classified by income, they are middle class. The husband is employed and earns about $11,000 a year. They have an automobile, a television set, a radio, a washing machine, a refrigerator, and a telephone. They own[1] their own home and spend about 55 percent of their income for

---

1. This home may not be completely paid for, but is being purchased with regular monthly payments made over a period of years—the mortgage payments. In addition to mortgage payments, the costs of owning a home include property taxes, and maintenance and repair costs.

housing and food. Clothing accounts for almost 10 percent of their expenditures, and medical care amounts to 6 percent. Transportation, including maintenance and gasoline for their car, costs about 8 percent.
Taxes account for 15 percent of their yearly expenditures. The rest of
their income is used for such items as insurance, savings, gifts, and
recreation.

Most families consist of a mother, a father, and a maximum of two
children living at home. There may be relatives—grandparents, aunts,
uncles, cousins, and in-laws in the same community, but American
families usually maintain separate **households.** This familial structure
is known as the "nuclear family." It is unusual for members of the
family other than the husband, wife, and children to live together. Occasionally an aging grandparent may live with the family, but this arrangement is usually not considered desirable. Although the nuclear
family unit is economically independent of the rest of the family, members of the whole family group often maintain close **kinship** ties. Visiting between parents and their married children and between married
sisters and brothers is frequent when they live close to each other. If
they live in different communities, they **keep in touch** by writing letters
and by telephone.

Marriage in the United States is considered a matter of individual
responsibility and decision. Young people frequently **fall in love** and
marry even if their parents disapprove of their choice. American marriages are usually based on romantic love, rather than on social class,
education, money, or religion. In fact, there has been a steady increase
in intermarriage between young people of different religious backgrounds. On the other hand, marriages between Blacks and whites are
rare. They probably account for fewer than 1 percent of all marriages
each year. Most American men marry by the time they are 25, and the
husband is usually two or three years older than his wife.

Marriage is preceded by **dating,** that is, young men and young
women going out together. **Casual** dating usually begins in the early
teens, and by the late teens a pattern of steady dating develops. This
pattern involves two young people going out together for some length
of time. Steady dating is often followed by marriage or by a formal
engagement, which is, in effect, a public statement of the intention to
marry. If the engaged couple change their minds, the engagement is
broken. Broken engagements are not unusual and are completely acceptable.

What is called the "new morality" among young people is a controversial development of the 1960s and early 1970s. Practiced largely
by young, college-educated people, this pattern accepts premarital

sexual relationships and even living together before marriage. However, many Americans do not approve of this behavior pattern and uphold a double standard in sexual behavior. This means that it is acceptable for young men to have sexual experiences before marriage, but young women are expected to be virgins before marriage. Many social scientists claim that premarital sexual relations were not unusual among both men and women before the 1960s. They say that what is different today is the open acceptance by many young people of a single standard for both sexes before marriage.

Although serious dating with a commitment to marriage is the familiar style of **courtship** in many cultures, what seems unusual to many foreign observers is the casual American dating system. Very often young Americans who hardly know each other go out on dates. For example, it is perfectly respectable for a young man to call up a young woman, introduce himself by telephone, and arrange a date. Usually they have a friend in common. It is equally acceptable for friends to arrange a "blind date," that is, a date between two young people who have not met before.

After their marriage the young couple is free to decide where to live and when to start a family. Most newlyweds set up their own household immediately. In the early 1970s only 1.5 percent of all married couples were not living on their own—independently and by themselves. Most married people practice some kind of birth control. They plan the number of children they are going to have and when their children will be born. Birth-control information is easily available in most states, and the practice of limiting the size of families has general approval. The birth **rate** has been declining steadily in recent years.

If the couple finds that their marriage was a mistake, they are free to get a divorce. The divorce rate has almost doubled in the past fifty years, and current statistics indicate that one of every three marriages will end in divorce. Many people view these figures with alarm. They fear that the institution of marriage is disintegrating—falling apart. A number of sociologists, on the other hand, say that this increase in divorces does not indicate more unhappy marriages. Instead, they point to changes in the laws that have made divorce easier and to changes in attitudes that have made divorce more acceptable than it had been years ago. They also claim that, since more than two-thirds of all divorced people marry again, divorce marks a temporary, rather than a permanent, break in marital relations.

Many families have labor-saving conveniences such as dishwashers, washing machines and dryers, and vacuum cleaners. In addition, they can purchase prepared foods in conveniently located super-markets, and they have a large choice of ready-made clothes. Their children attend school five days a week, which gives mothers some free time. On the other hand, very few families employ full-time do-mestic help, and most women do their own cooking and cleaning and **take care of** their young children when the children are not at school. In addition, over 40 percent of all married women work. Many are also active in community affairs.

When parents want to go out together, they usually arrange for a baby-sitter to take care of their young children. Baby-sitters are employed at an hourly rate, and high-school and college students often earn money in this way.

In the American family the husband and wife usually share im-portant decision making. When the children are old enough, they par-ticipate as well. Foreign observers are frequently amazed by the **per-missiveness** of American parents. The old rule that "children should be seen and not heard" is rarely followed, and children are often allowed to do what they wish without strict parental control. The father seldom expects his children to obey him without question, and children are encouraged to be independent at an early age. Some people believe that American parents carry this freedom too far. Others think that a strong father image would not suit the American values of equality and independence. Because Americans emphasize the importance of independence, young people are expected to break away from their parental families by the time they have reached their late teens or early twenties. Indeed, not to do so is often regarded as a failure, a kind of weak dependence.

This pattern of independence often results in serious problems for the aging parents of a nuclear family. The average American is expected to live beyond the age of 70. The job-retirement age is usu-ally 65. The children have left home, married, and set up their own households. At least 20 percent of all people over 65 do not have ade-quate retirement incomes. But the major problem of many widows, widowers, and elderly couples is not economic. They feel useless and lonely with neither an occupation nor a close family group.

Many communities and church groups sponsor social **centers** for "senior citizens." At these centers older men and women can make friends and participate in a variety of planned activities, including games, trips, lectures, and discussion groups. These programs may help some old people, but they do not provide the complete solution to the problems of old age. In recent years the situation has been re-ceiving increasing attention. Doctors, social workers, psychologists, and government officials are looking for ways to help lonely, elderly people meet the psychological and physical difficulties of growing old in our society.

Another subject that has been receiving considerable attention recently involves the position of women in the United States. Supporters of what is called the women's **liberation** movement claim that men control American society. They want women to achieve equality with men. Their major concerns are economic and social. They want to improve job opportunities for women, and they believe that women and men should receive the same rate of pay for the same kind of work. They also support the establishment of government-financed centers that would provide daytime care for the children of working parents.

Many members of the women's liberation movement also believe that equality of men and women requires changing the traditional roles of women and men in the home. They say that men should take on some of the responsibilities of child care and household work. In other words, they believe that men should perform some of the home-making duties that women have traditionally performed. Although there is disagreement on how influential this movement may become, there is general agreement that the basic structure of the American family will continue for a long time.

VOCABULARY

an ancestor *ancestry*	a person from whom one's grandparents are descended
	The parents of George Washington, the first President, were born in America, but his great-grandparents were English. Washington was an American of English **ancestry.** His **ancestors** were English.
casual *casually*	informal, relaxed
	He wore **casual** clothes. He did not wear a jacket or a tie. He was dressed **casually.**
*a center	a meeting place for certain activities
	A social **center** is a place where people meet to participate in social activities. Many churches sponsor social **centers** for young people. Usually located in church buildings, these **centers** provide young people with the opportunity to meet, talk, dance, and listen to records under pleasant, casual conditions.

in common

having the same interests or attitudes

Happily married people usually have a great deal **in common.** They frequently have similar educational backgrounds, and they agree on political questions.

a courtship
to court

the act of trying to win a person's affection for the purpose of marriage

The **Courtship** *of Miles Standish* is a famous poem by the American poet, Henry Wadsworth Longfellow. It tells the story of Miles Standish, an early colonial leader. He loved a young woman, Priscilla Mullens, but was too shy to **court** her himself. He asked his friend, John Alden, to **court** Priscilla for him. When John Alden spoke to her for Standish, Priscilla replied, "Why don't you speak for yourself, John?" That was the end of Miles Standish's **courtship.** John and Priscilla married soon after.

*to date
a date*

to have a social meeting

Sally and Richard go out together every Saturday night. They **date** each other every week. They always have a Saturday night **date.**

to fall in love

to begin to love

Do you think people usually **fall in love** when they first see each other, or do they have to know each other for a long time before they **fall in love?**

a household

a home and all the people who live in it

Household expenses include the costs of maintaining a house or apartment and of feeding and clothing the people who live in it.

to keep in touch

to remain in communication

Whenever he goes on a trip, he **keeps in touch** with his family by telephone and by mail. He calls or writes almost every day.

To keep in touch with what is happening in the world, you should read a newspaper every day.

kinship

a family relationship, the state of being related by blood or marriage

Studies indicate that black families have closer **kinship** ties than white families do. Black families frequently take relatives, children and adults, into their households.

| liberation | being set free |
| *to liberate* | One of the issues of the Civil War was the **liberation** of the slaves. They were **liberated** by an official act of President Lincoln. They were set free by the President. |

permissiveness	the act of allowing people to do what they want
to permit	to do
permissive	American parents often **permit** their children a great deal of independence. The parents are **permissive.** They believe in **permissiveness.**

a rate	a measured amount
	An hourly **rate** of pay is the amount of money that an employee receives for each hour of work.
	The **rate** of speed of an auto is the number of miles the car travels during a specified length of time.

| to take care of | to watch over or protect |
| | Small children should not be left alone. Someone should protect them. Someone should **take care of** them. |

Vocabulary Review

A. Fill in the blanks with the appropriate words from the vocabulary list of Chapter 16.

EXAMPLE   1. He was not worried about the situation. His attitude was relaxed and <u>casual</u>.

2. It was "love at first sight." They _____ when they met for the first time.

3. They shared many interests. They had many interests _____.

4. While he was away he wrote and phoned his wife almost every day. He _____ with her almost every day.

5. His father allowed him to drive the car. His father _____ him to drive the car.

6. In 1975 federal law provided that workers had to be paid at least $2.10 an hour. The minimum hourly _____ of pay was $2.10.

B. Match the words in column I with the definitions in column II.

	I		**II**
EXAMPLE	1. household	f. home and the persons living there	a. watch over
	2. date	_____	b. set free
	3. center	_____	c. meeting place
	4. take care of	_____	d. social engagement
	5. liberate	_____	e. descend
			f. home and the persons living there

Comprehension and Thought Questions

1. Give some examples of the diversity of American society.
2. Describe the characteristics that many middle-class American families have in common: size, religion, income, ancestry, education, etc. Describe a "typical" family in your country in terms of size, religion, income, ancestry, and education.
3. Read each of the following sentences aloud. Is the sentence true or false? If it is incorrect, change it so that the sentence is accurate.
   a. Although young Americans rarely marry persons of different religious beliefs, there is a great deal of intermarriage between Blacks and whites in the United States.
   b. Casual dating is common in the United States.
   c. Most young couples set up independent households when they get married.
   d. The divorce rate is increasing.
   e. Because most married women have maids who do domestic work and take care of the children, large numbers of them work.
4. Why do some people believe that permissiveness in raising children suits certain American values?
   a. Do you think this reasoning is correct? Why?
   b. Will you be a permissive parent? Why?
   c. How permissive were your parents?
5. How does the nuclear family structure affect the life-style of old people in the United States? Compare the situation of the elderly in the United States with that of the elderly in your country.
6. Discuss some of the aims of the women's liberation movement. What is your opinion of the women's liberation movement in the United States? in other countries? Describe the social, political, and economic status of women in your country. What are the career opportunities for

women in your country? Have there been any important changes in recent years?

Discussion and Composition Topics

1. In earlier times and in other cultures marriages have been based on social position, religion, education, and financial arrangements. Today in the United States marriage is based on romantic love. Many sociologists believe that romance alone cannot lead to lasting marriage and that the logical result of marriage founded on romance is divorce. They say that romantic love leads to unrealistic expectations in a marital relationship. Only in fairy tales do people fall in love, get married, and live happily ever after. A lasting marriage, they believe, depends on communication, respect, and values held in common.
   a. Give your opinion of the relationship between romantic love and successful marriage and compare it with the opinion of many sociologists as described in the preceding paragraph.
   b. How free are young men and women to choose their mates in your country?
   c. What is the attitude toward divorce in your country?
2. If possible, visit a day-care center in your community.
   a. Before you go, plan the questions you will ask on subjects such as the method of financing, the number and ages of children who are enrolled, the qualifications of the people who take care of the children.
   b. Would you want your child to attend a day-care center? Explain your answer.

Library Assignment 1

Find the following statistical information about your country: the birth rate, the infant mortality rate, and the death rate.

Library Assignment 2

Listed below are several books that portray life in different kinds of American families. Read one book and write a report on it. Include a summary of the story and a description of one major character, and comment on the family relationships described in the book.

Each of these books is available in a paperback edition. Your librarian may suggest additional books on American family life.

1. Agee, James, *A Death in the Family,* New York, Bantam, 1971.
   This novel about a loving and closely knit family in Knoxville, Tennessee, presents a remarkably sensitive picture of the relationships of a young married couple and their two small children. Many contemporary critics regard *A Death in the Family* as a modern American classic.

2. Fermi, Laura, *Atoms in the Family,* Chicago, University of Chicago Press, 1957.

   The author was the wife of Enrico Fermi, winner of the Nobel Prize for physics. The Fermis and their two children emigrated from Italy to the United States shortly before World War II. Mrs. Fermi has written an amusing and interesting account of their experiences during their early years in America—including a description of life as a non-English-speaking mother of children who learned English much more quickly and easily than she did.

3. Grau, Shirley Ann, *The Keepers of the House,* New York, Fawcett, 1965.

   This is the story of an interracial marriage in a small southern town and the violent consequences of Black-white confrontation. The time is the twentieth century, from the years before World War II until the late 1950s.

4. Horgan, Paul, *Things as They Are,* New York, Warner, 1971.

   Life in a small eastern town is seen through the eyes of a young boy. His relations with his family and his friends are sensitively presented as he describes the happiness and sorrows of growing up in the early decades of the 1900s.

5. Jackson, Shirley, *Life Among the Savages,* New York, Scholastic, 1969.

   This is a sophisticated and amusing autobiographical account of family life in a small Vermont town. The "savages" are the author's four children, who range in age from 1 to 10.

6. Richter, Conrad, *Light in the Forest,* New York, Bantam, 1953.

   Based on actual experiences in early America, this book tells the story of a white boy who was born in a frontier town and captured by Indians when he was 4 years old. He was raised as an Indian, and for eleven years he lived as a full member of an Indian family. Then the Indians agreed to return all white captives to their own people. Thus True Son, born John Butler, faces the terrible conflicts of different ways of life, values, and beliefs.

7. Rölvaag, O. E., *Giants in the Earth,* New York, Harper & Row, 1964.

   During the second half of the nineteenth century many Scandinavians migrated to the United States. Rölvaag, a descendant of Norwegian immigrants, has written an historical novel about his ancestors, who settled on the lonely frontier of what was then called the Dakota Territory.

8. Wright, Richard, *Black Boy,* New York, Signet, 1951.

   The late Richard Wright describes his childhood and youth in Mississippi. His mother, deserted by her husband, struggled to support her children on the inadequate wages of a domestic. Richard became an alcoholic before he was six years old. But, despite the destructive forces he faced, this black boy grew to be one of the outstanding American writers of this century.

Listening Exercises for Chapter 16 begin on p. 266.

VOCABULARY EXERCISES FOR SECTION V

Exercise I   Noun Suffixes

A. The suffix **-hood** is added to certain nouns to make other nouns. The stress of the original noun does not change. Add **-hood** to the following nouns and pronounce each new word.

EXAMPLE   father, fatherhood

1. adult	5. boy
2. neighbor	6. girl
3. mother	7. brother
4. child	8. widow

B. The suffix **-ship** is another suffix that is added to certain nouns to create new nouns without changing the stress. Add **-ship** to the following nouns and pronounce each new word.

EXAMPLE   scholar, scholarship

1. kin	4. court
2. relation	5. member
3. friend	6. citizen

C. The suffix **-ity** may be added to some adjectives to form nouns. The stress falls on the vowel sound preceding the **-ity** suffix. Pronounce each adjective from the list below and then pronounce the new noun with the **-ity** suffix. All these words appeared in Section V in noun or adjective form.

EXAMPLE   diverse, diversity

1. individual	10. rigid	
2. formal	11. ethnic	(Note the pronunciation
3. uniform	12. public	change)
4. municipal	13. real	
5. moral	14. eligible	
6. equal	15. entire	
7. personal	16. available	(Note the spelling)
8. local	17. respectable	
9. general	18. responsible	

D. Change the italicized verb in each of the following sentences to a noun by adding the suffix **-ment**. The stress does not change when **-ment** is added. Using the new noun, change the sentence, but keep the same meaning.

EXAMPLE   Students **advance** from one class to the next automatically when they receive satisfactory grades.

Advancement from one class to the next is automatic when students receive satisfactory grades.

1. The foundation **endowed** the university with $1 million.
2. Forty students were **enrolled** in the class.
3. People usually **retire** from their jobs when they reach the age of 65.
4. Many people are concerned because students do not **achieve** satisfactory reading ability.

Exercise II   More Suffixes

A. The suffix **-ly** is added to many adjectives and a few nouns to form adverbs. The stress does not change.

EXAMPLE   comprehensive, comprehensively

1. Find ten adjectives in Chapter 16 that can be changed to adverbs by adding the suffix **-ly.**

EXAMPLE   public, publicly

2. Find five adverbs in Chapter 16 that end in **-ly.**

B. The suffix **-ly** is also added to a few nouns and adjectives to form new adjectives. The stress remains the same. Here are some examples.

1. kind	a. kindly
2. love	b. lovely
3. scholar	c. scholarly
4. elder	d. elderly
5. lone	e. lonely
6. week	f. weekly
7. month	g. monthly
8. day	h. daily

(These words can also be used as adverbs)

C. The suffix **-able** (or **-ible**) is added to some verbs to form adjectives. The stress usually does not change. Here are some examples from Section V.

1. to achieve	a. achievable
2. to accept	b. acceptable
3. to read	c. readable
4. to suit	d. suitable
5. to prefer	e. preferable
6. to compare	f. comparable
7. to understand	g. understandable
8. to comprehend	h. comprehensible

(Note the stress change)

(Note the spelling change)

Exercise III

Verbs may be made into nouns (gerunds) by adding **-ing** to the simple form of the verb.

EXAMPLE   *Applying* to college involves *taking* examinations and *filling* out application forms.

Change the verbs in the list below to gerunds, and write a short paragraph on one of the subjects.

1. To Finance Schools Properly
2. To Retire at 65
3. To Take Care of Children
4. To Keep in Touch With My Family
5. To Fall in Love
6. To Date

Exercise IV

Underline the word or phrase from column II that is closest in meaning to the word in column I.

	I	II
EXAMPLE	retire	come back; <u>stop working</u>; answer again
1.	vocation	a. holiday; occupation; departure
2.	board	b. disinterested; wide; group of administrators
3.	comprehensive	c. costing a large amount of money; worried; including a lot
4.	discipline	d. field of knowledge; emphasis; student
5.	rigid	e. very cold; poor and unhappy; not changing

VI
AMERICAN POLITICAL PARTIES AND THE ELECTION PROCESS

Political Parties

"The United States has a two-party system, but is there any real difference between the parties? Why do voters get so excited and emotionally involved in elections that offer them no clear, sharp policy choices?"

These questions are frequently asked by foreigners who view the American political scene with puzzled interest. They are also puzzled by the fact that some members of opposing parties seem to have more in common with each other in terms of political philosophy and legislative programs than do some members of the same party. In Congress, for example, **liberal** Democrats and certain Republicans may vote alike, while **conservative** Democrats and other Republicans may unite in opposition to the same issue.

It is true that the American two-party system may fail to present sharp policy choices to the voters. On the other hand, this overlapping of philosophy and programs encourages **moderate** policies and political stability. It eases the transfer of presidential and legislative power from one party to the other following an election. In the U.S. political system it is not unusual for the President to belong to one party and the majority of the members of one or both houses of Congress to belong to the other party. Even in this situation, because deep party divisions over policy are rare, the system continues to function smoothly.

The two parties, the Republican and the Democratic, are organizations of **compromise.** Within each party, groups of citizens with somewhat different—but not completely opposite—aims unite to gain political power that they could not win separately. Party programs are constructed as statements of practical compromises. Each party tries to reach consensus, which means general agreement, among different groups on important issues.

Occasionally a special issue produces a third party, but, although the question may not be settled, the party itself usually does not last long. Often one of the two major parties **takes over** the issue and its supporters. During this century several minor parties, such as the Socialist, Socialist Labor, Communist, and Prohibition parties, have been on the **ballot** at one time or another. However, these parties have had little practical importance. For example, Communist party presidential **candidates** have never received more than three-tenths of 1 percent of the total votes in any election. The most important third party in recent years has been the extremely conservative American Independent party. In 1968 its presidential candidate was the well-known governor of Alabama, George Wallace. He received approximately 12 percent of the total votes. In 1972, however, a relatively unknown candidate **ran** for President on the American Independent party's ticket. He received only 1.4 percent of all the votes that year.

Although it is difficult to make sharp distinctions between the Democratic and Republican parties, a majority of American voters find enough differences to classify themselves as members of one party or the other. A **poll** conducted a year before the 1972 presidential election found that approximately 25 percent of all **eligible** voters de-

George Wallace campaigning as a "third party candidate" in 1968. *Wide World*

scribed themselves as Republicans, 40 percent as Democrats, and 35 percent as independents. An independent is someone who does not belong to any political party. A poll taken in the year following the 1972 election indicated that party preferences remained unchanged,[1] although the Republican candidate for President, Richard M. Nixon, had won an overwhelming victory.

Individuals identify with a particular party for many reasons. These reasons include the party's position on issues, the traditions of the social and economic group to which the voter belongs, his **ethnic** and geographic origins, and the personal charm and attractiveness (charisma) of the party's candidates. Recent studies show that family may be the most important influence in determining party membership. Two out of three Americans follow their parents' voting patterns. Among married couples, 95 percent vote alike.

The parties differ to the extent that they attract different groups of voters, although these groups often overlap. For example, most businessmen are Republicans. However, many businessmen are active Democrats for reasons other than economic ones—such as religion, national, racial, or geographic origin, or specific policy issues. People who have relatively large incomes, live in the suburbs, are in business or industrial management, are farmers, or are over 45 years old usually vote Republican. By contrast, lower-income city dwellers, union members, and those under 45 usually vote Democratic. Blacks, Catholics, and Jews have generally supported the Democrats during the past forty years. Since the early 1930s the Democratic party has been considered the more liberal party, speaking for labor and lower-income groups. The Republican party has been regarded as comparatively conservative, representing business and upper- and middle-income groups.

Great and dramatic events have influenced the choice of party by large groups of voters. The Civil War in the 1860s and the Great Depression in the 1930s have been most important. In general, people in the South have remained Democratic since the Civil War, when a Republican administration led the victorious northern army against the southern forces. Social and economic reforms introduced by a Democratic President, Franklin Roosevelt, in the 1930s won the continuing support of working people, especially trade-union members. Some of these reforms included legislation to regulate the wages and hours of American workers. For the first time a law guaranteed the right of workers to join unions and to bargain for better working conditions. Other new legislation provided financial help for elderly people and for workers who were unemployed.

1. The Gallup Poll, reported in the *Boston Globe,* April 5, 1973, p. 8.

Recently there have been signs that Democratic party loyalty in the South and among unionists is beginning to weaken. In the 1972 presidential election, for example, Richard Nixon, the Republican candidate, won the majority of votes in every southern state. It is estimated that approximately half of all the trade unionists who voted supported Mr. Nixon. If these developments continue, there will be important changes in the strength and **composition** of the two parties.

Independents are voters without firm loyalty to either party. They frequently **split** their **ticket,** which means that in the same election they choose Democrats for some offices and Republicans for others. Voting the **straight ticket** is the pattern of a loyal party member who votes only for members of his party and never crosses party lines.

Recent national elections point to a steady increase in ticket splitting even by voters who describe themselves as Democrats or Republicans. In the 1972 presidential election, for example, the majority of voters in every state but Massachusetts voted for Richard Nixon, the Republican candidate. At the same time, half the senators and more than half the representatives and governors who were elected that year were Democrats. Massachusetts, the only state that supported the Democratic candidate for President, chose a Republican governor.

How are political parties organized? Most important, they are local—which means that they are state or county groups. There are no special requirements for membership. Members do not have to vote for party candidates or give money to pay for party expenses. There are no membership cards, no dues, no initiation ceremonies, no required attendance at meetings. Actually, party membership is nothing but an expression by the voter of which party he prefers.

National political parties come into existence only once every four years, when the local groups combine to try to win the presidency. The single force that unites these local groups is their desire to gain national public **office.** It is important to note that the President and Vice-President are the only nationally elected public officials. All other elective offices from senator to mayor are chosen from a state or smaller area.

The only permanent national political organizations are the Democratic and Republican national committees. State party organizations choose the national committee members. The major function of these committees is to organize the party's national meetings, which are called conventions. At these conventions the presidential candidates are chosen. The committees also assist in election **campaigns.** Between elections, the committees provide services, such as research and publicity materials, to local party groups; and they help in various activities such as organizing women's clubs, young people's clubs, and working with minority groups.

VOCABULARY

a ballot *to ballot*	an official paper that the voter uses to indicate his choices in an election He wanted to be elected mayor, and his name was on the **ballot.** At the national presidential conventions delegates **ballot** for their favorite candidate. They vote for the person they want to win.
to campaign *a campaign*	to take part in planned activities for a special purpose such as winning an election He **campaigned** for the presidency throughout the country. He gave speeches, appeared on TV, shook voters' hands, and did everything he could to win the presidential election. He won the election. His **campaign** was successful.
a candidate	a person who actively seeks a position or a political office Richard M. Nixon and George McGovern were the presidential **candidates** in 1972. They actively campaigned to win the presidential election.
to be composed of **composition*	to be made up of; to consist of The Senate **is composed of** 100 members, two from each state. The **composition** of the Democratic party is changing. Southern voters who used to be loyal Democrats are beginning to vote for Republican candidates.
to compromise *a compromise*	to settle a disagreement by means of each side giving up some things it has asked for and neither side getting all it wants. The factory strike was settled when the union and management reached a **compromise** on the question of wages. The workers had demanded $3.00 an hour. The management had offered $2.00. They **compromised** on $2.50.

conservative
conservatism

opposed to change. (In some countries this is described as politically right-of-center)

"What is **conservatism?** Is it not belief in the old and tried rather than the new and untried?"

Abraham Lincoln, President, 1861–1865, speech, 1860

eligible
eligibility

having the necessary requirements

The Constitution requires a senator to be at least 30 years old and to have been a citizen for not less than nine years. To be **eligible** to serve in the Senate, a person must be a United States citizen for not less than nine years and must be at least 30 years old. The Constitution sets certain **eligibility** requirements to serve in the United States Senate.

ethnic

referring to racial, religious, or national origin

The American people belong to many religious, racial, and national groups. The American population is composed of people of different **ethnic** backgrounds.

Political journalists often use the term **ethnic** in a narrower sense, to refer to certain European national groups, especially those from southern and eastern Europe.

liberal
liberalism

favoring some change or reforms. (In some countries this is described as politically left-of-center)

"The Democratic Party will live and continue to receive the support of the majority of Americans just so long as it remains a **liberal** party."

Franklin D. Roosevelt, President, 1933–1945, speech, 1938

President Roosevelt believed that the Democratic party should support **liberalism.**

moderate
moderation

not extreme; within reasonable limits

"Real liberty is not found in the extremes of democracy, but in **moderate** government."

Alexander Hamilton, first Secretary of the Treasury, in Federal Convention Debates, 1787

*an office
an official
official

a public position of authority

He has had several **official** jobs. He has been a representative, a senator, and a cabinet secretary. He has been a government **official** for many years. He has held **office** in the federal government for many years.

a poll	a sample of public opinion; a record of votes
to poll	The Gallup **Poll** reports public opinions and attitudes on major issues by questioning a representative selection of people.
	A **polling** place is where people vote in an election.
	The chairman took a **poll** of the party members to determine their choice for presidential candidate. He **polled** the party members to determine their choice for presidential candidate.
*to run	to seek election
	George McGovern **ran** against Richard Nixon in 1972. He competed with Mr. Nixon for the office of President. They **ran** for the office of President.
a running mate	The vice-presidential candidate **runs** with his party's presidential candidate. They **run** together. They are **running mates.**
to take over	to assume control or responsibility for
	If the President is too ill to perform his duties, the Vice-President **takes over** the presidential role and acts as President.
*a ticket	a list of candidates of one party who are running in an election
to balance the ticket	The party's candidates included a Roman Catholic, a Protestant, a Jew, and a Black in order **to balance the ticket** and attract voters of different ethnic backgrounds.
to split the ticket	A loyal party member votes for the candidates of his party. He never votes for a candidate of the opposing party. He never **splits his ticket.**
to vote the straight ticket	A loyal party member votes for the candidate of his party. He never votes for a candidate of the opposition party. He always **votes the straight ticket.**

Vocabulary Review

Answer the following questions, which contain words (printed in heavy type) from the vocabulary list.

1. This class **is composed of** students who are studying American English. Describe the **composition** of the class in terms of nationality, age, and sex.

2. Who is **eligible** for the **office** of President of the United States? If you don't remember, look it up in Chapter 3.
3. Who was the winning **candidate** in the last U.S. presidential **campaign?**
4. In time of great economic difficulties would you expect a **liberal,** a **moderate,** or a **conservative** to be elected President? Why?
5. Think of some questions for a nonpolitical **poll.**

EXAMPLE   1. What is your opinion of public transportation in the United States?
2. What American food do you like best? least?

Comprehension and Thought Questions

1. What is a two-party political system?
   a. Even though there are often more than two political parties in the United States, we refer to the American two-party system. Why?
   b. List some of the advantages and disadvantages of the American two-party system. Compare these advantages and disadvantages with those of a one-party system and a multi-party system.
2. Over the years minor or third parties have frequently appeared on the American political scene. Do you think minor parties have any importance in American politics? Why?
3. What are some factors that influence an American voter's choice of party?
4. What name is given to voters who do not belong to a party? Why do they choose not to be party members?
5. To which party, if any, would you belong if you were a U.S. voter? Why?
6. What are the requirements for membership in the Democratic and Republican parties?
7. Explain the statement that American **national** parties come into existence only once every four years.

Discussion and Composition Topics

1. Describe the political party system in your country.
   a. How many parties are there?
   b. Do they represent sharp differences in philosophies and policies?
   c. Describe the political philosophies and policies of the leading party or parties.
   d. Describe minor parties, if any.
   e. How long do major or minor parties last in your country?
   f. How often does the party in control of the government in your country change? How is this change determined?
   g. How often are national elections held in your country? Are they held regularly? What national political offices are voted for?
2. a. What factors influence a voter's choice of party in your country? Compare these factors with those that influence an American voter's

choice of party membership (or nonmembership).
b. What requirements must you meet in order to belong to a party in your country?
c. Does everyone in your country belong to a political party? If not, how are nonparty members regarded by party members?
d. What influences a voter's choice of a candidate in your country? How important is party affiliation?

Listening Exercises for Chapter 17 begin on p. 268.

The Election Process

The **conventions** at which the two parties choose their presidential candidates take place in the summer of the election year. State **delegates** to these national meetings are chosen in various ways. About one-third of the states select their delegates at local party conventions. The other states elect their delegates in primaries held during the spring. Primaries are first, or preliminary, elections in which voters choose delegates who are pledged to support one of the announced presidential candidates of their party.

The number of delegates at each national convention varies with the number of voters in each state and certain party rules. In recent years the Democrats have required state delegations to reflect the composition of the voting population of their states, with adequate representation of women, youth, and certain minority ethnic groups.

The atmosphere at a national convention is theatrical. Delegates first approve their party **platform,** the statement of the party's position on various issues. Like the wood floor of a speaker's platform of the last century, the party platform is composed of individual "planks"— statements of party positions on such subjects as foreign relations, employment, education, and civil rights. The presidential candidate is expected to support the platform in his campaign.

The platform is supposed to unite the party, but sometimes a **controversial** issue may result in violent disagreement, and special efforts are necessary to reach a compromise. For example, in 1972 the issue of legalized abortion was highly controversial throughout the country. Abortion is the medical procedure used to end an unwanted pregnancy. At that time abortion was illegal in most states. Many delegates to the 1972 Democratic convention wanted to include a

Party delegates from each state attend national presidential conventions.
Al Kaplan, DPI

plank in the platform that would strongly support legalized abortion. Others, largely for religious reasons, wanted a plank that would oppose legalized abortion. The issue was debated into the early morning hours. Finally the delegates voted not to include any reference to abortion in the platform. Although neither the supporters nor the opponents of abortion were entirely satisfied, the issue was no longer a point of public conflict. By omitting all mention of abortion, they had reached a kind of compromise.

After the platform is **adopted, nominating** speeches for the various candidates are made, followed by enthusiastic noisemaking and demonstrations for each nominee. Next comes the voting. The convention chairman calls the roll, asking a representative of each state to report the number of votes cast, or given, by the delegates of that state to each nominee. The winner of more than 50 percent of the votes becomes his party's presidential candidate.

The presidential nominee usually selects his running mate, the vice-presidential candidate, who will campaign with him. He usually chooses someone who will balance the ticket, which means that the vice-presidential nominee may attract groups of voters who are different from those who support the presidential nominee. He often belongs to a different religious group and comes from a different part of the country.

Presidential campaigns begin in early September and continue until election eve in early November when the candidates make final television appeals for votes. Television and radio advertising is a major part of the campaign and represents the single largest cost. Other costs include travel of the candidate and his staff, salaries for the staff, newspaper advertising, and various kinds of publicity materials, such as campaign literature. This is printed information about the candidate and his position on issues, and it often includes requests for financial **contributions.** This literature is distributed to the voters during the campaign.

Two widely used publicity items are campaign pins and bumper stickers. On the pins, which may vary in diameter from one to six or eight inches, appear the name of the candidate, sometimes his picture, and often an eye-catching phrase about him. In 1972 some pins favoring the Republican candidate, Richard Nixon, read "Nixon's the

Delegates seek support for individual "planks" at the Democratic National Convention in 1972.   *Lawrence Frank, Rapho Guillumette*

one." Pins for the Democratic candidate, George McGovern, called for support of "Honest George." Pins are worn by supporters of the candidate to attract attention and to advertise his candidacy.

Bumper stickers are long strips of paper that are pasted on the bumpers, the protective metal bars across the front and back of an automobile. Like the pins, bumper stickers usually carry the name of the candidate and a short phrase or slogan supporting his candidacy. At the height of a presidential campaign thousands of bumper stickers appear on cars all over the country.

Campaigns are financed by contributions from individual citizens. In recent years the federal government and some states have enacted legislation to regulate campaign contributions and expenditures. A law passed before the 1972 election required that all presidential candidates report the names of the contributors to their campaigns and the amounts of their contributions. Following the disclosure of very serious illegal actions committed during the 1972 presidential campaign, Congress held extensive hearings on how to prevent illegal campaign contributions and expenditures, and in 1974 legislation was enacted that limits both contributions and expenditures. The law also provides for partial public financing of presidential campaigns. This legislation received strong bipartisan support (support by members of both parties).

Increasing attention has also been given to the use of radio and television time during campaigns. For many years federal regulations have specified that candidates must receive equal amounts of free time for political radio and TV broadcasts. In addition, candidates were allowed to purchase unlimited amounts of air time for campaign purposes. In the early 1970s Congress voted to limit the amount of money that a candidate could spend for radio and TV advertising. In 1968 presidential candidates had spent $28.5 million for TV and radio programs. In the 1972 election campaign, which followed the new legislation, the candidates spent approximately half that amount.

Because of the local structure of American political parties, no one knows exactly how much a national campaign costs. In addition to money expenditures, the value of **volunteers** must be considered. Every campaign attracts hundreds of unpaid workers at the **grassroots,** or local, political level. They perform various jobs, such as filling and mailing envelopes with campaign literature. Volunteers often go from house to house trying to persuade individual voters to support a particular candidate. Many students campaign in this manner, without pay, when they are interested in a certain candidate or a special issue.

Members of each party choose most of their candidates for local offices and for the federal legislature in primary elections. The rest are chosen at special party meetings. Winners are determined in the final, general elections.

By contrast, selection of the President involves an extra step, election by the Electoral College, a procedure established in the Constitution. Electors are representatives of each state party who vote on behalf of the voters of their state several weeks after the national popular election. The number of electors is based on the number of congressmen from the state. They are chosen according to laws of each state and are supposed to vote for the candidate who has won the majority of votes in that state. Even if a presidential candidate receives only slightly more than 50 percent of the votes in a particular state, he will receive all the electoral votes of that state. This system is known as the winner-take-all principle. As a result, although the national **popular** vote may be very close, one candidate may receive an overwhelming majority of Electoral College votes.[1] If a **deadlock** occurs in the Electoral College and neither candidate receives more than half the electoral votes, the Constitution provides that the House of Representatives should choose the next President. That has happened only twice, more than 150 years ago.

In recent years there has been much discussion about eliminating the Electoral College procedure. Many people think it is **awkward** and undemocratic. They also worry about the danger of a strong third-party candidate who might use his Electoral College votes **to bargain** for support on a particularly controversial issue. Opponents of the Electoral College favor the direct election of the President and Vice-President. Others believe that the system has worked well and should not be changed. They say that in a close popular election the Electoral College votes clearly establish the winner.

The election place—or polling place—is usually in a public building. Each state prints the ballots, which contain a list of the names of all the candidates. The voter makes his choice in secret in a private voting **booth.** Voters may mark paper ballots with pencils, pull levers on voting machines, or punch data cards. Most states have special mail arrangements for voters who are ill or must be away from home on Election Day. This is known as absentee voting.

Although the presidential election results are not official until the Electoral College has met, the American people consider the popular election totals to be final. Radio and television coverage gives election night some of the features of a horse race: high excitement dur-

1. In 1960 John Kennedy received 49.7 percent of the popular vote and more than 56 percent of the Electoral College votes. Eight years later Richard Nixon won 43.4 percent of the popular votes and approximately 56 percent of the Electoral College votes.

ing the running, uncertainty about the result, and important rewards to the winner. When the **outcome** is clear, the loser usually makes a public statement in which he accepts his defeat and offers his congratulations to the victor.

VOCABULARY

*to adopt
   an adoption

to vote acceptance of something

Each party **adopts** a platform at its national convention. It votes to accept this statement of party principles and aims. The **adoption** of a platform is an important part of the national convention program.

*awkward

not well designed for use

Many people believe the Electoral College procedure is inconvenient and inefficient. They think it is **awkward.**

*to bargain
   a bargain

to discuss exchanging or trading something for something else

One of the most famous political **bargains** in American history was made between Rutherford B. Hayes and the members of the Electoral College following the controversial election of 1876. Hayes, the Republican candidate, promised to withdraw federal troops that had been kept in southern cities since the end of the Civil War. In return, southern state electors cast their votes for Hayes, and he was declared President. Hayes **bargained** with the southern electors and won the presidency.

*a booth

a small enclosed area big enough for one person

A polling **booth** is a small enclosure where voters can vote in privacy.

A public telephone **booth** assures privacy when someone makes a telephone call.

to contribute
   a contribution
   a contributor

to give help or money

When someone makes a political **contribution,** he gives money to help finance a candidate's campaign. He **contributes** to the campaign. He is a campaign **contributor.**

controversial
   a controversy

causing considerable disagreement

He gave a **controversial** speech that created much disagreement. Many people thought he was wrong. He said his facts were correct and could not be disputed or denied. He claimed that his facts were beyond **controversy.**

*a convention
to convene

a conference or meeting of members of a society or political party

National **conventions** are held every four years to select presidential candidates. Delegates of each party meet to choose their candidates. They **convene** to choose their candidates.

a deadlock
to deadlock

a complete failure to reach an agreement

If opposing groups cannot agree and do not compromise, they have reached a **deadlock.** They are **deadlocked.**

a delegate
to delegate
a delegation

a person sent to a meeting or convention to represent others

The national convention **delegates** are chosen by party officials at state conventions or in special elections. Local party members **delegate** to them the responsibility of choosing good candidates. A state's **delegation** to the convention is composed of representatives of that state.

grass roots

the local level where the voters and the ordinary people are located

"We cannot depend on lords and noblemen. Our only hope lies in **grass-roots** heroes who come from the ordinary common people."

Yoshida Shoin, nineteenth-century Japanese educator and philosopher, in William T. DeBary, Ryusaku Tsunoda, Donald Keene, (eds.), *Sources of Japanese Tradition,* New York, Columbia University Press, 1958, p. 622

to nominate
a nomination
a nominee

to propose for election to a specific position

"I will not accept if **nominated** and will not serve if elected."

William T. Sherman, message to the Republican Convention, 1884

Sherman did not want the presidential **nomination** of the Republican party. He did not want to be the **nominee.**

an outcome
to come out

a result

The **outcome** of the election was not certain until the last vote was counted. No one was sure who had won the election until every vote was counted. Because the election was so close, no one knew how it would **come out** until all the votes had been counted.

*a platform	a program of a political party

"To me party **platforms** are contracts with the people."

Harry S. Truman, President, 1945–1953, *Memoirs*, Vol. II, New York, Doubleday, 1956, p. 182

*popular	of the people

The **popular** vote refers to all the votes cast by the people in an election.

a volunteer	someone who offers his services
to volunteer	

Volunteers help in many ways in an election campaign. They contribute unpaid time and work. They **volunteer** their assistance without pay.

Vocabulary Review

A. Put a plus sign (+) in front of each word in list II if it has a meaning that is the same as or similar to the corresponding word in list I. Put a minus sign (−) in front of the word in list II if it has a different meaning.

I	II
EXAMPLE 1. adopt	—— reject
2. awkward	_____ efficient
3. controversy	_____ agreement
4. grass roots	_____ highest level
5. outcome	_____ result
6. volunteer	_____ offer freely
7. convention	_____ political conference
8. contribution	_____ gift of money
9. platform	_____ political program

B. Special Class Assignment

The students should elect a class president. At least two candidates should be **nominated.** Each candidate should give a short speech describing his or her **platform.** The class should vote by secret ballot. As there are no voting **booths,** each student should write the name of his or her favorite candidate on a piece of paper. One person should **volunteer** to count the votes. When the **outcome** of the election is known, the winner should make a brief statement.

Comprehension and Thought Questions

1. a. What is a party platform? Do you have anything similar to party platforms in your elections? If so, explain.
   b. Are candidates for national office in your country limited to or re-

stricted by programs and policy statements of their parties? Explain your answer.

2. a. How are presidential candidates chosen in the United States?
   b. What factors usually influence the choice of the vice-presidential candidates?
   c. If you have elections in your country, how are the candidates for the office of the chief executive chosen?
3. a. How long do presidential campaigns last?
   b. How much do they cost?
   c. Who finances political campaigns?
   d. What are some major campaign expenses?
4. a. If you have political campaigns in your country, how are they financed?
   b. Does your government regulate campaign financing and expenditures in any way? If so, discuss this regulation.
5. How has the federal government attempted to regulate radio and television political broadcasts? Do you think such regulation is necessary? Why?
6. a. What is the role of volunteers in political campaigns in the United States?
   b. How important are political volunteers in your country?
   c. Describe the political role of students in your country.
7. All elected officials except the President and Vice-President are chosen in **direct** elections. The President and Vice-President are chosen in **indirect** elections. What is the difference between direct and indirect elections?
8. a. Why is the secret ballot considered the desirable method of voting?
   b. What is absentee voting? If you have absentee voting in your country, who is eligible to vote? Can you vote in an election in your country while you are in the United States? Explain your answer.

Discussion and Composition Topics

1. Young people are usually more liberal in politics than older people. Do you agree with this statement? Why?
2. Do you think election campaigns should be financed by the government or by contributions of private citizens? Why?
3. In recent years some American colleges have given their students time off from classes to work as volunteers in political campaigns. Do you think such arrangements are a good idea? Explain your opinion.
4. Do you think there is a particular "type" of person who enters politics? If so, what characteristics do you think are typical of politicians?

Listening Exercises for Chapter 18 begin on p. 269.

The Voters and the Political Process

Who is allowed to vote in elections? If a voter meets the legal require-ments, he is eligible to vote. He has **registered** when his name appears on the official list of eligible voters. Each state has its own regulations concerning voter eligibility and registration. All states require a voter to be a United States citizen and a **resident** for a specific length of time of the state where he votes. In 1920 the Constitution was amended to guarantee women the right to vote. In 1971 another constitutional amendment lowered the minimum voting age from 21 to 18 years. Some states require a **literacy** test for certain elections, but a federal law states that a voter is **qualified** if he has completed the sixth grade in a school in U.S. territory, even if the classroom language was not English. This law means that many Spanish-speaking citizens, espe-cially those who have come to the mainland from Puerto Rico, can vote. The federal law also provides that in a presidential election the voter does not have to meet a state's residence requirements.

The most painful and difficult problem in the history of voting in the United States has involved the black population. Until the Civil War, southern Blacks were nonvoting slaves. Following a brief post-war period of political liberation known as the Reconstruction, various organizations in the South used violence and threats of violence to keep Blacks away from the polls. Southern states also passed laws designed to restrict the voting eligibility of Blacks. These laws pro-vided literacy and education tests and required property ownership and the payment of poll taxes by those who wanted to vote. In addi-tion, registration was made exceedingly difficult. Registration offices were frequently located in out-of-the-way places and were open at inconvenient times or for too few hours to accommodate all the applicants.

Voters going to the polls. *Joel Gordon*

In recent years federal legislation and judicial decisions have resulted in dramatic increases in black voter registration and election **participation.** For example, the Voting Rights Act of 1965 suspended certain literacy tests and other restrictive voting requirements. It provided for the appointment, in areas where there was discrimination, of federal examiners who were authorized to register qualified voters. Within two years after the enactment of the Voting Rights Act, registration of the nonwhite population in eleven southern states[1] rose from 35.5 percent to 57.2 percent. Nonwhite registration in five southern states changed as follows:[2]

	Registration Before the Voting Rights Act of 1965	Registration in 1967
Mississippi	6.7 percent	59.8 percent
Alabama	19.3	51.6
Georgia	27.4	52.6
Louisiana	31.6	58.9
Arkansas	40.4	62.8

1. Alabama, Arkansas, Florida, Georgia, Louisiana, Mississippi, South Carolina, North Carolina, Tennessee, Texas, and Virginia.

2. © 1945, 1947, 1951, 1955, © 1960, 1964 by Claudius O. Johnson; © 1970 by Claudius O. Johnson, Daniel M. Ogden, Jr., H. Paul Castleberry, Thor Swanson, reprinted from *American National Government* by Claudius O. Johnson, Daniel M. Ogden, Jr., H. Paul Castleberry, Thor Swanson with permission of Thomas Y. Crowell Co., Inc.

As their interest and participation in the election process have grown, Blacks have won an increasing number of offices. Most recent gains have been on the state and city levels. The number of black state legislators more than doubled between 1964 and 1972. In 1968 there were twenty-nine black mayors. Four years later eighty-six Blacks headed city governments. In 1973 a Black, Thomas Bradley, was elected mayor of Los Angeles, the city with the second largest population in the country. What was particularly significant in that election was the fact that Bradley received wide support among white voters. Usually black candidates have been successful only when the majority of voters were black. Bradley's victory cut across this racial voting pattern.

Today there are more than 2000 elected black officials. Over half of them serve in the southern states that were once centers of segregation. In 1972 a total of thirteen Blacks were elected members of the U.S. House of Representatives. Two of these were the first Blacks elected from southern states in more than 100 years. There was also one black senator, Edward Brooke of Massachusetts, who was elected for his second term.

Another interesting political development occurred in 1972. Representative Shirley Chisholm, a black woman, ran as a presidential candidate in several Democratic primaries. Although she won relatively few votes, she received considerable attention, and her candidacy marked a change in the traditional American political scene. This was the first time that a Black or a woman was a candidate on a major party ticket in several presidential primaries.

Despite the encouraging gains by Blacks in recent years, difficulties remain. Perhaps the hardest problem is to change traditional **attitudes,** which are the result of years of fear, ignorance, and **prejudice.** Black people must recognize the importance of their votes and their participation in the election process. White voters must be willing to support black candidates and **to cooperate** with them when they are elected.

The political process does not stop after an election. Many organizations with special interests maintain paid representatives in the national and state capitals. These **lobbyists** try to influence government policy in favor of the organizations or **interest groups** that they represent. This is a recognized part of the American political system. Lobbying is directed at various government officials, particularly legislators who are scheduled to vote on bills affecting the interest groups.

In the early 1970s an example of this kind of lobbying involved airplane companies who wanted the government to finance the development of a new kind of plane. Called a supersonic plane, it would have carried 300 passengers at 1800 miles an hour. This lobbying effort was opposed by other interest groups, which were concerned about the environmental problems that might result from flying at such high speeds. Congress did not approve the financing of the plane, partly because of the opposition lobbies.

Lobbying methods usually involve talking to government officials in the legislature and the executive branch in order to persuade them to support the interest group's position. Lobbyists may appear at congressional committee hearings, and sometimes they propose bills for consideration by the committees.

Other interest-group methods include supporting sympathetic political candidates, taking legal action in the courts, and publicizing their views on special issues. In the late 1960s and early 1970s, for example, numbers of citizens organized to oppose U.S. military action in Vietnam. Their activities included visits and letter writing to their congressmen and senators in order to express their opposition to the war. They also held public meetings, which were attended by thousands of people. They placed antiwar advertisements in newspapers throughout the country, and they organized support for political candidates who opposed the war. This support consisted of financial contributions to the campaigns of these candidates and volunteer work as well. Some interest groups are specifically organized for such political action. Others, such as trade unions and professional and religious organizations, carry out various activities, of which lobbying is only one.

It is widely believed that lobbyists sometimes use improper methods in their efforts to influence government officials. One unusual example of the **abuse** of lobbying took place several years ago. In a dramatic statement on the floor of the Senate, Senator Francis R. Case of South Dakota revealed that he had been offered a $2500 campaign contribution by two lobbyists who represented a natural-gas interest group. The lobbyists wanted the Senator to vote for a bill having to do with natural gas. The lobbyists were tried in a federal court and found guilty of violating the Federal Regulation of Lobbying Act.

There have been some attempts by the government to regulate lobbying. The lobbying act just mentioned requires all lobbyists to register publicly and to report the money they receive and spend for lobbying purposes. Another law requires registration of certain non-diplomatic representatives of foreign countries who might lobby in an attempt to influence U.S. government policy.

Although it is generally recognized that this legislation has not been effective in doing away with all lobbying abuses, lobbying remains an essential part of the American governmental process. It provides an important means by which organized groups of citizens with special interests or problems can have a greater voice in government than they would have as individuals.

VOCABULARY

to abuse *an abuse*	the wrong use or misuse of something A lobbyist **abuses** the practice of lobbying when he offers money or other kinds of rewards in an attempt to influence a government official. This is against the law and is a serious **abuse** of lobbying privileges.
an attitude	a point of view; a way of thinking about something Public-opinion polls report people's **attitudes** on major social, economic, and political issues. The polls report what people think about these issues.
to cooperate *cooperation*	to work or act together The President expects legislators who are members of his party to **cooperate** with him in carrying out his legislative program. He expects their **cooperation.**
an interest group	a group of people who share interests and concerns on particular issues and who work together on these issues The U.S. Chamber of Commerce is an organization composed of businessmen and women throughout the United States. It is an **interest group** that represents people in business. One of its most important functions is to work for government policies that favor its members.
literacy *literate*	the ability to read and write The **literacy** rate in the United States is higher than 95 percent. More than 95 percent of all Americans can read and write. They are **literate.**
*a lobby to lobby	a group of people who try to influence government action for or against certain programs and policies Common Cause is an organization that acts as a citizens' **lobby** to improve government policies and procedures. Representatives of Common Cause **lobbied** for the regulation of political campaign contributions.

to participate

    participation

to take part in something

Many volunteers **participated** in the campaign. They contributed time and money. Their **participation** helped the candidate.

a prejudice

    prejudiced
    to prejudge

an opinion formed without adequate knowledge

John F. Kennedy was the first Roman Catholic President. Before his election many political observers thought Americans were **prejudiced** against Roman Catholics and would not vote for him. These observers believed that **prejudice** against Roman Catholics would prevent Kennedy from winning the election. They thought people would **prejudge** Kennedy and vote against him without knowing his ability. Since Kennedy's victory in 1960, Roman Catholicism has not been an issue in American politics.

to qualify

    a qualification

to meet specific requirements

Each state establishes its own voter-**qualification** requirements. A voter must **qualify** according to state regulations in order to vote in state elections.

to register

    registration

to place someone's name on an official list

No one can vote unless he **registers** with the proper election officials. **Registration** is necessary before one can vote.

a residence

    to reside
    a resident

the place where a person lives

The White House is the President's **residence.** He **resides** in the White House. He is a **resident** of the White House. His legal **residence** is the state in which he **resided** before he was elected.

Vocabulary Review

Briefly answer the following questions, which contain words from the vocabulary list of Chapter 19.

1. Must foreign students **register** with a U.S. government official when they arrive in this country?
2. a. What is the name of the President's **residence?** Is there a special name for the **residence** of your chief executive?
   b. What city do you **reside** in now?
3. Have you ever **participated** in a political campaign? If so, describe your **participation.**
4. What is your **attitude** toward physical exercise? Do you think it is important? If so, what kind of exercise do you prefer?

5. Do you **qualify** for admission to an American college? If not, what **quali-fications** do you need?
6. Do you think small children have racial or religious **prejudices?**
7. What would you do if you saw someone **abusing** a dog?
8. What is the approximate **literacy** rate in your country?

Comprehension and Thought Questions

1. a. What are some requirements that a voter must meet in order to be eligible to vote in the United States? Are these requirements the same in state and federal elections?
   b. Compare these requirements with voting requirements in your country.
2. In what ways has recent federal legislation affected voting eligibility requirements for young people? for minority groups?
3. a. What changes must occur in the political attitudes of Blacks and whites in order to improve political participation among black citizens?
   b. What recent developments seem to be encouraging signs of increased political activities among Blacks?
4. a. What are lobbies? What is their purpose? How do lobbies provide citizens with an opportunity to influence government policies?
   b. How do citizens influence government policies in your country?
   c. If you were a paid lobbyist who represented your country in the United States, what would you lobby for? against? Why?

Discussion and Composition Topics

1. Slightly fewer than 55 percent of all eligible voters actually voted in the 1972 presidential election.
   a. How do you think this compares with the voting pattern in your country or any other country you know about?
   b. Do you think voting should be compulsory? In other words, should eligible voters be required to vote in every election? Explain your answer.
2. What qualifications do you think a person should have in order to be eligible to vote? age? literacy? length of residence? other?
3. Have you ever voted? If so, tell about it. How old were you? What office was the election for? Was there a secret ballot? Where was the polling place? Did you have to present any special identification to prove your eligibility?
4. Here are some quotations on politics and politicians. Comment on each of them. Do you agree with the statement? Why or why not?
   "The ballot is stronger than the bullet."
   > Abraham Lincoln, President, 1861–1865, speech, 1856

   "Politics makes strange bedfellows."
   > Charles D. Warner, American writer, *My Summer in a Garden, 1870*

   "Politics is so expensive, it takes a lot of money just to get defeated."
   > Will Rogers, American humorist, newspaper article, 1931, Bartlett, *Familiar Quotations,* 14th ed., Boston, Little Brown, 1968, p. 954A

"You have all the characteristics of a popular politician: a horrible voice, bad breeding, and a vulgar manner."

Aristophanes, Greek playwright, *Knights,* 424 B.C.

"Man is by nature a political animal."

Aristotle, Greek philosopher, *Politics,* 342 B.C.

Library Assignment

1. Find the name and official title of the chief executive of each of the following countries:
   a. Albania
   b. Argentina
   c. Indonesia
   d. Kenya
   e. South Korea
2. Find the literacy rate of
   a. Australia
   b. Brazil
   c. Egypt
   d. U.S.S.R.
   e. Your country
   Be sure to note the exact sources of your data.

Listening Exercises or Chapter 19 begin on p. 270.

VOCABULARY EXERCISES FOR SECTION VI

Exercise I

The following words from the text can be used as nouns or verbs. Use each word as a noun in a sentence. Then use the same word as a verb in a sentence.

EXAMPLE   He cast his **vote** for Franklin Roosevelt in 1932.

He **voted** for Harry Truman in 1948.

1. balance   5. abuse
2. compromise   6. volunteer
3. bargain   7. lobby
4. campaign

Exercise II

From the vocabulary lists of Section VI choose a word, phrase, or idiom that means the opposite of each of the words listed here.

1. to vote the straight ticket   5. a quick, easy agreement
2. high level   6. to reject or refuse
3. unqualified   7. conservative
4. extreme   8. efficient and well designed

Exercise III   More Noun Suffixes

A. The suffix **-ment** is added to some verbs to form nouns. The stress remains the same. Change the verbs listed below to nouns by adding **-ment.** Then use each noun in a sentence.

EXAMPLE   govern, government

The United States has a constitutional **government.**

1. amend
2. require
3. judge (note the optional spelling change)
4. adjourn

B. The suffixes **-cy** or **-sy** may be used to form abstract nouns. The stress may be affected. Add the suffix **-cy** or **-sy** to the following words. Pronounce each new noun, and use it in a sentence. Note the spelling changes.

EXAMPLE   accurate, accuracy

He shot the gun with great **accuracy.**

1. president   5. bureaucrat
2. candidate   6. democrat
3. literate
4. controversial

C. The suffix **-er** or **-or** is often added to verbs to form nouns that indicate the agent of the verb. The stress remains unchanged. Use each verb listed below in a sentence. Then add the agent suffix and use the noun in a sentence with a similar meaning.

EXAMPLE   review

He **reviews** books.

He is a book **reviewer.**

1. campaign   4. bargain
2. compromise   5. legislate
3. contribute   6. vote

Exercise IV

Fill in the blanks in the following paragraph from the following list of words from Section VI. Make the words plural when necessary. You may use the same word more than once.

1. office   5. candidate
2. delegate   6. platform
3. compromise 7. interest group
4. convention

EXAMPLE   The national political (4) <u>conventions</u> of both parties follow similar schedules.

First the _____ adopt the _____.

This statement of party policies often includes _____ on

important issues in order to win support of various _____

_____ and the majority of voters. Then the

_____ choose their party's _____ for the

_____ of President and Vice-President.

VII
CONCLUSION

As Others Saw Us

During the first half of the nineteenth century three foreigners spent time in the United States and later wrote books describing their impressions. One visitor was Mrs. Frances Trollope, a writer and the mother of the English novelist Anthony Trollope. She arrived in 1827, hoping to open a "bazaar," or department store, and to make her fortune. She did neither, but she wrote a detailed and highly critical account of the United States in *The Domestic Manners of the Americans*. Several years later a young Frenchman, Alexis de Tocqueville, came here to study the American prison system. He traveled extensively and wrote *Democracy in America*, which has become a widely read commentary on the United States. In 1842 Charles Dickens, the famous English novelist, sailed from England on one of the early trans-Atlantic passenger steamships. He hated the ocean voyage, and he did not like the United States much either. His description of his trip, *American Notes*, is filled with criticisms of the people and their country, and especially of slavery.

At the time of these visits the nation was very young. Numbers of people who remembered the Revolutionary War were still alive. The United States had not yet become an industrial giant. Slavery existed throughout the South and continued for several more decades. The frontier was steadily moving west, but great areas of the country remained wild and undeveloped. What these three foreign visitors saw and what they thought about what they saw is recorded, in part, in the following (slightly edited) quotations from their books.

On equality

de Tocqueville

In the United States the well-to-do citizens take care not to stand apart from the people; on the contrary, they constantly keep on easy terms with the lower classes; they listen to them and they speak to them every day. They know that the rich in democracies always stand in need of the poor.

. . .

Nothing struck me more forcibly than the general equality of condition among the people. . . . The influence of this equality extends far beyond the political character and laws of the country. . . . It creates opinions and affects the ordinary practices of life.

Trollope

The tone of equality puts the lower classes in a false position and they must feel it. The fact that they can enter a drawing room [parlor or living room] and dirty the carpet with tobacco and mud does not produce the slightest change in their own dwellings. And among the truly poor the reality of inequality exists in America exactly as much as it does elsewhere.

On women

Trollope

The women are certainly by far . . . handsomer than those either of France or England. . . . They are quiet and orderly in their manners and habits . . . and are constantly occupied about their household concerns. But generally speaking they lack [do not have] intelligence. What is far worse, they lack grace.

de Tocqueville

If I were asked to what the remarkable prosperity and the growing strength of the Americans ought to be attributed, I should reply: to the superiority of their women.

On the press

Dickens

Any man who reaches a high place, from the President, downwards, may mark his downfall from that moment; for any printed lie that any villain writes about him in the newspapers appeals at once to Americans and is believed.

. . .

While the newspaper press remains in its present lowly state, high moral improvement in America is impossible. Some excuse these journals by saying their influence is not so great. I must be pardoned for saying that every fact leads me to the opposite conclusion.

de Tocqueville

The more I consider the independence of the press in America, the more convinced am I that it is the chief and basic element of liberty. . . . The power of the press is second only to that of the people.

. . .

The number of periodical publications in the United States is unbelievably large. In America there is scarcely a village that does not have its newspaper.

. . .

The only true American authors are the journalists. They are not great writers, but they speak the language of the country and they make themselves heard.

On politics and government

Dickens

The feature of political speeches in the legislature seems to be the constant repetition of the same ideas in different words. The inquiry outside the halls of the legislature is not "What did he say?" but "How long did he speak?"

. . .

Politics are much discussed. There will be a presidential election in three years and a half, and party feeling runs very high. The great feature of this institution is that as soon as the bitterness of the last election is over, the bitterness of the next one begins: which is a great comfort to all strong politicians and true lovers of their country: that is to say, ninety-nine men and boys out of every ninety-nine and a quarter.

Trollope

There are some points on which Americans all agree—namely, that the American government is the best in the world . . . that America has produced the greatest men that ever existed . . . that all the nations of the world look upon them with a mixture of wonder and envy and that in time they will all follow their great example and have a President. . . . Americans are all strongly attached to their government.

. . .

When a candidate for any office begins his campaign, his party endows him with every virtue and ability. They are ready to pick out the eyes of those who oppose him; but as soon as he succeeds, his virtues and abilities vanish, and except for those who hold office under him, everyone is off to elect his successor.

de Tocqueville

The institutions are democratic; the people elect their representatives to insure their independence. The people, therefore, are the real directing power, and the opinions, the prejudices and the interests . . . of the people exercise a constant influence on the daily conduct of affairs.

. . .

Politics enjoys a prominent place in the interests of a citizen of the United States; and almost the only pleasure which an American knows is to take part in the government and discuss its activities.

. . .

The basis of the American democratic government consists in the absolute power of the majority. . . . But the main evil of the present democratic institutions may be the lack of protection against the majority. . . . In America the majority sets limits to the liberty of opinion; within these limits an author may write whatever he pleases, but he will regret it if he steps beyond them.

On personal habits

Dickens

I wish to offer a remark on public health. Much of the disease one finds here could be avoided. Greater personal cleanliness is absolutely necessary; the custom of hastily swallowing large quantities of animal food three times a day, and rushing back to work after each meal must be changed; the gentler sex must dress more wisely and take more healthful exercise. Above all, in public institutions and throughout every town and city, the system of ventilation and removal of impurities must be completely changed.

Trollope

Whiskey flows everywhere at the cheap rate of twenty cents a gallon and its horrible effects are visible on the face of every man you meet.

. . .

Americans rarely dine in society except in taverns [restaurants] and boarding houses. They eat with the greatest possible rapidity, and in total silence.

. . .

They consume an extraordinary quantity of bacon. Ham and beef-steaks appear morning, noon, and night. In eating they mix things together strangely: ham with applesauce; salt fish with onions. They eat horrible half-baked hot rolls both morning and evening. The flour of Indian corn is made into a dozen different sorts of cakes, but in my opinion it is all bad.

de Tocqueville

Americans prefer serious and silent amusements. In a free hour instead of going to dance merrily . . . an American shuts himself up at home to drink. He enjoys two pleasures simultaneously; he can go on thinking of his business and can get drunk decently by his own fireside. . . . Americans are the most serious people on the face of the earth.

On education

Trollope

At sixteen, often much earlier, education ends, and money-making begins; the idea that more learning is necessary is laughed at . . . very little learning is thoroughly gained beyond reading, writing, and book-keeping [commercial arithmetic].

On general characteristics

de Tocqueville

In America I saw the freest men . . . placed in the happiest circumstances in the world; but it seemed to me that a cloud hung over them, and I thought them serious, almost sad, even in their pleasures.

Trollope

I do not like their principles, I do not like their manners, I do not like their opinions.

On values and beliefs

de Tocqueville

Although the travelers who have visited North America differ on many points, they all agree . . . that morals are far more strict there than anywhere else.

. . .

The love of physical well-being and physical comfort is the predominant taste of the nation. The love of wealth is the basis of all that Americans do.

. . .

In the United States work is considered the necessary, natural, and honest condition of human existence. . . . It is held in honor.

. . .

The Americans prefer the useful to be beautiful, and they require that the beautiful should be useful.

Discussion and Composition Topics

1. De Tocqueville and Trollope discussed equality in terms of economic class. Do you think their observations apply to contemporary American society? Explain your opinion.
2. Read Trollope's comments on American women. Do you think her comments accurately describe American women today? Explain your opinion.
3. De Tocqueville stated that the press was the chief and basic element of liberty in the United States. Do you think his opinion would be valid today? Explain your answer.

4. Both Dickens and de Tocqueville commented on the Americans' intense interest in politics. Do you think contemporary Americans are more interested in politics than the people in your country? If possible, give examples to illustrate your answer.
5. Choose one quotation from Chapter 20 that you think most accurately describes contemporary Americans. Choose one that you think does not apply to contemporary Americans. Explain your choices.

As Others See Us: Modern Views

In 1972 a series of articles by scholars and writers from several countries appeared in the American journal *Daedalus*. These articles presented the authors' opinions of the contemporary United States. The country that they discussed was far different from the young nation that had been visited by de Tocqueville, Dickens, and Trollope. America had become a world power, facing serious and complex problems at home and abroad. Included here are some edited excerpts from *Daedalus*, as well as comments by a few other twentieth-century foreign observers.

The authors quoted are:

Achille Albonetti, Italy, economist
Raymond Aron, France, authority on international affairs
Jagdish Bhagwati, India, economist
Constantinos Doxiadis, Greece, architect and city planner
Omar Grine, Algeria, sociologist and economist
Annie Kriegel, France, political sociologist
Richard Llewelyn-Davies, England, architect
Octavio Paz, Mexico, diplomat and poet

Other writers quoted are:

Denis Brogan, England, political scientist
Simone de Beauvoir, France, writer
Robert Conquest, England, political writer
John Maynard Keynes, England, economist
Gunnar Myrdal, Sweden, social economist
George Bernard Shaw, Ireland, playwright and satirist

On national characteristics

Constantinos Doxiadis

I have not met an American who could not have come from any other country: honest and dishonest, realist and dreamer, and any other type I could imagine. People are the same everywhere.

> In *Daedalus,* Journal of the American Academy of Arts and Sciences, Fall 1972, Vol. 101, No. 4

Denis Brogan

Americans like things big.

. . .

The American is optimistic, cheerful, energetic—convinced that if not all is for the best in the best of all possible countries, it is on the way to becoming so.

> In *American Aspects,* London, Hamish Hamilton, 1964

Omar Grine

The American people have always impressed me with their optimism.

> In *Daedalus, op. cit.*

Octavio Paz

Americans like speed, alcohol, horror films, and sensational news. They constantly demand new things and ever new things; they find no rest in anything.

. . .

The Americans have a fear and horror of anything that is not clean.

. . .

Americans are lonely. They are open and friendly . . . but they rarely know how to create deep love or lasting friendship . . . few want anything more than to rise a few rungs on the social ladder . . . they have no inner fire.

. . .

North Americans are capable of self-criticism—and this criticism is what leads to change. It keeps the country modern.

> In *Daedalus, op. cit.*

George Bernard Shaw

An American has no sense of privacy. He does not know what it means. There is no such thing in the country.

> Speech, 1933, in Bartlett, *Familiar Quotations,* 14th ed., Boston, Little, Brown, 1968, p. 838a

On values and beliefs

Jagdish Bhagwati

The U.S.A. is a strange puzzle. The distinct and dramatic disregard of basic human values which has marked its recent foreign and domestic political policies contrasts with the evidence of growing concern by a number of Americans with the moral content and influence of their institutions and policies.

. . .

There are vast numbers of young students who are seeking to direct their society to a better purpose. They have breathed life and vitality into most of the great issues of the day: pollution, population control, environment, the role of science in society, consumer protection, and women's liberation. . . .

The values of these young people contrast sharply with foreign and domestic programs of leading government officials. For example—Americans bombing Southeast Asia, support of anti-democratic governments throughout the world, reduction in aid to poor nations, and the appointment of a former segregationist to the Supreme Court.

In *Daedalus, op. cit.*

Omar Grine

Americans have lost faith in the stability of their society. They have begun to realize that they are like others; moreover, they are not at all certain about what they want.

. . .

America was founded on change. The people have made change a kind of religion.

In *Daedalus, op. cit.*

Octavio Paz

Americans want to believe that Good and Evil can be defined in precise categories, and that Good already is or can be easily achieved.

. . .

They believe in science, and science has a high place in their system of beliefs and values.

. . .

Pleasure is not part of the U.S. tradition. Duty and work are the key words.

In *Daedalus, op. cit.*

Achille Albonetti

The experience of intervention in Europe during the two World Wars led Americans to believe that they were the people who were chosen to extend peace and stability to the four corners of the earth. Their faith has now been shaken, but they are still building foreign policy on that traditional belief.

In *Daedalus, op. cit.*

Denis Brogan

There are two basic American beliefs. First, all technical progress, or nearly all, is the work of Americans—that knowhow, mastery of tools and machines, is what it takes to get ahead in this competitive world.

Second, and closely connected with this belief, is the respect given to the businessman who is . . . the man who organizes the great human and physical resources of the United States to produce "the American way of life." It is believed that the businessman is the representative American.

. . .

Nothing could be sillier than to think that all Americans have one attitude in common or that there is such a thing as "What Americans are thinking."

In *American Aspects, op. cit.*

On equality

Gunnar Myrdal

In 1962 prejudice against Negroes was still common in the United States, but racism as a comprehensive ideology was maintained by only a few. The change from earlier years has been so rapid that I predict the end of all formal segregation . . . within a decade, and the decline of informal segregation . . . to just a shadow in two decades. The attitude of prejudice might remain, but it will be . . . minor . . . within three decades. These changes would not mean that there would be equality between the races within this time, for the heritage of the past . . . would still operate to give Negroes lower "life chances." But the . . . social forces creating inequality will, I predict, practically disappear in three decades.

In *An American Dilemma*, New York, Harper & Row, Rev. ed., 1962

On youth

A Czech student

What surprises me most about American students is not that they take themselves seriously—students always do—but that their elders take them seriously. In the West it seems possible to grow quite old without having to grow up.

In the *New York Times*, October 10, 1970, VI: 28

On women's liberation

Annie Kriegel

It is not surprising that the women's liberation movement is marked by its vitality and survival, since it has settled upon an area where America has failed most completely.

In *Daedalus, op. cit.*

On food

Octavio Paz

Traditional North American cooking is food with no mysteries—simple, spiceless, and healthful. There are no tricks—the carrot is an honest carrot; the potato is not ashamed of being a potato; the steak is a bloody giant. Americans love cream and butter and sugar. They combine a simple lunch with ice cream and milk shakes. Their food fears spices. Pleasure is absent from American cooking. They prefer health to pleasure.

In *Daedalus, op. cit.*

On politics and government

John Maynard Keynes

In the United States it is almost unbelievable what nonsense a public man has to say today if he wishes to remain respectable.

1932, in Bartlett, *Familiar Quotations, op. cit.*, p. 777a

Denis Brogan

American boys are continuously told they can, when they grow up, become President of the United States. (Girls are not yet told they can.)

In *American Aspects, op. cit.*

On cities

Constantinos Doxiadis

Americans may have the best skyscrapers and highways, but they also have the worst cities in the world.

In *Daedalus, op. cit.*

Richard Llewelyn-Davies

For most Europeans it is hardly believable that the innercity slums can exist in a society as wealthy as America.

In *Daedalus, op. cit.*

A summing up

Richard Llewelyn-Davies

America's size and diversity make most generalizations questionable.

In *Daedalus, op. cit.*

Omar Grine

America has long been admired for both its potential and its achievement. . . . One of America's great qualities as a nation—certainly the one that was most admired—was its self-confidence. But over the years a crisis has developed. Americans have less confidence in America and in each other.

In *Daedalus, op. cit.*

Raymond Aron

The United States remains the laboratory of a people uncertain of its own destiny.

In *Daedalus, op. cit.*

Simone de Beauvoir

In America life flows away in an effort to survive.

In *America Day by Day*, New York, Grove Press, 1953

Robert Conquest

The phrase "America has gone mad" has been in constant use in Europe for years.

In the *New York Times, op. cit.*

Achille Albonetti

Europeans are constantly rediscovering America; it is good for them to do so, since it gives them an opportunity to rediscover themselves and, in the process, to reflect on where the Old World itself may be going.

In *Daedalus, op. cit.*

Discussion and Composition Topics

1. Compare the statements of Trollope and Dickens (Chapter 20) and of Paz (Chapter 21) about American food. Do you think they agree? What is your opinion of American food?
2. Myrdal wrote his comments on racial equality more than ten years ago. On the basis of your observations, do you think his predictions about the decline of racial inequality have proved accurate? Why?
3. The Czech student says that in the West it seems possible to grow quite old without having to grow up. What do you think he means? What factors in American society might delay growing up? Do young American adults seem more or less mature than young adults in your country? Explain your opinion.
4. Comment on Doxiadis's statement on American cities. Do you think American cities are different from cities in other countries? Why?
5. Paz states that pleasure is not part of the U.S. tradition and that "duty" and "work" are the key words. De Tocqueville thought that Americans were the most serious people on the face of the earth. Brogan and Grine find that the Americans are optimists. Which, if any, of these opinions do you think accurately describes contemporary Americans? Why?
6. What statements by these twentieth-century observers are closest to your opinions of contemporary Americans? What statements seem inaccurate? Why? Basing your opinions on your reading and your personal experiences, what comments would you add?
7. Since you came to the United States, what aspects of American life have

you found most difficult? most pleasing? most surprising? most disappointing?

8. Briefly describe some of the characteristics, values, and beliefs of the people from your country.

9. If an American who did not speak your native language fluently spent a year as a student in your country, how easily do you think he could adjust? What difficulties might he have?

VIII

LISTENING EXERCISES

I. Libraries

Chapter 1. Public and Private Libraries

Dictation 1

The public librarian has a number of different jobs. He must choose and catalog all books, periodicals, and other materials for the library collection. He must know the community that uses the library. He serves all kinds of people—those who use the library for pleasure and those who use it for research.

Dictation 2

The Educational Research Information Center, known as ERIC, is a government program that collects and publishes reference materials on research and developments in such different fields of education as library science, teaching English, and teaching foreign languages.

Listening Comprehension

Libraries of Tomorrow

Adapted from "Librarianship," *The Encyclopedia of Careers,* New York, Doubleday, 1972, I, 372.

What important change can we expect to see in libraries during the next several years? There will be a great increase in the number of publications which a library must have for research and for general circulation. In 1920 there were about 5000 books published in the United States. In the early 1970s more than 30,000 books and over 50,000 periodicals were published each year.

Libraries will also have to expand their collections to include important publications from all parts of the world. Because no single library can store and circulate so many publications, libraries must work together. Recently several large research libraries set up a program that provides that one copy of every important book published in any of 137 countries must be bought by at least one of these libraries. The Library of Congress records the location of the book and each library in the plan is informed where the book is kept. Then all the libraries can arrange to use it.

Comprehension Questions

1. What is the important change that we can expect to see in libraries in the next several years?
2. How many books were published in the United States in 1920?
3. Approximately how many more books were published annually in the early 1970s than were published in 1920?
4. Approximately how many periodicals were published in 1972?
5. Several large research libraries recently set up a plan to include foreign publications in their collections. From how many countries are books bought under this plan?
6. How does the plan work?

Chapter 2. How to Use a Library

Dictation 1

The main card catalog is a bibliography of the library collection. It is organized into three classifications: subject, author, and title.

Dictation 2

From the Regulations of the Mugar Library, Boston University

Periodicals may be used only in the library. They do not circulate outside the library. Bound volumes are kept in the closed stacks and may be requested by filling out a call slip.

Special Assignment

Dictation 2 is taken from the regulations of the Boston University Library. Find out what rules and regulations apply in your library. Are there restrictions on eating? smoking? You may have to talk to the librarian at the information desk to find out.

Listening Comprehension 1

Most students who do library research take notes on three-by-five cards on which they record important facts and information. (Three-by-five cards are three inches wide and five inches long.) The students note the source of each item: author, title, publication data, and call number, in case they need to look up the book again.

Comprehension Questions

1. What are three-by-five cards? How are they used in library research?
2. What information should be recorded on these cards?

Listening Comprehension 2

The following new word is introduced in this exercise: **decimal,** a dot or point used to divide a whole number from parts of a number.

EXAMPLE   14.7

Melville Dewey (1851–1931)

Melville Dewey established the Dewey Decimal System for library book cataloging. Many libraries in the United States use this method to determine the call number of each volume in the library collection. Dewey used numbers from 000 to 999 to cover such general categories of knowledge as history, literature, and geography. These numbers are made more specific by use of decimal points and supplemented with letters of the alphabet to indicate classification and subclassification.

Dewey played an important part in the early days of library organization. In 1883, while still a young man, he established the first school for librarians at Columbia University. He also introduced the first traveling, or mobile, libraries to bring books to rural communities. He is undoubtedly more responsible than any other individual for the development of library science in this country.

Comprehension Questions

1. What is the official name of one system used to determine library book call numbers?
2. How is that system organized?
3. How old was Dewey when he established the first school for librarians? Where was it located?
4. What other important contribution did Dewey make to library development in the United States?

II. The American Government

Chapter 3. The Constitution and the Presidency

Dictation

The President is the most important figure in the United States government. The Constitution gives him the authority to carry out specific duties. He and the Vice-President are the only elected officials who represent all the people.

Listening Comprehension 1

The following word is introduced in this exercise: **address,** to indicate someone's special official position or title. **Address** is also used here in its more familiar meaning: to write information on an envelope to assure delivery to the correct person.

A letter sent to the chief executive is addressed, "The President, The White House." One of the earliest debates in the legislature concerned the title of the chief executive. Some legislators recommended that he be addressed, "His Highness, the President of the United States of America and Protector of Their Liberties," but it was decided to follow the Constitution, which specifically refers to him as "The President of the United States." Over the years the President has never had an official title. A governor is addressed as "Your Excellency," a judge as "Your Honor," but the chief executive is simply "Mr. President."

Comprehension Questions

1. How is a letter to the President addressed?
2. What title did some legislators propose?
3. How is a governor addressed? a judge?
4. What is the official title of the President?
5. How do news reporters address the President when they ask questions at a news conference?

Listening Comprehension 2

The following new word is introduced in this exercise: **impeachment,** a procedure in which a government official is brought to trial for high crimes or improper acts.

The Constitution provides that the President of the United States may be removed from office if he is impeached and found guilty of high crimes or other improper acts. Indeed, impeachment is the *only* way in which the President can legally be removed from office. If the majority of the members of the lower house of the legislature, the House of Representatives, find reason to believe that the President is guilty of misconduct, they vote to refer the matter to the Senate, which is the upper house of the legislature. The Senate then tries the President for the crimes or improper acts reported by the House. During the trial the Senate is presided over by the Chief Justice of the Supreme Court, which is the highest court of the land. If two-thirds of the Senate votes that the President is guilty, he is removed from office. It is important to note that impeachment is designed only to remove an unfit official from his office. There is no punishment involved.

Impeachment proceedings may be brought against other government officials in addition to the President. Throughout United States history there have been impeachments of one Senator, a member of the cabinet, and several federal judges. Of these, only three—all of them judges—were found guilty. In 1868 President Andrew Johnson was impeached on charges of improper use of presidential power. The Senate vote was one short of the necessary two-thirds, and he was not removed from office. Thereafter, for more than one hundred years, no president faced impeachment until proceedings were begun in 1974 against Richard Nixon, who resigned before the House voted.

Comprehension Questions

1. How can the President be removed from office? Describe the procedures in the House of Representatives and the Senate.
2. What punishment is involved if the President is impeached and found guilty?
3. What President was impeached? When? What was the Senate vote on his case?
4. What other government officials have been impeached?
5. How many have been found guilty?

Chapter 4. The Legislature

Dictation

Many bills never become laws. Often congressional committees do not report them. Other bills are defeated by a majority of votes in either house of Congress. Still others may be vetoed by the President.

Listening Comprehension

Adapted from the *New York Times,* August 10, 1972, p. 19.[1] (Christmas, which occurs on December 25, is a national holiday.)

A Pocket Veto

In 1972 Senator Edward Kennedy, testing a President's pocket veto powers, asked a United States court to order the Nixon administration to carry out a $225 million legislative program to educate doctors. Congress had passed this medical education act in 1970 and had sent it to the President for approval. But President Nixon had used a pocket veto to kill the bill. The veto had become effective on December 24, 1970 while Congress was on a four-day Christmas holiday.

The Senator claimed Mr. Nixon's veto was an unconstitutional attempt to avoid a congressional vote which would have overridden a regular veto. A two-thirds vote in each house is necessary to override a regular veto. The Senator said he was sure the veto would have been defeated because the bill had received such strong support in both houses. It had been approved 64 to 1 by the Senate and 346 to 2 by the House.

A pocket veto may be used if Congress adjourns within ten days after the President receives a bill from Congress. If the President does not sign the bill within that ten-day period, the bill dies. But the Constitution is not clear about whether a short holiday represents an adjournment. The issue is whether a President may properly use the pocket veto authority when Congress is out of session for only a few days.

Comprehension Questions

1. What kind of bill was killed by President Nixon's pocket veto?
2. When did the veto become effective?
3. Who raised the legal question?
4. a. Did Senator Kennedy think Congress would have defeated a regular veto?
   b. What size vote is necessary to override a presidential veto?
   c. What were the original votes for and against this bill in the Senate? in the House?
5. What constitutional issue was raised in the court action?

Chapter 5. The Judicial Branch

Dictation

Judicial review of legislative and executive actions is within the jurisdiction of the Supreme Court. This court may declare any of these actions unconstitutional and, therefore, invalid.

1. © 1972 by The New York Times Company. Reprinted by permission.

Listening Comprehension

Adapted from the *New York Times,* June 20, 1972, p. 1.[2] The following new word is introduced in this exercise: **to wiretap,** to use electronic listening devices or equipment in order to listen to private conversations, especially telephone conversations.

> WASHINGTON, JUNE 19. The Supreme Court declared unconstitutional today the federal government's use of wiretapping without court approval. The Court rejected the Nixon Administration's position that the President's authority gives the government the constitutional power to wiretap without court permission.
>
> The Court declared that free speech and other civil liberties under the Bill of Rights cannot properly be guaranteed if wiretapping is carried out entirely under the jurisdiction of the executive branch and without court approval.

Comprehension Questions

1. When was this Supreme Court decision announced?
2. Which branch of government was limited by the decision?
3. Who was President at the time?
4. On what part of the Constitution did the Court base its decision?
5. How does this decision illustrate judicial review of actions by the executive branch?

2. © 1972 by The New York Times Company. Reprinted by permission.

III. The News Media

Chapter 6. Newspapers

Dictation

The American Association of Newspaper Editors is an organization of the editors of most of the newspapers published in the United States. They take the position that there must be a sharp division between editorials and news reports.

Listening Comprehension 1

The typical daily newspaper publishes its most important stories on the first page. Each article is briefly summarized in short headlines. The leading story appears in the far right-hand column, and the next most important article is printed in the first column on the left.

The names of the publisher and editors are usually listed on the editorial page. Responsible editors make a careful effort to separate fact from opinion and to avoid sensational presentation of the news. Facts appear in the news accounts. Opinions appear in the editorials and special columns.

Comprehension Questions

1. Where do the two most important news stories appear in the typical daily paper?
2. How are news stories summarized?
3. Whose names appear on the editorial page?
4. Where do the personal opinions of editors and columnists appear?

Listening Comprehension 2

Journalism Schools

There is no general agreement on the best method of training journalists. Some people believe that a reporter should get his education on the job—to learn to report by actually reporting. Others believe that special academic instruction is necessary preparation.

Today almost fifty colleges and universities offer professional training in journalism. These schools are an important source of the writers and editors of today's newspapers and magazines. Although most instruction in journalism takes place at the undergraduate level, there are graduate programs in many universities as well.

The first regular four-year program in journalism was offered by the University of Illinois in 1904. At about the same time Joseph Pulitzer, the famous newspaper publisher, gave $2 million to Columbia University to establish a school of journalism. Courses emphasized training in writing methods—reporting and editing—and also included instruction in newspaper management and various aspects of advertising.

In the past several years many new courses have reflected the complicated world about which journalists must write. Today journalism students combine their study of writing and research with work in the arts, economics, sociology, and politics. Many schools offer courses in such fields as government relations and the press, problems of the press and free speech, and theories of communication and public opinion. A good reporter must have wide knowledge in many areas in order to present the news accurately.

Comprehension Questions

1. What is the best method of training journalists?
2. How many colleges and universities offer professional training in journalism?
3. What two universities established the first regular journalism programs?
4. Describe the programs of the first journalism schools.
5. What kinds of courses have been added in recent years?
6. Why is it important for a journalist to have wide knowledge in many areas?

Chapter 7. The News Media Before Television

Dictation 1

Most newspapers publish domestic and foreign news and special stories of local interest. They also include articles of analysis and comment by well-known columnists.

Listening Comprehension 1

Vocabulary Quiz

Broadcasting stations are licensed by the Federal Communications Commission to serve **the public interest.** They are permitted to **compete** with each other for profit. Over the years broadcasting has become **commercialized** and **competitive.** Advertising occupies a large amount of broadcasting time. Today **local** advertising accounts for more than half the income of radio stations. Nationally **sponsored programs,** on the other hand, account for over 90 percent of TV income.

See comprehension questions on page 88.

Listening Comprehension 2

The following new term is introduced in this exercise: **Black Panthers,** a controversial, militant organization of young urban Blacks.

The Caldwell Decision

Several years ago some members of the Black Panthers were on trial. During the trial a *New York Times* reporter, Earl Caldwell, wrote several articles containing information that the judge decided was related to the trial. He ordered Caldwell to give the court the names of the people who had supplied the information to the reporter, as well as his notes. Caldwell refused. He claimed that the judge was violating the Constitutional guarantee of freedom of the press. The case was taken to the Supreme Court.

In June, 1972 the majority of the justices of the Supreme Court ruled that a reporter must give up his notes and the sources of his news if certain federal courts request this information in connection with a criminal law case. If the reporter refuses, he can be sent to jail.

One of the justices who opposed the decision charged that it violated the first amendment of the Constitution. He also said that the decision would interfere with the function of the press to investigate events and inform the people about what is going on. He stated that many persons would not give information to a reporter if they thought their names might be made public.

The majority of the members of the Court thought newsmen should be required to answer questions which were related to a criminal investigation. They stated that it was more clearly in the public interest to reduce crime than to permit news stories about crime.

Since this decision, several reporters have gone to jail because they refused to supply information requested by the courts.

Comprehension Questions

1. What did Caldwell refuse to do?
2. What was his reason?
3. a. What was the Supreme Court decision in the Caldwell case?
   b. Was the decision unanimous?
4. One of the judges who opposed the decision gave several reasons for his opposition. What were they?
5. What have several reporters done since the decision was made?

Chapter 8. Television, Radio, and the Press

Dictation 1

The Federal Communications Commission is forbidden by law to censor radio and television programs. Although the FCC cannot set program standards, it requires licensed stations to serve the "tastes, needs, and desires" of their communities.

Dictation 2

Some people believe that government-sponsored television would improve the quality of TV programs. Others fear that this might bring official censorship, which would affect the traditional freedom of the mass media.

Listening Comprehension

Adapted from an article by Nicholas Johnson,[1] Federal Communications Commissioner, "What Do We Do About Television?" *Saturday Review,* July 11, 1970, p. 14.

Television is the greatest communication medium ever designed and operated by man. It sends into the human brain an unending amount of opinions and information and sets moral and artistic standards for all of us. Every minute of a television program teaches us something. It is never a neutral influence. For example, how and when public issues are handled depends in large part on how they are treated by the television networks in entertainment as well as news and public affairs programing.

What the American people think about government and politics in general, as well as a favorite candidate in particular, is largely influenced by television.

Unfortunately commercial television seldom contributes anything of value to our lives. Many Americans express a deep hostility toward television because they know most TV programs are of poor quality and that sometimes these programs are even harmful.

The question is: how can television be improved? There are many things the ordinary viewer can do. For example, he can complain to his local station about offensive advertising. He can organize citizens' groups to urge local stations to improve their programing and to urge the FCC to review its licensing procedures. In addition, these groups should propose regular analyses of specific TV commercials and programs by educators, psychologists, doctors, etc. to determine the influence of these programs on children and adults. Television can be our most exciting medium if we just think about ways to improve it.

---

1. Mr. Johnson is also the author of *How to Talk Back to Your Television Set,* Boston, Atlantic-Little Brown, 1970, and *Test Pattern for Living,* New York, Bantam, 1972.

Comprehension Questions

1. This article was written by a man named Nicholas Johnson. What was his official position?
2. Commissioner Johnson mentions some specific attitudes that are influenced by television. What are they?
3. What is his opinion of commercial television?
4. According to Commissioner Johnson, why are many Americans hostile toward television?
5. He proposes several ways in which viewers can improve television. What are they?

IV. The Arts

Chapter 9. American Painting

Dictation

What is abstract art? Each artist will answer that question differently. That is because abstract art is alive. It seems to change, move, and grow. Abstract art is not a precise representation of nature. It reflects the artist's feelings about nature and his understanding of it.

> Adapted from an essay by Stuart Davis, twentieth-century American painter, *Readings in American Art Since 1900*, edited by Barbara Rose, New York, Praeger, 1966 pp. 123–124

Listening Comprehension 1

Jackson Pollock (1912–1956)

Jackson Pollock was one of the most important American artists of the mid-twentieth century. He introduced new techniques and a new approach to abstract painting. His work was the result of improvisation rather than planning. He often laid his canvases on the floor and with quick movements of his wrist and arm, he dropped paint. His brush seldom touched the canvas. He said he liked this technique because he could work on the canvas from four sides and feel that he was inside his painting.

Comprehension Questions

1. Why was Pollock an important American painter of the mid-twentieth century?
2. How did Pollock often paint?
3. Why did he prefer that method?
4. How old was Pollock when he died?

Listening Comprehension 2

The following new words are introduced in this exercise: **tepees,** cone-shaped tents of skins used as houses by some North American

Indians, and **sand,** very fine grains of rock found along the edge of the ocean and in deserts.

Painting by American Indians

As the American Indian did not have a written language, art was very important. Painting was used to tell stories and to record personal experiences; above all, it was religious.

The Indians used dried animal skins for their canvases. These painted skins were made into clothing, and they also served as the material from which tepees were built.

Different colors had special meanings. For example, among some Indians red represented the east, black the south, yellow the west, and blue the north. Realistic pictures portrayed people, animals, and birds. Other designs were completely abstract and expressed religious beliefs.

One of the most unusual examples of Indian art was the sand-painting by Indians in the southwest region of the United States. Religious artists created pictures on the ground by an unusual technique. They let colored sand run through their fingers, and, with controlled, precise hand movements, they made realistic figures, as well as abstract designs. Time was an important part of the sand-painting process. The paintings were supposed to be begun, finished, used for a religious ceremony, and destroyed within twelve hours. Therefore it is difficult to find examples of this art today.

Different kinds of historical American Indian art can be seen in museums throughout the United States. The most complete collection is in the Museum of the American Indian in New York City. The U.S. Bureau of Indian Affairs in Washington has lists of shops and galleries where contemporary Indian art can be seen and bought.

Comprehension Questions

1. In what different ways did American Indians use painting?
2. What served as canvases? How were these canvases used?
3. What did certain colors represent? Were all Indian paintings abstract?
4. Where did sand painting occur?
5. a. How was sand painting done?
   b. Why is it difficult to find examples of sand painting today?
6. Where can you see examples of historical Indian art? contemporary Indian art?

Chapter 10. American Theater

Dictation 1

There is much discussion in the United States today about the need for the government to subsidize the theater. New playwrights often find it difficult to get their writing produced, and many actors suffer from long periods without work. But some people fear that government sponsorship would bring censorship or some kind of control.

Dictation 2

During the depression of the 1930s the federal government financed many theater productions in order to provide work for actors and playwrights. More than 30 million people attended these subsidized performances of dramas, musicals, and special children's shows.

Listening Comprehension 1

The following new words are introduced in this exercise: **transistor,** an electronic device used in radio sets and the like, **earphone,** a device worn over the ear through which sounds are received, **microphone,** an instrument into which a person talks, which carries his voice to the earphone.

Understanding Foreign Plays

In recent years many foreign plays have been performed for American audiences in the language of traveling theater groups. Naturally, this practice has created a serious production problem. How can American theatergoers understand plays in Japanese, French, Polish, Russian, or Thai? A play depends on words to carry its meaning. If the theater does not bring meaning to its audience, it has not succeeded.

There have been several different experiments with ways to solve this language problem. Possibly the most successful is simultaneous translation while the play is being performed. The translator sits in the balcony, watches the peformance, and simultaneously translates it into a microphone. Members of the audience, wearing earphones, hear his voice by means of tiny transistor receivers. This method is not completely satisfactory. It is difficult to "see" one language with your eyes and "hear" a different one with your ears. In addition, the translator often gives his own interpretation of the play, which may be different from what the playwright or the actors intend. However, until theatergoers learn all languages, transistor translations are probably the best method that can be developed.

Comprehension Questions

1. This article is about the problem of language comprehension. Why is it a serious theater problem?
2. What method has been developed to meet the situation?
3. How well does it work?

Listening Comprehension 2

When you go to a commercial theater, you are given a program at no cost. It is a small pamphlet that contains different kinds of information about the play. It lists the members of the cast, usually in the order in which they appear on the stage. It also contains brief biographies of the main actors and actresses and mentions other plays in which they have appeared. In addition, there is usually a short biography of the playwright. The program also explains where and when the action of the play takes place.

Some programs include general articles on the theater, as well as advertisements of plays that are being performed in other local theaters.

Comprehension Questions

1. What is a theater program? How much does it cost?
2. What information does it contain about the cast? the playwright?
3. What other information may it contain?

Chapter 11. A History of American Architecture

Dictation 1

An architect is always having to make some adjustments between the facts of money, the requirements of function, and his own aesthetic standards.

> Ian McCallum, contemporary architect, in *Architecture in America: A Battle of Styles,* William A. Coles and Henry Hope Reed, Jr. (eds.), New York, Appleton, 1961, p. 282

Dictation 2

A building should look on the exterior the way it actually is in the interior. Perhaps this is the major difference between modern architecture and the architecture of other periods.

> Adapted from a statement by Philip Johnson, contemporary architect, in Seldman Rodman, *Conversations with Artists,* New York, Devin-Adair, 1957, p. 65

Listening Comprehension

Architects are professional designers of buildings. Often they specialize in specific kinds of architecture, such as residential, commercial, industrial, educational, or governmental. As many building projects involve whole communities, new professions are developing in the fields of urban and regional planning. These professions are closely related to architecture.

The first college course in architecture in the United States was established at the Massachusetts Institute of Technology in 1866. Today there are approximately sixty schools of architecture that combine the study of liberal arts with technical courses. A bachelor's degree in architecture usually requires five years of study. Graduate programs are also available at many universities. After an architectural student has completed his university preparation, he must spend three years working in an architect's office. Then he must pass a national examination in order to obtain his architect's license.

Comprehension Questions

1. a. What are some specific fields of architecture?
   b. Name two new professions that are closely related to these fields.
2. Where and when was the first college course in architecture established in the United States?
3. About how many schools of architecture are there today?
4. How many years does it usually take to earn a bachelor's degree in architecture?
5. In addition to university training, what must an architect do in order to obtain his architect's license?

Chapter 12. Modern American Architecture

Dictation 1

Architecture is the most available and public of the arts. It surrounds us in our daily lives, houses the complex and diverse functions of our civilization, and symbolizes the extent to which man can manage his natural environment.

Adapted from Coles and Reed, *op. cit.*, p. viii

Dictation 2

Architectural style means a type or manner of architecture, characterized by distinct patterns of structure or decoration and a special form of skilled construction. What is called the Modern Style dominates contemporary building. This style emphasizes function with certain innovations in construction techniques, design, and materials.

Ibid., p. vii

Dictation 3

Modern technology has had a great influence on our architecture. Without it we would never have had the towering skyscraper or buildings constructed out of prefabricated, mass-produced parts. New materials offer us opportunities for innovation of which we have not yet taken full advantage.

Adapted from Eero Saarinen, *ibid.*, p. 123

Listening Comprehension 1

The following new word is introduced in this exercise: **client,** one who receives professional services (as from an architect or a lawyer).

Adapted from the *New York Times,* January 21, 1973, Section 6, p. 6.[1]

Architects use the word "program" to describe what clients tell them they need in a house. From this information architects plan the interior and the exterior to produce an environment designed to meet that family's way of living—its life style. For example, one family told the architectural company which was to build their summer house by the ocean, that they were an active family, with three children who liked sports, especially swimming. They often entertained weekend guests, both children and adults. They needed a room for a maid. And the parents needed to be alone occasionally; they wanted a place where they could be by themselves.

The architect who designed the house said, "It was a complex program, yet the house is remarkably simple, a rectangle that honestly expresses the program." The house has few windows on the entrance side. This gives a sense of privacy. The back is a wall of windows opening on an outdoor place for dining, a swimming pool and a view of the ocean. The interior is modern. Some of the furniture, such as beds and chests, is built into the rooms. The colors are clear and bright.

Comprehension Questions

1. What is an architectural program?
2. How do architects use this information?
3. Describe the life style of the clients in this article.
4. What was the architect's opinion of the program?
5. Describe the house that was built.

Listening Comprehension 2

The following new words are introduced in this exercise: **Secretariat,** the building where United Nations officials and staff have their offices, and **marble,** a hard stone used in sculpture and architecture.

The Secretariat of the United Nations is a tall, thin building rising directly from the ground for thirty-nine stories. The narrow end-walls are covered with grayish-white marble. The two other sides, facing the East River on one side and New York's skyscrapers on the other, are entirely covered by green-colored glass. The building is like a great vertical mirror in a white marble frame.

As there were such diverse styles of architecture existing in the fifty-nine nations of the United Nations at the time the Secretariat was to be constructed, an international group of expert architects and engineers from many countries designed the building together in 1946. They represented Australia, Belgium, Brazil, Canada, China, Czecho-

1. © 1973 by The New York Times Company. Reprinted by permission.

slovakia, France, Greece, Poland, Sweden, the Soviet Union, the United States, the United Kingdom, Uruguay, and Yugoslavia.

The building's simple, rectangular shape is supposed to symbolize unity and peace among nations.

Comprehension Questions

1. In what city is the Secretariat located?
2. How tall is it?
3. What are the views from two sides?
4. Why does the text describe the building as a great vertical mirror in a white marble frame?
5. When was the building designed?
6. How many countries were UN members at that time?
7. Name at least six countries that were represented in the group that designed the building.
8. What is the building supposed to symbolize?

V. Education and the Family

Chapter 13. The School Years

Sentences for Dictation

1. By 1860 a majority of states had elementary public schools, and secondary schools were beginning to appear. At least half of all school-age children were getting some public school education.
2. Public education is expected to offer equality of educational opportunity, including free tuition and free books, to everyone.
3. In 1889 twenty-six states had compulsory school-attendance laws.
4. American public schools educate children of all social, economic, and religious backgrounds.
5. In colonial times only poor children attended public schools. In the years following the Revolution city people who could pay the tuition continued to send their children to private schools; usually these were church schools.
6. Public schools introduced a secular approach to education.
7. Many people believe that high schools must change their curricula to meet the needs of today's industrial society. They believe that there should be more emphasis on practical vocational training programs for students who plan to go to work after high school.

Listening Comprehension

Financing Schools

A serious problem in American schools is the inequality of primary and secondary school financing. Approximately 40 percent of the money for schools comes from state taxes. Seven percent comes from the federal government. The remaining 53 percent comes from taxes in local school districts. Because each school district spends the money it raises from local taxes on its own schools, rich communities can spend much more on their schools than poor communities in the same state can. For example, in 1973 one small town in Texas could afford only $36 per pupil annually. A well-to-do nearby district spent $412 per pupil. In Massachusetts the richest school district spent more than ten times as much money per pupil than the poorest school district in the same state did. In other states the differences in expenditures by school districts were even greater.

Many citizens are deeply concerned about this inequality in school financing. They believe that schools in poor areas cannot offer children education that is as good as the education offered to children in rich communities. Poor school districts cannot afford adequate school construction and maintenance, school facilities such as science laboratories, and they often cannot pay high salaries to their teachers. These citizens believe that the method of school financing must be changed in order to offer all children equal educational opportunities.

Because education is the responsibility of each state, many people believe that each state must pass a law to change the method of financing its schools. In the early 1970s a committee appointed by the President studied the situation and recommended that each state take over the collection of all educational taxes from individual school districts. Then all money for education should be distributed equally to local school boards. This would mean that each school within the state would receive the same amount of money per pupil. Although there would still be differences in the expenditures by each of the fifty states for the education of each student, at least there would be equal educational opportunities for students within the same state.

Comprehension Questions

1. What problem does this article describe?
2. What percentage of the money for schools comes from the states? the federal government? local school districts?
3. Give two examples of unequal expenditures for school children.
4. How are such differences reflected in the quality of education offered by schools in poor districts and by schools in rich communities?
5. a. What recommendation was recently made by a committee that had been appointed by the President?
   b. How would this recommendation affect school expenditures for each student in the United States? for each student within the same state?

Chapter 14. Colleges and Universities

Dictation 1

During the twenty-five years between 1947 and 1972 the number of college students rose from approximately 2.5 million to more than 8 million. Graduate school enrollment more than tripled from about 225,000 to over 900,000, and the number of doctorates awarded annually increased from 4,000 to over 30,000.

Dictation 2

American institutions of higher learning cover a broad range from community and junior colleges and technical institutes to small private colleges and enormous state and private universities.

Dictation 3

Across the country this year nearly 1.5 million students will take the Scholastic Aptitude Test and a variety of achievement tests in subjects ranging from English to physics. The results of the examinations will be sent to the colleges and universities to which the students have applied for admission.

Listening Comprehension

The following new names are introduced in this exercise: **Mount Holyoke,** a private women's college in Massachusetts; **Oberlin,** a private coeducational college in Ohio; and the **University of Iowa,** a coeducational state university.

Harvard, the first American college, was founded in 1636 to train religious leaders. During the years before the American Revolution several other institutions of higher learning were founded by church groups, and during the first half of the nineteenth century many more religious colleges and universities were established. Today more than half of all private colleges have some kind of church connection, but very few of these schools are now devoted to religious education. Students and faculty usually come from many different religious groups, and large numbers belong to no religious group at all.

In the first half of the nineteenth century several states established publicly financed colleges and universities, and many secular private colleges were also founded. For the first time serious attention was given to the higher education of women. The first coeducational college program was established at Oberlin in 1833, and in 1837 the first women's college, Mount Holyoke, was founded. Ten years later the University of Iowa became the first state university to accept women. By 1860 women were attending many state universities, as well as private schools.

During the second half of the nineteenth century the federal government encouraged public higher education by giving large amounts of land to the states. Money from these land grants was used to found new public institutions or to improve existing state colleges and universities. During this period there was also a great increase in the number of privately endowed schools.

The rise of the university as we know it today was gradual rather than sudden. The first Ph.D. was awarded in 1861, and in the years that followed several other important changes in the organization of American universities took place. Universities instituted systems that did away with rigid curricula and permitted students to select the subjects that they wanted to study. Separate departments were made responsible for the teaching of different disciplines such as biology, history, and philosophy. In the 1890s medicine and law became serious subjects of graduate study.

Probably the most dramatic development in recent years has been the steady increase in graduate student enrollment. In 1960 approximately 350,000 students attended graduate and professional schools. By 1970 this number had more than doubled to almost 900,000 students.

Comprehension Questions

1. What was the first American college? When was it founded?
2. a. What proportion of private colleges have church connections?
   b. How important are those connections in terms of faculty and curricula?
3. a. When was the first coeducational college program established?
   b. When were women first admitted to a state university?
4. What were federal land grants? How were they used?
5. How long ago was the first Ph.D. awarded?
6. What important changes at universities took place in the last part of the nineteenth century?
7. How much did graduate school enrollment increase between 1960 and 1970?

Chapter 15. The Role of the Government: Issues and Problems in Education Today

Dictation 1

More than 140,000 foreign students from 176 countries are currently studying at American colleges and universities. Of these students, about three-fourths are men. The most popular disciplines among both graduates and undergraduates are engineering, physical sciences, literature, language, and history.

Dictation 2

Adapted from the *New York Times,* April 17, 1973, p. 20.[1]
A new report on the financial condition of institutions of higher education finds that colleges and universities are reaching a balance between rapidly rising costs and slowly growing incomes. They are saving money by reducing building maintenance, not increasing faculty salaries, expanding enrollments, and cutting down the number of teachers.

Listening Comprehension

Adapted from an editorial in the *New York Times,* April 17, 1973, p. 38.[2]

The Reading Question

A 25-man committee has been set up to study why so many children in New York City cannot read and what can be done about this situation. These questions asked about New York schoolchildren are troubling cities across the country.

The New York City committee plans to examine the educational programs in "low achievement" schools. The editors of this newspaper hope that the committee will not find that the entire cause of the children's poor records is their "deprived" or "disadvantaged" background; the committee's emphasis should be on efforts to find programs that have proved successful. The committee must look for classrooms in inner-city schools where some children do learn to read. The problem is to locate teachers, programs, attitudes, and other factors responsible for.a student's satisfactory achievement despite the handicap of a poor home situation.

Comprehension Questions

1. In what city will the reading question be studied?
2. Who will make the study? in what kind of schools?
3. What do the editors think the committee should emphasize?
4. Specifically what do the editors think the committee should look for?

Chapter 16. The Family

Sentences for Dictation

1. Members of a nuclear family live together in one household. After the children grow up, fall in love, and get married, they usually keep in touch with each other and with their parents.
2. Casual dating is a common social pattern among young people.
3. The birth rate in the United States has been steadily declining. In 1955 there were 25 births for every 1000 people. In 1972 the rate was 15.6.

Listening Comprehension

Some influences that have shaped family life in the United States have been the physical environment, the slave system, industrial development, modern science, immigration, and the rapid growth of the cities.

Frontier life in early days encouraged individualism and independence. Early courtship and marriage and large families were encouraged, in order to provide labor on the farms. The father was the head of the household, and he applied strict discipline.

In the second half of the nineteenth century industrialization brought changes to the American family. Young people became wage earners at an early age. Factory employment also brought the opportunity for economic independence to women. This development was followed by their political and social freedom.

The development of black families followed a different pattern. The ancestors of most American Blacks were slaves. In the slave economy that existed in the South for more than 200 years, the father and mother were sometimes sold to different owners. It was often impossible for the parents to keep in touch with each other. The children remained with the mother, and she became the strong central figure around whom family relationships were built. This pattern of the mother centered family continued after the slaves were liberated in the 1860s. In the years following liberation many Blacks moved to the cities, looking for employment. Generally it was easier for the women to find jobs than it was for the men. Both were unskilled, but women could work as domestic, or household, helpers. In this way the woman often became the main source of financial support of the family. The men were often unemployed, and marriages frequently broke up.

High unemployment rates for men, working mothers, and broken marriages continue to be the pattern among a large number of poor black families. Black family incomes are 40 percent lower than the incomes of white families. The unemployment rate for black men is approximately double that for whites, and almost one-third of all black families are headed by women.

Statistics indicate, however, that when black families enter the middle- and upper-income levels of American life, the patterns that emerge are similar to those of white families with the same income. The father is the main source of financial support, although the black mother works in order to supplement the family income more often than the white mother of the same economic group. One interesting difference between black and white families of all economic levels is the closeness of kinship ties. Kinship relations seem to be considerably stronger among Blacks than among whites, and black families take relatives, both children and older people, into their households more frequently than white families do.

Comprehension Questions

1. What are some of the influences that have affected the development of American family life?
2. What were some of the characteristics of frontier family life?
3. How did the factory system affect the position of women?
4. Why was the black mother the central family figure in the slave economy? Why did she often remain the central figure after the end of slavery? What proportion of black families are headed by women?
5. Compare the family patterns of Blacks and whites of middle- and upper-income levels.
6. What point does the text make about the difference in kinship ties among black and white families?

VI. American Political Parties and the Election Process

Chapter 17. Political Parties

Dictation

A nation has a two-party system if there are only two major parties that regularly run candidates for public office at most levels. Even if minor parties or third parties occasionally win some votes in a national campaign, we still refer to a two-party system.

Listening Comprehension

Voting in the United States

The percentage of eligible voters who took part in presidential elections gradually increased in the years between 1920 and 1968. In 1920, 43.5 percent of all eligible voters cast their votes for presidential candidates. In 1968, 61.8 percent voted. In 1972, however, fewer than 55 percent of the 139.6 million eligible voters cast their ballots for a presidential candidate.

There was also a great deal of ticket splitting in the 1972 election. Almost one-third of the Democrats voted for Mr. Nixon, the Republican candidate, who won approximately 61 percent of all the votes and a majority of votes in 49 states. In more than half these states, however, the voters chose Democratic candidates for Congress. As a result, although the Republican presidential candidate won a great victory, Democrats won the majority of seats in the House and Senate.

Because of this ticket splitting, some political observers described the 1972 election as a "nonparty" election. Many people believe that party structure is becoming weak and that ticket splitting will increase. They believe that although most voters may continue to describe themselves as Democrats or Republicans, they will actually vote as independents.

Comprehension Questions

1. In terms of the percentage of eligible voters who vote in presidential elections, how was the 1972 election different from the election in 1968? Give specific voting percentages.
2. How many people could have voted in 1972?
3. What percentage of the votes did Mr. Nixon win in 1972?
4. Give an example of ticket splitting in 1972.
5. How do some political observers describe the 1972 election? Why do they think it was a "nonparty" election?
6. How do some people think Americans will vote in the future?

Chapter 18. The Election Process

Dictation

There is much controversy over election contributions and costs. In 1972 more than $400 million was spent in campaigns for offices at all levels of government. Although many grass-roots voters contributed small amounts, most of the money came from a very small percentage of all eligible voters.

Listening Comprehension 1

What the Platform Really Means

The platform should not be taken too seriously as a guide to what a presidential candidate would do if he won the election. A new President's program depends on his personal philosophy, popular reactions to his election campaign, his relations with Congress, and the events of history—and very little on the planks of the platform.

Although the platform does not tell us much about what a new President may do, it tells us a lot about what the people want. The 1972 Democratic platform, for example, reflected the popular feeling that there was something wrong with some American institutions, such as the tax system and the election process, and that more was needed than new faces in political office.

Comprehension Questions

1. According to this article, what determines the program of a new President?
2. How important is the platform?
3. What specific platform is mentioned?
4. What popular attitudes did it reflect?

Listening Comprehension 2

In July 1973 the Senate approved a bill called the Federal Elections Campaign Act of 1973. The bill was then sent to the House of Representatives for consideration and debate. Its purpose was to control and regulate contributions to election campaigns and also to regulate the use of these contributions. The bill limited the amount of money that could be given to any candidate for federal office by a single contributor. No one was permitted to give a candidate more than $3000 for a primary election campaign and more than $3000 for a general campaign. This would have been a great change from other years. Some candidates in previous campaigns—President Nixon in 1972, for example—received single contributions of $1 million or more and many other gifts of $100,000 and more. The bill also provided that all contributions amounting to more than $100 had to be publicly reported, with the name, address, and occupation of the contributor.

In addition, the bill limited the amount of money a candidate could spend in a campaign for the presidency, the Senate, or the House of Representatives.

Some opponents of the bill declared that the bill was not strong enough. They wanted to include legislation that would shorten the length of campaigns, change the process by which delegates are selected for national nominating conventions, and do away with the Electoral College. Other opponents found the bill too strong.

In the summer of 1974 the House voted for a version of the Campaign Act that lowered the level of campaign contributions to $1000 in a primary and $1000 in a general election. The House and Senate versions then went to conference. A compromise was worked out and became law. This law limits contributions and expenditures in all campaigns for national office and provides for some government financing of presidential campaigns.

Comprehension Questions

1. What was the name of the Senate bill described here?
2. What limits would the bill have set on the size of individual campaign contributions in a primary election? in a general election?
3. What would have been the requirements for contributions of more than $100?
4. What did the bill say about spending campaign funds?
5. Why did some people oppose the bill? What additional legislation did others want?
6. What is the current status of the Federal Elections Campaign Act?

Chapter 19. The Voters and the Political Process

Dictation

Adapted from *Ethnic Group Politics,* Harry Bailey and Ellis Katz (eds.), Columbus, Ohio, Charles Merrill Publishing Co., 1969, p. 126.

In southern communities where black voter registration has greatly increased, a new group of black politicians is appearing. They are such good campaigners that they can bargain with white politicians who want their support.

Listening Comprehension 1

Lobby is a word that was first used as a political term about 150 years ago. Representatives of interest groups used to stand in the lobbies (the halls outside meeting rooms) of national and state legislatures hoping to speak to the legislators in order to influence their votes. The word now refers to organized efforts to influence policy decisions of government officials.

Comprehension Questions

1. When was the word **lobby** first used as a political term?
2. Explain the origin of the word.
3. What is the current political meaning of **lobby?**

Listening Comprehension 2

Some interesting examples of the differences between American-English and British-English are found among words referring to government and politics. For example, in Great Britain a candidate **stands** for office; in the United States he **runs.** In Britain the Cabinet is composed of **ministers;** here the Cabinet is made up of **secretaries.** The British legislature is the **Parliament;** the United States legislative body is the **Congress.** In Britain the party out of power is the **opposition;** in this country we refer to the **minority party.** What Americans call a **vote** in Congress is called a **division** in the British legislature.

    Some American political words and concepts are not found in British-English at all; for example, **primary elections, straight ticket** and **split a ticket, plank,** and **platform.** Some American words such as **caucus** and **lobby** have been borrowed by the British and are now in general use in Great Britain.

Comprehension Questions

1. List some different British-English and American-English political words that mean the same thing.
2. Mention some American-English political words not found in Great Britain.
3. Name two political terms of American origin that are now used in Britain.

Bibliography

General Sources

Dictionaries

The Advanced Learner's Dictionary of Current English, 2nd ed., London, Oxford University Press, 1970.
The American Heritage Dictionary, Boston, Houghton Mifflin, 1971.
Webster's Third International Dictionary, Springfield, Mass., Merriam, 1966.

Newspapers

The *Boston Globe*
The *New York Times*

Other

Bartlett, John, *Familiar Quotations,* 14th ed., Emily M. Beck (ed.), Boston, Little, Brown, 1968.
International Encyclopedia of the Social Sciences, David Sills, (ed.), New York, Macmillan, 1968.
U.S. Bureau of the Census, *Statistical Abstract of the United States, 1972,* Washington, D.C., U.S. Government Printing Office, 1972.
U.S. Department of Labor, Bureau of Labor Statistics, *Handbook of Labor Statistics,* Washington, D.C., U.S. Government Printing Office, 1970.

Section I

Hessel, Alfred, *A History of Libraries,* Washington, D.C., Scarecrow Press, 1950.
Rose, Ernestine, *The Public Library in American Life,* New York, Columbia University Press, 1954.
Shores, Louis, *Origins of the American College Library,* Nashville, Peabody College Press, 1934.
The Public Library and the City, Ralph W. Conant (ed.), Cambridge, Mass., M.I.T. Press, 1965.

273

Section II

Carman, Harry J., and Harold C. Syrett, *A History of the American People,* New York, Knopf, 1955.

Johnson, C. O., D. M. Ogden, Jr., H. P. Castleberry, and T. Swanson, *American National Government,* New York, Crowell, 1970.

Schlesinger, Arthur M., *The Imperial Presidency,* Boston, Houghton Mifflin, 1973.

U.S. Congress, *Our American Government,* 92nd Congress, 1st session, House Document No. 92–31, Washington, D.C., U.S. Government Printing Office, 1971.

U.S. Department of Justice, *Our Government: Book 3,* Washington, D.C., U.S. Government Printing Office, 1971.

Section III

Barnouw, Eric, *The History of Broadcasting,* 3 vols., New York, Oxford University Press, 1966–1970.

Barnouw, Eric, *Mass Communication,* New York, Holt, Rinehart and Winston, 1965.

Mott, Frank L., *American Journalism,* New York, Macmillan, 1941.

Mott, Frank L., *The News in America,* Cambridge, Mass., Harvard University Press, 1952.

Siepman, Charles A., *Radio, Television and Society,* New York, Oxford University Press, 1950.

Section IV

Painting

Goodrich, Lloyd, *Art of the United States: 1670–1966,* New York, Praeger, 1966.

Larkin, Oliver, *Art and Life in America,* New York, Rinehart, 1949.

Pierson, William H., and Martha Davidson, *Arts of the United States,* New York, McGraw-Hill, 1960.

Readings in American Art Since 1900, Barbara Rose (ed.), New York, Praeger, 1968.

Rose, Barbara, *American Art Since 1900,* New York, Praeger, 1967.

Theater

Brockett, Oscar G., *The Theater,* New York, Holt, Rinehart and Winston, 1964.

Esslin, Martin, *The Theater of the Absurd,* New York, Doubleday, 1969.

Fuller, Edmund, *Pageant of the Theater,* New York, Crowell, 1965.

Patterson, Lindsay, *Black Theater,* New York, New American Library, 1967.

Theater in the Twentieth Century, Robert W. Corrigan (ed.), New York, Grove Press, 1963.

Toohey, John L., *A History of the Pulitzer Plays,* New York, Citadel Press, 1967.

Architecture

Larkin, Oliver, *Art and Life in America,* New York, Rinehart, 1949.

McCallum, Ian, *Architecture, U.S.A.,* New York, Reinhold, 1960.

Mumford, Lewis, *Roots of Contemporary Architecture,* New York, Grove Press, 1959.

Sullivan, Louis, *Autobiography of an Idea,* New York, Dover, 1924.

Whiffen, Marcus, *American Architecture Since 1780,* Cambridge, Mass., M.I.T. Press, 1969.

Section V

Education

Cremin, Laurence, *The Transformation of the School,* New York, Random House, 1964.

Encyclopedia of Education, L. C. Deighton (ed.), New York, Macmillan, 1971.

Lee, Gordon, C., *An Introduction to Education in Modern America,* New York, Holt, 1957.

Mayer, Martin, *The Schools,* New York, Doubleday, 1963.

On Equality of Educational Opportunity, Frederick Mosteller and Daniel P. Moynihan (eds.), New York, Random House, 1972.

Silberman, Charles, *Crisis in the Classroom,* New York, Random House, 1971.

The Family

The Family: Its Function and Destiny, Ruth N. Anshen (ed.), New York, Harper and Row, 1959.

Bell, N., and E. Vogel, *A Modern Introduction to the Family,* rev. ed., New York, Free Press, 1968.

Coles, Robert, *Children of Crisis,* 3 vols., Boston, Little, Brown, 1967–1973.

The Negro American, Talcott Parsons and Kenneth B. Clark (eds.), Boston, Beacon, 1966.

Reiss, Ira A., *The Family System in America,* New York, Holt, Rinehart and Winston, 1971.

Section VI

Campbell, A., P. Converse, W. Miller, and D. Stokes, *The American Voter,* New York, Wiley, 1964.

DeVries, Walter, and V. Lance Tarrance, *The Ticket Splitter: A New Force in American Politics,* Grand Rapids, Mich., Eerdmans, 1972.

Ethnic Group Politics, Harry A. Bailey and Ellis Katz (eds.), Columbus, Ohio, Merrill, 1969.

Johnson, C. O., D. M. Ogden, Jr., H. P. Castleberry, and T. Swanson, *American National Government,* New York, Crowell, 1970.

Key, V. O., *Politics, Parties and Pressure Groups,* 5th ed., New York, Crowell, 1964.

Morison, Samuel E., *Oxford History of the American People,* New York, Oxford University Press, 1965.

78 79 80   10 9 8 7 6 5 4